Jaguar XJ6 & XJ Owners Workshop Manual

by J H Haynes
Member of the Guild of Motoring Writers
and Peter Strasman
MISTC

Models covered

UK:
Jaguar XJ6 2.8 Litre Saloon
Jaguar XJ6 4.2 Litre Saloon (Series 1)
Jaguar XJ6 4.2 Litre Saloon & Coupe (Series 2)
Jaguar XJ 3.4 Saloon
Jaguar XJ 4.2 Saloon & Coupe
Daimler Sovereign 2.8 Saloon
Daimler Sovereign 3.4 Saloon
Daimler Sovereign 4.2 Saloon (Series 1)
Daimler Sovereign 4.2 Saloon & Coupe (Series 2)

USA:
Jaguar XJ6 4.2 Litre Saloon (Series 1)
Jaguar XJ6 4.2 Litre Saloon & Coupe (Series 2)

*Covers standard and long wheelbase models, Vanden Plas bodied cars,
automatic and manual transmission. Does not cover twelve cylinder
models (XJ12 and XJ5.3).*

ISBN 0 85696 242 2

ABCDE 242
FGHIJ
KLMNO
PQR

Printed in England

HAYNES PUBLISHING GROUP
SPARKFORD YEOVIL SOMERSET ENGLAND
distributed in the USA by
HAYNES PUBLICATIONS INC
861 LAWRENCE DRIVE
NEWBURY PARK
CALIFORNIA 91320
USA

Acknowledgements

Thanks are due to the Special Car Division of British Leyland Limited for their assistance in the provision of technical information. Castrol Limited provided lubrication data.

We are indebted to Reg Hawkins who was kind enough to lend his car for our project.

Thanks are due to the Champion Sparking Plug Company for the provision of spark plug photographs. The bodywork repair photographs used in this manual were provided by Lloyds Industries Limited who supply 'Turtle Wax', 'Dupli Color Holts' and other Holts range products.

Lastly we are grateful to all of those people at Sparkford who helped in the production of this manual. Particularly, Martin Penny and Les Brazier who carried out the mechanical work and took the photographs respectively; Stanley Randolph who planned the layout of each page, Terry Davey who drew the line illustrations and Rod Grainger the editor.

About this manual

Its aims

The aim of this book is to help you get the best value from your car. It can do so in two ways. First it can help you decide what work must be done, even should you choose to get it done by a garage, the routine maintenance and the diagnosis and course of action when random faults occur. However, it is hoped that you will also use the second and fuller purpose by tackling the work yourself. This can give you the satisfaction of doing the job yourself. On the simpler jobs it may even be quicker than booking the car into a garage and going there twice, to leave and collect it. Perhaps most important, much money can be saved by avoiding the costs a garage must charge to cover their labour and overheads.

The book has drawings and descriptions to show the function of the various components so that their layout can be understood. Then the tasks are described and photographed in a step-by-step sequence so that even a novice can cope with complicated work.

The jobs are described assuming only normal tools are available, and not special tools. However, a reasonable outfit of tools will be a worthwhile investment. Many special workshop tools produced by the makers merely speed the work, and in these cases guidance is given as to how to do the job without them. On a very few occasions special tools are essential to prevent damage to components, then their use is is described. Though it might be possible to borrow the tool against a deposit, such work may have to be entrusted to the official agent.

To avoid labour costs a garage will often give a cheaper repair by fitting a reconditioned assembly. The home mechanic can be helped by this book to diagnose the fault and make a repair using only a minor spare part.

Using the manual

The book is divided into twelve Chapters. Each Chapter is divided into numbered Sections which are headed in **bold type** between horizontal lines. Each Section consists of serially numbered paragraphs.

There are two types of illustration: (1) Figures which are numbered according to Chapter and sequence of occurrence in that Chapter. (2) Photographs which have a reference number on their caption. All photographs apply to the Chapter in which they occur so that the reference number pinpoints the pertinent Section and paragraph number.

Procedures, once described in the text, are not normally repeated. If it is necessary to refer to another Chapter the reference will be given in Chapter number and Section number.

If it is considered necessary to refer to a particular paragraph in another Chapter the reference is given in this form: 1/5:5. Cross-references given without use of the word 'Chapter' apply to Sections and/or paragraphs in the same Chapter (eg; 'see Section 8') means also 'in this Chapter'.

When the left or right side of the car is mentioned it is as if looking forward from the rear of the car.

Great effort has been made to ensure that this book is complete and up-to-date. However, it should be realised that manufacturers continually modify their cars, even in retrospect.

Whilst every care is taken to ensure that the information in this manual is correct no liability can be accepted by the authors or publishers for loss, damage or injury caused by any errors in, or omissions from, the information given.

Contents

Note: *In addition each Chapter contains, where applicable, Specifications General description and Fault diagnosis*

Introduction to the Jaguar XJ6 and Daimler Sovereign

The car was originally introduced as the Jaguar XJ6 in 1968 with a six cylinder (type XK) twin overhead camshaft engine, which was offered in 2.8 or 4.2 litre capacity.

The transmission was a four-speed manual gearbox with optional overdrive or three-speed automatic transmission.

Power steering was standard on de-luxe models but optional on standard models.

In October 1972, a long wheelbase model was introduced. This had the 4.2 litre engine and was known as the XJ6L and provided extra space in the rear passenger compartment.

In September 1973, the Series 2 range was introduced offering only the 4.2 litre engine, the 2.8 litre version being discontinued. The new car included ventilated front brake discs, laminated windscreen and revised interior and instrumentation. Overdrive could be specified as a standard fitting and full air-conditioning was offered as an option.

In January 1974, the Series 2, two door coupe was launched and designated the XJ6C.

In April 1975, a 3.4 litre version of the XJ6 was introduced, having an engine which had a re-designed cylinder block which was torsionally stronger. Overdrive or automatic transmission was offered at no extra cost.

The Daimler range has followed closely the Jaguar model introductions and as the car differs only in detail (such as the radiator grille), it is designed to cater for the brand loyalty which exists among Daimler owners.

There is a great difference in equipment between early cars and Series 2 models, also there is a wide variation in accessories and emission control systems according to the model, the date of production and the territory for which the car is destined.

Generally, the overhaul and repair operations are not difficult to carry out but many of them are rather protracted due to the number of components which have to be removed. This is to be expected on such a well constructed, lavishly equipped car.

General dimensions, weights and capacities

Dimensions (early cars)

Overall length	15 ft 9½ in (4.812 m)
Overall width	5 ft 9 ¾ in (1.762 m)
Overall height	4 ft 8 7/8 in (1.44 m)
Wheelbase	9 ft 0 7/8 in (2.765 m)

Weights (early cars)

2.8 litre (manual)	30¼ cwt (1536.8 kg)
2.8 litre (overdrive)	30½ cwt (1549.5 kg)
2.8 litre (automatic)	30¼ cwt (1536.8 kg)
4.2 litre (manual)	30¾ cwt (1562.2 kg)
4.2 litre (overdrive)	31 cwt (1574.9 kg)
4.2 litre (automatic)	31½ cwt (1600.3 kg)

Dimensions (Series 2)

	XJ6	XJ6L (LWB)	XJ6C (Coupe)
Overall length *	190.7 in (4.844 m)	194.7 in (4.945 m)	190.7 in (4.844 m)
Overall width	69.7 in (1.760 m)	69.7 in (1.760 m)	69.7 in (1.760 m)
Overall height	54.1 in (1.374 m)	54.1 in (1.374 m)	54.1 in (1.374 m)
Wheelbase	109.1 in (2.771 m)	113.1 in (2.873 m)	109.1 in (2.771 m)

Weights (Series 2)

	XJ6	XJ6L (LWB)	XJ6C (Coupe)
3.4 litre	3717 lb (1686 kg)	—	—
4.2 litre	3867 lb (1754 kg)	3907 lb (1772 kg)	3879 lb (1759 kg)
4.2 litre (N. American Specification) **	4074 lb (1848 kg)	—	4086 lb (1853 kg)

* Add 4.2 in (107 mm) for impact bumpers   ** Includes automatic transmission and air-conditioning.

Capacities

Fuel tank:

Not N. America	Each tank 12 Imp. gals. (54.6 litres/14.5 US gals.)
N. America	11 Imp. gals. (50 litres/13.2 US gals.)
Series 2 cars	10.5 Imp. gals. (47.75 litres/12.6 US gals.)

Cooling system (including heater):

2.8 and 3.4 litre	30 Imp. pints (17 litres/36 US pints)
4.2 litres	32 Imp. pints (18 litres/38 US pints)
Gearbox (without overdrive) - early cars	2½ Imp. pints (1.5 litres/3 US pints)
Gearbox (with overdrive) - early cars	4 Imp. pints (2.25 litres/4¾ US pints)
Gearbox (without overdrive) - later cars	3 Imp. pints (1.6 litres/3¼ US pints)
Gearbox (with overdrive) - later cars	4½ Imp. pints (2.4 litres/5 US pints)

Automatic transmission:

Model 8	16.5 Imp. pints (9.4 litres/19.8 US pints)
Model 12	16.5 Imp. pints (9.4 litres/19.8 US pints)
Model 35	16.5 Imp. pints (9.4 litres/19.8 US pints)
Model 65	14.5 Imp. pints (8.2 litres/17.4 US pints)
Rear axle	2¾ Imp. pints (1.5 litres/3¼ US pints)
Engine (including new filter)	14½ Imp. pints (8.25 litres/17½ US pints)

Jaguar Series Two XJ6 Coupe (UK Specification)

Jaguar XJ6 Saloon (North American Specification)

As this book has been written in England, it uses the appropriate English component names, phrases, and spelling. Some of these differ from those used in America. Normally, these cause no difficulty, but to make sure, a glossary is printed below. In ordering spare parts remember the parts list will probably use these words:

Glossary

English	American	English	American
Accelerator	Gas pedal	Layshaft (of gearbox)	Counter shaft
Alternator	Generator (AC)	Leading shoe (of brake)	Primary shoe
Anti-roll bar	Stabiliser or sway bar	Locks	Latches
Choke/venturi	Barrel	Motorway	Freeway, turnpike etc.
Battery	Energizer	Number plate	Licence plate
Bonnet (engine cover)	Hood	Paraffin	Kerosene
Boot lid	Trunk lid	Petrol	Gasoline
Boot (luggage compartment)	Trunk	Petrol tank	Gas tank
Bottom gear	1st gear	'Pinking'	'Pinging'
Bulkhead	Firewall	Quarter light	Quarter window
Camfollower or tappet	Valve lifter or tappet	Retread	Recap
Carburettor	Carburetor	Reverse	Back-up
Catch	Latch	Rocker cover	Valve cover
Circlip	Snap ring	Roof rack	Car-top carrier
Clearance	Lash	Saloon	Sedan
Crownwheel	Ring gear (of differential)	Seized	Frozen
Disc (brake)	Rotor/disk	Side indicator lights	Side marker lights
Propellor shaft	Driveshaft	Side light	Parking light
Drop arm	Pitman arm	Silencer	Muffler
Drop head coupe	Convertible	Spanner	Wrench
Dynamo	Generator (DC)	Sill panel (beneath doors)	Rocker panel
Earth (electrical)	Ground	Split cotter (for valve spring cap)	Lock (for valve spring retainer)
Engineer's blue	Prussion blue	Split pin	Cotter pin
Estate car	Station wagon	Steering arm	Spindle arm
Exhaust manifold	Header	Sump	Oil pan
Fast back (Coupe)	Hard top	Tab washer	Tang; lock
Fault finding/diagnosis	Trouble shooting	Tailgate	Liftgate
Float chamber	Float bowl	Tappet	Valve lifter
Free-play	Lash	Thrust bearing	Throw-out bearing
Freewheel	Coast	Top gear	High
Gudgeon pin	Piston pin or wrist pin	Trackrod (of steering)	Tie-rod (or connecting rod)
Gearchange	Shift	Trailing shoe (of brake)	Secondary shoe
Gearbox	Transmission	Transmission	Whole drive line
Halfshaft	Axle-shaft	Tyre	Tire
Handbrake	Parking brake	Van	Panel wagon/van
Hood	Soft top	Vice	Vise
Hot spot	Heat riser	Wheel nut	Lug nut
Indicator	Turn signal	Windscreen	Windshield
Interior light	Dome lamp	Wing/mudguard	Fender

Miscellaneous points

An "Oil seal" is fitted to components lubricated by grease!

A "Damper" is a "Shock absorber" it damps out bouncing, and absorbs shocks of bump impact. Both names are correct, and both are used haphazardly.

Note that British drum brakes are different from the Bendix type that is common in America, so different descriptive names result. The shoe end furthest from the hydraulic wheel cylinder is on a pivot; interconnection between the shoes as on Bendix brakes is most uncommon. Therefore the phrase "Primary" or "Secondary" shoe does not apply. A shoe is said to be Leading or Trailing. A "Leading" shoe is one on which a point on the drum, as it rotates forward, reaches the shoe at the end worked by the hydraulic cylinder before the anchor end. The opposite is a trailing shoe, and this one has no self servo from the wrapping effect of the rotating drum.

Buying
spare parts and vehicle identification numbers

Buying spare parts

Spare parts are available from many sources, for example: Leyland garages, other garages and accessory shops, and motor factors. Our advice regarding spare parts is as follows:

Official appointed Leyland garages - This is the best source of parts which are peculiar to your car and otherwise not generally available (eg; complete cylinder heads, internal gearbox components, badges, interior trim etc). It is also the only place at which you should buy parts if your car is still under warranty; non-Leyland components may invalidate the warranty. To be sure of obtaining the correct parts it will always be necessary to give the storeman your car's engine and chassis number, and if possible, to take the old part along for positive identification. Remember that many parts are available on a factory exchange scheme - any parts returned should always be clean! It obviously makes good sense to the specialists on your car for this type of part for they are best equipped to supply you.

Other garages and accessory shops - These are often very good places to buy material and components needed for the maintenance of your car (eg; oil filters, spark plugs, bulbs, fan belts, oils and grease, touch-up paint, filler paste etc). They also sell general accessories, usually have convenient opening hours, charge lower prices and can often be found not far from home.

Motor factors - Good factors will stock all of the more important components which wear out relatively quickly (eg; clutch components, pistons, valves, exhaust systems, brake cylinders/pipes/hoses/seals/ shoes and pads etc). Motor factors will often provide new or reconditioned components on a part exchange basis - this can save a considerable amount of money.

Vehicle identification numbers

When buying spare parts, always quote the car model, chassis or engine number, as necessary, to the partsman. This will ensure that the

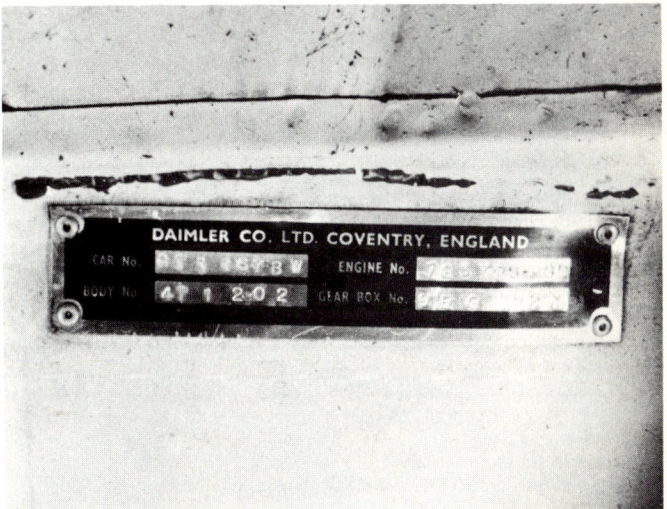

Engine and car number index plate

correctly fitting item is supplied for your particular car.

The *engine and car numbers* are located on a plate attached to the left-hand wing valance within the engine compartment.

On cars destined for operation in *North America*, the *chassis number* is repeated on the top of the fascia panel just inside the windscreen.

Routine maintenance

Maintenance is essential for ensuring safety and desirable for the purpose of getting the best in terms of performance and economy from the car. Over the years the need for periodic lubrication - oiling, greasing and so on - has been drastically reduced if not totally eliminated. This has unfortunately tended to lead some owners to think that because no such action is required the items either no longer exist or will last for ever. This is a serious delusion. It follows therefore that the largest initial element of maintenance is visual examination. This may lead to repairs or renewals.

Every 250 miles (400 km) or weekly

Brakes
Check reservoir fluid level (photo).
Check foot and handbrake movement for increased travel or falling off in efficiency.

Engine
Check oil level.
Check coolant level.
Check battery electrolyte level.

Lights
Check for operation.
Clean lenses.

Steering
Check tyres for pressure and wear characteristics.

General
Clean windscreen.
Top-up washer reservoir.

At first 1000 miles (1600 km) - new cars only

Brakes
Check fluid level in reservoir.
Check travel of footbrake and handbrake lever.

Engine
Check torque of cylinder head nuts.
Check for oil, water or fuel leaks.
Top-up carburettor dampers.
Top-up battery.
Check coolant level in header tank or expansion tank.
Drain and refill engine oil.
Check tension of all drivebelts.
Check contact breaker gap and ignition timing.

Topping-up the brake master cylinder reservoir

Windscreen washer reservoir

Steering/suspension
Check level of power steering reservoir fluid.
Check all suspension bolts and nuts.
Check wheel alignment.
Check tyre pressures.
Grease all suspension nipples.

Transmission
Check clutch fluid level.
Check clutch free-movement
Check gearbox (or automatic transmission) fluid level (photo).
Adjust rear brake band (model 12 automatic transmission only).
Adjust front brake band (model 8 and 35 automatic transmission only).
Check oil level in final drive unit.

General
Check all lights and headlamp alignment.
Check locks and controls and adjust, if necessary.
Top-up screen washer reservoir.

Every 3000 miles (4800 km)

Brakes
Check disc pad wear.
Check handbrake and foot pedal travel.
Check fluid lines for leaks.

Engine
Check drivebelt tension.
Check exhaust system for leaks.
Top-up carburettor dampers.

Steering
Check condition of steering joints and gaiters.

Every 6000 miles (9600 km)

Clutch
Check reservoir fluid level.
Check free-movement.

Engine
Change engine oil and filter element.
Renew fuel filter.
Clean carburettor gauze filters (SU type only).
Clean and adjust contact breaker points.
Clean and re-gap spark plugs.
Check ignition timing.
Lubricate distributor.
Clean automatic enrichment device (AED) filter. SU - HS8 carburettor only.
Check and adjust carburettors and lubricate linkage.
Adjust upper timing chain (if necessary).

Steering
Check power steering fluid level.
Lubricate grease nipples on trackrod ends and rack and pinion assembly.

Transmission
Check fluid level in manual gearbox or automatic transmission.
Check fluid level in final drive unit.

Suspension
Lubricate all grease nipples including those on wheel bearings.

Topping-up the automatic transmission

Clutch fluid reservoir

Location of engine drain plug

Every 12000 miles (19300 km)

Engine
Renew spark plugs.
Renew air cleaner element (photo).
Clean EGR system orifice of carbon (emission control systems only).
Renew contact breaker assembly.
Check tightness of cylinder head nuts.
Check tightness of manifold nuts.
Clean crankcase ventilation filter.
Check exhaust system for leaks or deterioration.

Steering
Check front wheel alignment and security of all steering and suspension nuts and bolts.

Transmission
Change final drive unit oil (use special oil if limited slip differential).
Change manual gearbox/overdrive oil.
Clean overdrive unit filter.

Location of power steering fluid reservoir

Every 24000 miles (38600 km)

Brakes
Drain hydraulic system, flush and refill with new fluid.

Engine
Renew charcoal canister (fuel evaporative control system).
Check fuel filler cap seal and renew if defective.

Transmission
Adjust rear brake band (model 12 automatic transmission only).

Every 48000 miles (77200 km)

Brakes
Drain hydraulic system and renew all seals. Refill with fresh fluid and bleed.

Air cleaner cover unclipped showing disposable element

Annually

Renew coolant with fresh antifreeze mixture.

Jacking and towing

Use the jack supplied with the car only for wheel changing during roadside emergencies.

Whenever underbody repairs are being carried out, use a hydraulic, screw or trolley jack placed under the body side or crossmembers or under the suspension wishbones. Always supplement the jacks with axle stands.

If the car has to be towed in an emergency, and it is equipped with automatic transmission, observe the following procedure:

Model 8 transmission - restrict towing speed to 25 mph (40 kph).
All other automatic transmissions - disconnect propeller shaft so that rear wheels do not transmit drive to transmission unit.

Final drive unit drain plug

Recommended lubricants and fluids

Component		Castrol product
1 Engine		Castrol GTX
2 Gearbox (manual)		Castrol Hypoy
(automatic)		Castrol TQF
3 Rear axle		Castrol Hypoy
Front wheel bearings Rear wheel bearings Rear suspension Final drive halfshafts Steering tie-rods and wheel swivels Steering rack housing	... ...	Castrol LM Grease
4 Power steering reservoir		Castrol TQF
5 Clutch and Brake reservoirs		Castrol Girling Universal Brake and Clutch Fluid
Door locks, hinges, linkages etc.		Castrol Everyman

Chapter 1 Engine

Contents

Specifications

Engine (general)

Number of cylinders 6

	2.8 litre	3.4 litre	4.2 litre
Bore	3.2687 in (83.0 mm)	3.2687 in (83.0 mm)	3.625 in (92.07 mm)
Stroke	3.3857 in (86.0 mm)	4.1732 in (106.0 mm)	4.1732 in (106.0 mm)
Cubic capacity	170.38 cu in (2792 cc)	208.82 cu in (3422 cc)	258.43 cu in (4235 cc)

Compression ratio ... ... 8 : 1 (L), 7.8 1 : 1 (S3/3.4), 9 : 1 (S), 8.4 : 1 (Series 2)
Firing order ... ... 1 — 5 — 3 — 6 — 2 — 4 (No. 1 cylinder at rear)

Camshaft

Number of bearings ... ... 4 per shaft
Journal diameter ... ... 1.00 in (25.4 mm)
Running clearance ... ... 0.0005 in to 0.002 in (0.013 to 0.05 mm)
Endfloat (maximum) ... ... 0.004 to 0.006 in (0.10 to 0.15 mm)

Connecting rods

	2.8 litre, 3.4 litre	4.2 litre
Length (centre to centre)	5 5/8 in (14.28 cm)	7 3/4 in (19.68 cm)
Big-end bearing bore	2.2330 to 2.2335 in (56.72 to 56.73 mm)	
Big-end bearing running clearance	0.0015 to 0.0033 in (0.037 to 0.083 mm)	

Big-end side clearance	0.0058 to 0.0087 in (0.15 to 0.22 mm)
Small end bush bore diameter	0.875 in (+ 0.0002 in) (22.22 mm + 0.005 mm)

Crankshaft

Number of main bearings	7
Journal diameter	2.75 to 2.7505 in (69.85 to 69.86 mm)
Thrust washer thickness	0.092 in ($\pm$ 0.001 in) (2.33 $\pm$ 0.025 mm) 0.096 in ($\pm$ 0.001 in) (2.43 $\pm$ 0.025 mm)
Endfloat	0.004 to 0.006 in (0.10 to 0.15 mm)
Main bearing running clearance	0.0025 to 0.0042 in (0.063 to 0.106 mm)
Crankpin diameter	2.086 + 0.0006 in (52.98 + 0.015 mm)
Regrind undersizes	0.010, 0.020, 0.030, 0.040 in (0.25, 0.51, 0.76, 1.02 mm)
Minimum journal diameter after regrind	2.05 in (52.07 mm)

Cylinder block

Material	Cast-iron

Cylinder head

Material	Aluminium alloy
Valve seat angle	45°

Gudgeon pin

Type	Fully floating
Outside diameter:	
Green	0.8750 to 0.8751 in (22.225 to 22.228 mm)
Red	0.8751 to 0.8752 in (22.228 to 22.230 mm)

Pistons and piston rings (except Series 2)

Type	Alloy, solid skirt
Skirt clearance in bore	0.0007 to 0.0013 in (0.018 to 0.032 mm)
Number of piston rings	2 compression, 1 oil control
Ring width (compression)	0.0770 to 0.0780 in (1.97 to 2.00 mm)
Ring thickness:	
2.8 litre, 3.4 litre compression	0.124 to 0.130 in (3.15 to 3.30 mm)
4.2 litre compression	0.151 to 0.158 in (3.775 to 3.95 mm)
Ring end-gap:	
Compression	0.015 to 0.020 in (0.38 to 0.51 mm)
Oil control	0.015 to 0.033 in (0.38 to 0.82 mm)
Ring side-clearance:	
Compression	0.0025 in (0.064 mm)
Oil control	0.004 in (0.102 mm)

Pistons and piston rings (Series 2)

As for other models except:

Compression ring width	0.0781 in (2.0 mm)
Compression ring thickness	0.171 to 0.188 in (4.35 to 4.60 mm)
Compression ring side-clearance in groove	0.0015 to 0.0035 in (0.038 to 0.089 mm)
Top compression ring end-gap	0.015 to 0.020 in (0.38 to 0.51 mm)
Second compression ring end-gap	0.009 to 0.014 in (0.23 to 0.35 mm)
Oil control ring end-gap	0.015 to 0.045 in (0.38 to 1.14 mm)

Tappets

Material	Cast-iron
Outside diameter	1.3738 to 1.3742 in (34.89 to 34.90 mm)
Running clearance	0.0008 to 0.0019 in (0.02 to 0.048 mm)

Timing chains and sprockets

Type	Duplex
Pitch	3/8 in (9.5 mm)
Number of pitches:	
Top chain	100
Lower chain	82
Crankshaft sprocket (teeth)	21
Intermediate sprocket (teeth)	Outer 28, Inner 20
Camshaft sprocket (teeth)	30
Idler sprocket	21

Valve timing

Inlet valve opens	17° BTDC
Inlet valve closes	59° ABDC
Exhaust valve opens	59° BBDC
Exhaust valve closes	17° ATDC

Valves

Material:	
Inlet	Silicon chrome steel
Exhaust	21 − 4 − NS
Valve head diameter:	
Inlet	1.75 in ± 0.002 in (44.45 ± 0.05 mm)
Exhaust	1.625 ± 0.002 in (41.28 ± 0.05 mm)
Valve stem diameter (inlet and exhaust)	0.3125 in (7.94 mm)
Valve lift	0.375 in (9.53 mm)
Valve clearance (cold) - inlet and exhaust	0.012 to 0.014 in (0.30 to 0.35 mm)

Valve springs

Free-length, except Series 2	(Inner) 1 21/32 in (42.0 mm); (Outer) 1 15/16 in (49.2 mm)
Free-length, Series 2	(Inner) 1.734 in (44.04 mm); (Outer) 2.103 in (53.42 mm)

Valve guides

Material	Cast-iron
Length:	
Inlet	1.86 in (47.24 mm)
Exhaust	1.95 in (49.53 mm)
Inside diameter:	
Inlet	5/16 in (7.94 mm)
Exhaust	5/16 in (7.94 mm)
Interference fit in cylinder head	0.0005 to 0.0022 in (0.013 to 0.055 mm)

Valve seat inserts

Material	Sintered iron
Inside diameter:	
Inlet	1½ + 0.003 in (38.1 + 0.076 mm)
	− 0.001 in − 0.025 mm
Exhaust	1.379 to 1.383 in (35.03 to 35.13 mm)
Interference (shrink) fit in cylinder head	0.003 in (0.076 mm)

Lubrication system

Pump type	Eccentric rotor
Lobe to lobe tip clearance (max.)	0.006 in (0.15 mm)
Rotor to body clearance (max.)	0.010 in (0.25 mm)
Rotor end-clearance (max.)	0.0025 in (0.06 mm)
Oil pressure (hot) at 3000 rev/min	40 lb/sq in (2.81 kg/sq cm)
Oil capacity (including new filter)	14½ Imp. pints (8.25 litres/17½ US pints)

Torque wrench settings

	lb ft	Nm
Cylinder head nuts	54	75
Camshaft bearings	9	12
Main bearing bolts	72	100
Connecting rod nuts	37	51
Flywheel bolts	67	93
Oil filter centre bolt	20	28
Torque converter to driveplate bolts	30	41
Driveplate to crankshaft	67	93
Torque converter housing to engine bolts	35	48
Clutch to flywheel bolts	20	28
Clutch bellhousing to engine bolts	35	48
Oil filter bolt	20	28
Rear mounting bracket to body:		
Small bolts	18	25
Large bolts	32	44
Front mounting bracket to crossmember	18	25
Rear mounting peg	30	41
Rear flexible mounting pads	32	44

1 General description

1 The engines fitted to the models covered by this manual are very similar in design but vary slightly in the style of some small components.

2 All engines are of six cylinder twin overhead camshaft design and may be of high or low compression ratio.

3 The cylinder block is of cast-iron construction while the cylinder head is of aluminium alloy. The cylinder block on Series Two, 4.2 litre engines is of modiified, torsionally stronger construction with dry type cylinder liners.

4 The crankshaft is supported in seven main bearings.

5 Duplex camshaft chains are used and the camshafts have four bearings each.

6 Pressure lubrication is by means of an eccentric rotor type pump.

2 Major operations possible with the engine in the car

1 The following operations can be carried out without removing the engine from the car:

Removal and installation of the cylinder head.

Removal and refitting of the sump (after first withdrawing the front suspension - see Chapter 11).

Removal and installation of the piston/connecting rod assemblies (after having first removed cylinder head and sump).

Removal and refitting of the timing gear (after first having removed cylinder head and sump).

Removal of the engine mountings (weight of engine supported on a hoist).

3 Major operations only possible with the engine removed from the car

1 The following operations can only be carried out after the engine has been removed from the car:
Removal and refitting of the main bearings and crankshaft.
Removal and refitting of the flywheel

4 Method of engine removal

1 The engine should be removed from the car complete with manual gearbox or automatic transmission and the two units separated afterwards.
2 The power train is hoisted upwards from the engine compartment and in view of its weight, a substantial hoist or lifting tackle must be employed.

5 Engine/manual gearbox - removal

1 Remove the bonnet, as described in Chapter 12.
2 Remove the crossbraces from the engine compartment bulkhead and inner wings (photos).
3 Disconnect the lead from the battery negative terminal.
4 Drain the cooling system and remove the radiator as described in Chapter 2. *On cars equipped with full air-conditioning,* the condensor must be unbolted and carefully supported before the radiator can be withdrawn. On no account disconnect any of the air-conditioning system hoses.
5 Drain the engine oil.
6 Remove the air cleaner.
7 Disconnect the lead from the starter motor solenoid.
8 Disconnect the right-hand engine wiring harness at the plug and socket connector.
9 Disconnect the high tension and low tension cables from the ignition coil.
10 Disconnect the brake vacuum servo pipe from the underside of the inlet manifold. Refer to Section 26, Chapter 3 for disconnection details of manifold used with Stromberg carburettors.
11 Disconnect the flexible hoses from the power steering pump and plug the hoses.
12 Release the power steering pump adjuster nuts and push the pump as far as it will go towards the engine.
13 Disconnect the heater flow and return hoses from the nozzles on the engine compartment rear bulkhead.
14 Close the fuel tap and then disconnect the fuel inlet pipe from the carburettor.
15 Detach the throttle cable from the accelerator pedal, release the nut on the cable conduit and pull the assembly through the engine compartment rear bulkhead. Disconnect the choke cables or leads from the starter device.
16 Disconnect the leads from the alternator.
17 Disconnect the exhaust downpipes from the exhaust manifold.
18 *On cars fitted with air-conditioning,* unbolt the compressor and pull it to one side of the engine compartment and tie it securely. **On no account disconnect any of the air-conditioning system hoses.**
19 Disconnect the leads to the overdrive switch (where fitted) and remove the gearshift control lever knob.
20 Disconnect the remaining gearbox electrical leads.
21 Unbolt the clutch slave cylinder from the clutch bellhousing and tie it up out of the way. There is no need to disconnect the clutch hydraulic lines.
22 Attach a suitable hoist to the engine and take its weight.
23 Remove the engine rear mounting. To do this, place a jack under the mounting and then remove the four setscrews. Lower the jack until the tension in the mounting spring plate is released. Extract the mounting components which include four spacers which are located between the body and the mounting. Two types of engine rear mounting may be encountered but the removal procedure is identical. (Figs. 1.1 and 1.2).
24 Disconnect the propeller shaft at its front flange and tie it carefully to one side.
25 Remove the engine front mountings by unscrewing the top and bottom nuts which secure the flexible components. (Fig. 1.3)

5.2A Engine compartment rear bulkhead brace attachment

5.2B Engine compartment wing valance brace attachment

H.5647

Fig. 1.1. Engine rear mounting (earlier cars) (Sec. 5)

Fig. 1.2. Engine rear mounting (later cars) (Sec. 5)

Fig. 1.3. Engine front mounting (Sec. 5)

26 Disconnect the speedometer cable.
27 Lower the rear of the engine/gearbox until the gearshift control lever clears the console grommet and then hoist the engine/gearbox forward and up and out of the engine compartment at a steeply inclined angle.

6 Engine/automatic transmission - removal

1 The procedure is similar to that described in the preceding Section but carry out the following operations as substitutes for those concerning the clutch and gearshift knob.
2 Disconnect the kick-down cable from the carburettor.
3 Disconnect the speed selector cable from the lever on the side of the transmission housing.
4 Disconnect the speed selector cable clamp from the torque converter housing.
5 Disconnect vacuum pipes and electrical leads (refer to Chapter 6, Part 2).

7 Engine/manual gearbox - separation

1 Unbolt and withdraw the bolts which secure the clutch bellhousing to the engine.
2 Pull the gearbox from the engine in a straight line, supporting the weight of the gearbox to prevent strain or distortion to the clutch components while the gearbox primary shaft is still in engagement with the clutch driven plate. The use of a trolley jack will facilitate this operation. If the overdrive must be removed, refer to Chapter 6.

8 Engine/automatic transmission - separation

1 Unbolt and remove the semi-circular plate from the lower half of the torque converter housing.
2 Unbolt and remove the starter motor.
3 Unscrew and remove each of the four setscrews which retain the torque converter to the driveplate. These are accessible through the starter motor aperture but the crankshaft will have to be turned (by applying a spanner to the crankshaft pulley bolt) to bring each of the torque converter screws into view in sequence.

4 Unscrew and remove the bolts which secure the torque converter housing to the engine and then withdraw the automatic transmission. Be prepared for some loss of fluid and keep the torque converter pressed towards the transmission to prevent its disengagement from the oil pump drive tangs.
5 In view of the weight of the transmission, the use of a trolley jack will be an advantage during the foregoing operations.

9 Engine ancillaries - removal

1 With the engine removed from the car and separated from the transmission unit, remove the following external components before attempting to dismantle the engine:
   The alternator (Chapter 10)
   The distributor (Chapter 4)
   The clutch (Chapter 5)
   The water pump (Chapter 2)
   The starter motor (Chapter 10)

10 Preparation for dismantling the engine

1 During the dismantling process, the greatest care should be taken to keep the exposed parts free from dirt. To that end, thoroughly clean down the outside of the engine, removing all traces of oil and congealed dirt. Use paraffin or proprietary solvent. The latter will make the job much easier for after the solvent has been applied and allowed to stand for a time a vigorous jet of water will wash off the solvent with all the dirt. If the dirt is thickly and deeply embedded, work in the solvent with a stiff brush.
2 Finally wipe down the exterior of the engine with rag and only then when the engine is quite clean, should the dismantling process begin. As the engine is stripped, clean each part in a bath of paraffin or solvent.
3 Never immerse parts with oilways (for example the crankshaft) in the cleaning bath. To clean such items, carefully wipe down with a clean paraffin soaked rag and then wipe dry. Oilways can be cleaned out with wire or blown through with an air blast.
4 Re-use of old engine gaskets, copper washers etc is false economy and will, in all probability, lead to oil or water leaks. Always use new items throughout.
5 Retain the old gaskets until the job is finish - for it sometimes happens that a replacement is not always immediately available and in such cases the old one will come in handy for use as a template.
6 When stripping the engine it is best to work from the top down - the underside of the crankcase, when supported on wooden blocks, makes a firm base from which to work. We always recommend, therefore, that the sump is removed at an early stage.
7 Whenever possible, replace nuts, bolts and washers finger tight from wherever they were removed. This helps to avoid loss and muddle later; if they cannot be replaced lay them out in such a fashion that it is clear from whence they came.

11 Cylinder head (engine in car) - removal

1 Disconnect the lead from the battery negative terminal.
2 Remove the two bulkhead to inner wing braces.
3 Drain the cooling system.
4 Remove the air cleaner and the backplate which is secured to the carburettor flanges.
5 Close the fuel tap and disconnect the fuel inlet pipe from the carburettor.
6 Disconnect the high tension leads from the coil and from the spark plugs and then unclip the distributor cap and remove it to one side of the engine compartment.
7 Disconnect the vacuum pipe from the distributor and from the front carburettor.
8 Disconnect the accelerator cable from the pedal and draw the cable into the engine compartment.
9 Release the power steering pump adjustment bolt, push the pump towards the engine and remove the drivebelt. Now pull the pump away from the engine as far as possible.
10 Disconnect the heater hose from the connection on the water pump.

11 Disconnect the heater hoses from the nozzles on the engine compartment rear bulkhead.
12 Disconnect the brake servo vacuum pipe from the inlet manifold.
13 Disconnect the lead from the carburettor solenoid.
14 Disconnect the lead from the thermostatic switch on the inlet manifold water jacket.
15 Disconnect the carburettor overflow pipe support brackets from the engine sump.
16 Remove the top coolant hose and the bypass hose from the front of the inlet manifold water jacket.
17 Disconnect the exhaust manifold from the cylinder head.
18 Disconnect the two camshaft oil supply pipe unions from the rear of the cylinder head.
19 Remove the spark plugs.
20 Remove the dome nuts (and countersunk screw 4.2 litre) from each camshaft cover and then lift off the covers.
21 Remove the four nuts which secure the breather housing to the front of the cylinder head and withdraw the housing.
22 Release the tension on the camshaft chain by slackening the nut on the eccentric idler sprocket shaft, depressing the spring-loaded stop peg and rotating the serrated adjuster plate in a clockwise direction (viewed from the front of the engine).
23 Cut the locking wire on the two setscrews which secure each of the sprockets to their camshafts. Extract one setscrew from each sprocket and then rotate the crankshaft to bring the remaining bolts into view. Unscrew and remove these bolts. (photos)
24 Slide the camshaft sprockets up the slots in their support brackets. Do not turn the crankshaft once the camshaft sprockets have been disconnected.
25 Working in a diagonal pattern from the centre outwards, remove the fourteen dome nuts and six ordinary nuts (these are at the front of the cylinder head). If the car is equipped with an air-conditioning system, the compressor and mounting bracket will have to be unbolted and moved to one side to gain access to the cylinder head nuts. **On no account, disconnect the air-conditioning system hoses.**
26 Lift the cylinder head complete with inlet manifold and carburettors from the cylinder block.
27 Peel off the old gasket and discard it.
28 Support the cylinder head on blocks of wood to prevent damage to the open valves.

12 Cylinder head (engine out of car) - removal

1 The operations are identical to those described in the preceding Section, paragraphs 18 to 28.

13 Cylinder head - dismantling

1 Unbolt and remove the inlet manifold and carburettors (refer also to Chapter 3, Section 26).
2 Remove the four bearing caps from the camshaft, noting their mating marks for refitting in their original locations (Fig. 1.6).
3 Lift out the camshafts and their shell bearings (photo).
4 Make up a suitable tray or rack with compartments so that the valve components can be stored in order for refitting in their original locations (no. 1 cylinder at flywheel end).
5 Withdraw the hollow tappets and extract the adjustment shims. These may be stuck to the end of the valve stem or to the inside of the tappet by the adhesion of the lubricating oil. Keep the components in their original order, making sure not to mix them up (photo).
6 Insert a small wooden block into the combustion chamber at the front of the cylinder head and lay the cylinder head face down on a bench. The block will prevent the valves being displaced when the valve springs are compressed.
7 Using a valve spring compressor, compress the first valve spring collar and extract the split collets. Release the compressor and withdraw the collars, springs and spring seats (photos).
8 The inlet valves are fitted with valve stem oil seals and these should be removed, discarded and new ones obtained at time of major overhaul. An alternative method of dismantling the valves is to place a piece of tubing on the end of the valve collar and strike it hard in order to compress the spring and eject the split cotters (photo).

11.23A Cutting camshaft sprocket locking wire

11.23B Unscrewing camshaft sprocket bolt

Fig. 1.4. Camshaft sprockets disconnected (Sec. 11)

Fig. 1.5.

H.5646

Fig. 1.5. Exploded view of the cylinder head (Sec. 13)

1 Cylinder head	18 Inlet valve	33 Plug	49 Banjo bolt	65 Sealing ring
2 Stud	18a Seal	34 'O' ring	50 Washer	66 Inlet manifold
3 Dowel	19 Exhaust valve	35 Seal	51 Breather housing cover	67 Gasket
4 Core plug	20 Valve spring (inner)	36 Plug	52 Flame trap	68 Stud
5 Washer	21 Valve spring (outer)	37 'O' ring	53 Gasket	69 Stud
6 Valve guide	22 Valve spring seat	38 Setscrew	54 Dome nuts	70 Adaptor
7 Valve guide circlip	23 Valve spring collar	39 Washer	55 Spring washers	71 Washer
8 Inlet valve insert	24 Split cotters	40 Camshaft cover	56 Breather pipe	72 Manifold starting pipe
9 Tappet guide	25 Tappet	41 Gasket	57 Hose	73 Manifold starting pipe
10 Cylinder head gasket	26 Valve adjusting shim	42 Camshaft cover	58 Clip	74 Manifold starting pipe
11 Stud	27 Inlet camshaft	43 Gasket	59 Exhaust manifold	75 Neoprene tube
12 Stud	28 Exhaust camshaft	44 Dome nut	60 Exhaust manifold	76 Clip
13 Stud	29 Camshaft bearing	45 Washer	61 Gasket	77 Water outlet pipe
14 Stud	30 Oil thrower	46 Oil filler cap	62 Gasket	78 Gasket
15 Stud	31 Setscrew	47 'O' ring	63 Thermostat housing	79 Thermostat
16 Setscrew	32 Washer	48 Oil pipe	64 Stud	80 Automatic choke thermostat
17 Lifting lug				81 Gasket

Fig. 1.6. Camshaft bearing marks (Sec. 13)

Fig. 1.7. Camshaft, tappet, shim and valve arrangement (Sec. 13)

13.3 Extracting camshaft bearing shell

13.5 Extracting valve adjustment shim

13.7A Removing valve spring collar

13.7B Removing valve springs

13.8 Method of removing valve split cotters without compressor

14 Sump and oil pump - removal

The sump can be removed with the engine still in the car but the front suspension assembly must first be withdrawn, as described in Chapter 11.

1   Drain the engine oil.

2   Slacken the clip and disconnect the oil return hose at the base of the oil filter.

3   Remove all the setscrews which secure the sump to the crankcase. Note the location of the short screw at the right-hand front corner of the sump.

4   Withdraw the sump and peel or scrape off the gasket.

5   Remove the four nuts which secure the sump baffle plate and withdraw the plate.

6   Disconnect the filter screen and then unbolt the oil return pipe by unscrewing the two flange nuts.

7   Disconnect the suction and delivery pipes from the oil pump.

8   Flatten the lockplates on the bolts which secure the oil pump to the front main bearing cap.

9   Withdraw the oil pump and catch the coupling sleeve at the top of the pump driveshaft.

15 Oil filter - renewal of element

1   The oil filter is located on the right-hand side of the engine.

2   To gain access to it, remove the air cleaner and the support plate which retains the front carburettor overflow pipe to the sump and then detach the pipe from the carburettor float chamber.

3   Working from underneath the car, disconnect the flexible hose from the oil filter relief valve return pipe.

4   Unscrew the filter centre bolt and lift away the canister complete with element.

5   Discard the old element and sealing ring, wipe the interior of the canister clean and then install the new element.

6   Locate the new sealing ring (supplied with the element) in the groove in the filter base and then refit the canister and screw in and tighten the centre bolt (photo).

16 Piston/connecting rod - removal and dismantling

If the engine is in the car, the sump and cylinder head will first have to be removed as previously described.

1   Check that the connecting rods and big-end caps are numbered from 1 to 6 (from the flywheel end). The numbers should be adjacent and note to which side of the engine they face. If no marks are visible, dot punch both cap and rod before removal (photo).

2   Turn the crankshaft until the first connecting rod is at the lowest point of its travel and then unscrew the self-locking nuts from the big-end bolts.

3   Pull off the cap complete with its shell bearing and then push the piston/rod assembly up and out of the top of the cylinder bore. If there is a wear ridge at the top of the bore, this should be scraped away before attempting to remove the piston but take great care not to damage the surfaces of the bore (photo).

Fig. 1.8. Location of short sump securing setscrew (Sec. 14)

Fig. 1.9. Exploded view of the oil filter (Sec. 15)

1	Base	8	Relief valve
2	Sealing ring	9	Seal
3	Element	10	Felt washer
4	Canister	11	Washer
5	Sealing washer	12	Plate
6	Centre bolt	13	Spring clip
7	Spring		

15.6 Extracting oil filter canister sealing ring

16.1 Connecting rod and big-end cap markings

16.3 Withdrawing piston/connecting rod

Fig. 1.10. Crankcase and cylinder block components (Sec. 16)

1 Cylinder block
2 Core plugs
3 Blanking plate
4 Gasket
5 Timing cover
6 Dowel
7 Core plug
9 Dipstick guide tube
10 Plug
11 Hexagon plug
12 Copper washer
13 Dowel
14 Stud
15 Stud
16 Dowel stud
17 Rear oil seal cover
18 Dowel
19 Socket headed screw
20 Socket headed screw
21 Banjo bolt
22 Copper washer
23 Sealing ring
24 Filter gauze
25 Drain tap
26 Copper washer
27 Fibre washer
28 Crankshaft
29 Plug
30 Bush (clutch pilot)
31 Thrust washer
32 Main bearings
33 Damper
34 Cone
35 Distance piece
36 Oil thrower
37 Crankshaft sprocket
38 Oil pump drive gear
39 Woodruff key
40 Pulley
41 Bolt
42 Lockwasher
43 Bolt
44 Washer
45 Lockplate
46 Connecting rod
47 Big-end shell bearing
48 Flywheel
49 Dowel
50 Dowel
51 Setscrew
52 Lockplate
53 Piston
54 Top compression ring
55 Lower compression ring
56 Oil control ring
57 Gudgeon pin
58 Circlip
59 Sump
60 Gasket
61 Crankshaft front oil seal
62 Crankshaft rear oil seal (part)
63 Drain plug
64 Copper washer
65 Baffle assembly
66 Oil pump pipe
67 'O' ring
68 Stud
69 Hose
70 Hose clip
71 Dipstick
72 Ferrule
73 Ignition timing pointer
74 Engine mounting bracket
75 Engine mounting bracket
76 Flexible mounting pad
77 Washer

4   If the original bearing shells are to be refitted, mark them with tape or spirit pen in respect of both cylinder number and whether located in rod or cap.

5   Repeat the removal operations on the remaining five piston/rod assemblies.

6   The piston rings can be removed using a twisting action. Two or three old feeler blades slid behind the rings at equidistant points will prevent the rings dropping into an empty groove as they are withdrawn.

7   The gudgeon pins are a push fit in the piston and connecting rod small end. To dismantle the piston from the connecting rod, extract the circlips from both ends of the gudgeon pin and then stand the piston in hot or boiling water. The gudgeon pin can then be pushed out with thumb pressure.

Fig. 1.11. Exploded view of a piston/connecting rod assembly
Note alignment of piston (front) mark and rod numbers (Sec. 16)

This illustration also shows two types of oil control rings which are available

17 Crankshaft damper - removal

If the engine is still in the car, remove the steering pump and cooling fan drivebelts, also the alternator drivebelt and (if fitted) the compressor pump belt for the air-conditioning system.

1   Bend the tabs flat on the crankshaft damper bolt lockplate and extract the two setscrews which retain the lockplate. Mark the relationship of the damper to the pulley as they are balanced as an assembly and then extract the two remaining pulley bolts and withdraw the pulley from the damper assembly.

2   Unscrew and remove the large crankshaft damper bolt and extract the washer from behind it. In order to prevent the crankshaft turning as the bolt is unscrewed, place a block of wood between a crankshaft web and the crankcase wall (engine out of car) or jam the starter ring gear with a large screwdriver (engine in car). Alternatively, place a ring spanner or socket wrench on the bolt and strike it a sharp blow rather than attempting to lever the bolt undone.

3   Insert two levers behind the damper and lever it from the split cone. If necessary, give a sharp blow to the end of the cone to free the damper.

18 Timing gear - removal and dismantling

If the engine is in the car, remove the cylinder head, the sump, header tank, cowl, fan and radiator also the water pump and crankshaft damper assembly.

1   Remove the setscrews and withdraw the timing chain cover. Note that it is located by two dowels.

2   Withdraw the hexagon plug from the end of the bottom timing chain tensioner and insert an Allen key into the tensioner cylinder. Turn the Allen key clockwise until the cylinder is fully retracted and the timing chain tension released.

3   Unbolt the chain tensioner body and withdraw the tensioner complete with cone-shaped gauze which is located in the tensioner oil feed hole (photo).

4   Unscrew the four setscrews from the timing gear mounting bracket but do not remove them completely.

5   Remove the setscrews from the timing chain guides and remove the guides.

6   Now lift the complete timing gear from the cylinder block, disconnecting the lower chain from the teeth of the crankshaft sprocket as the assembly is withdrawn.

7   Remove the nut and serrated washer from the idler shaft and extract the plunger and spring.

8   Remove the four nuts which secure the front mounting bracket to the rear bracket.

9   Detach the lower timing chain from the intermediate sprocket.

10 Extract the circlip from the end of the intermediate sprocket shaft and press the shaft from the bracket.

11 Withdraw the two camshaft sprockets and upper chain.

18.3 Timing chain tensioner

Fig. 1.12. Timing lower chain and gears (Sec. 18)

Fig. 1.13. Timing upper chain and gear (Sec. 18)

19 Distributor drive - removal

1 With the oil pump already removed as described in Section 14, flatten the tab of the lockplate and unscrew the distributor drive gear nut. Remove the nut and the special washer.
2 Carefully tap the squared end of the distributor driveshaft upwards out of the helical driven gear.
3 Remove the helical driven gear and thrust washer and then withdraw the driveshaft (photo).
4 The drive gear on the front of the crankshaft can be removed if required after first pulling off the crankshaft timing sprocket (photo).

20 Flywheel (or driveplate - auto. transmission) - removal

1 Flatten the tabs of the securing bolt lockplates.
2 Mark the relationship of the flywheel to the crankshaft flange.
3 Unscrew and remove the flywheel bolts and lift the flywheel from its mounting flange (photos).

21 Crankshaft and main bearings - removal

1 Knock back the tab washers securing the fourteen main bearing cap

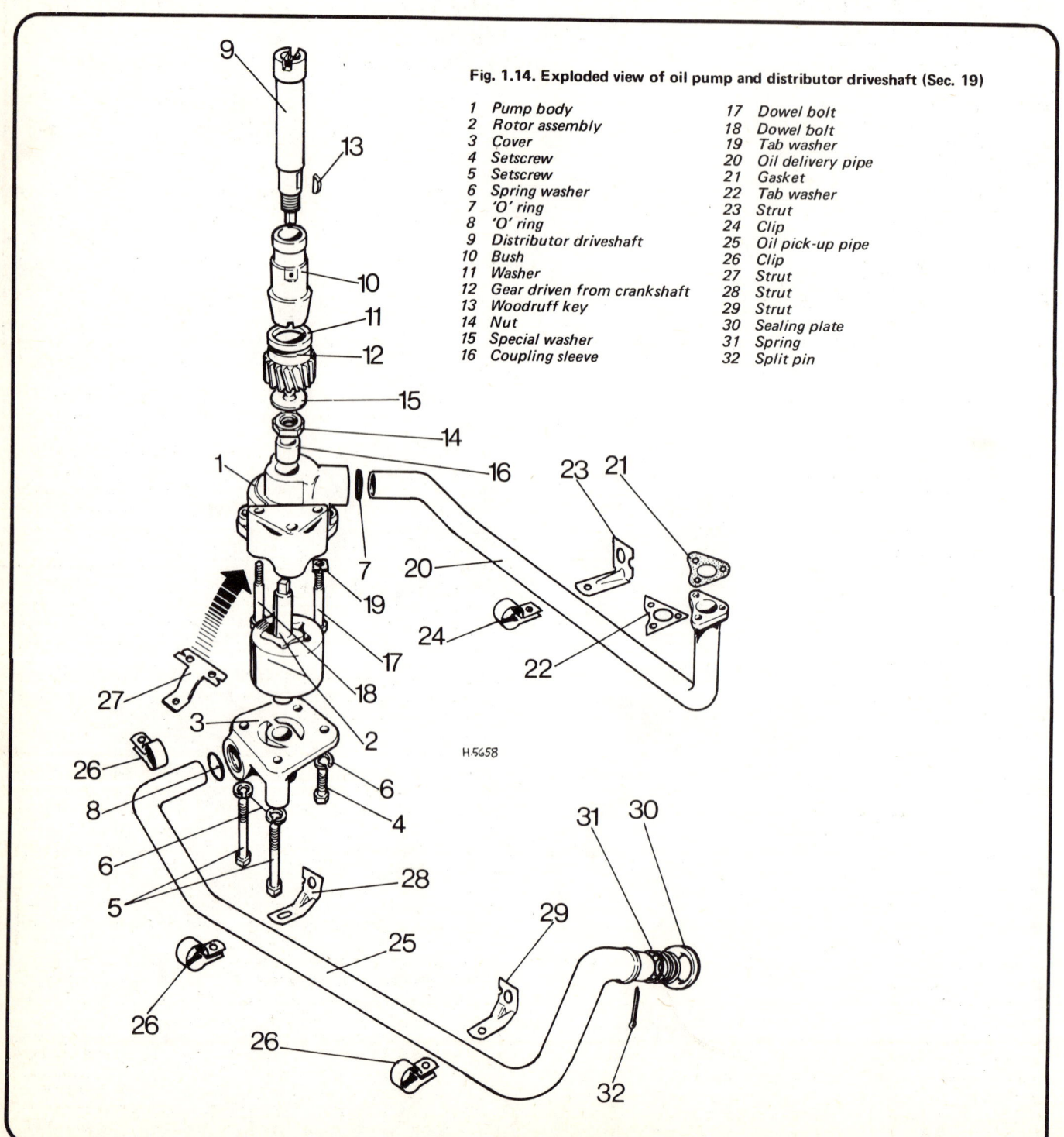

Fig. 1.14. Exploded view of oil pump and distributor driveshaft (Sec. 19)

1	Pump body	17	Dowel bolt
2	Rotor assembly	18	Dowel bolt
3	Cover	19	Tab washer
4	Setscrew	20	Oil delivery pipe
5	Setscrew	21	Gasket
6	Spring washer	22	Tab washer
7	'O' ring	23	Strut
8	'O' ring	24	Clip
9	Distributor driveshaft	25	Oil pick-up pipe
10	Bush	26	Clip
11	Washer	27	Strut
12	Gear driven from crankshaft	28	Strut
13	Woodruff key	29	Strut
14	Nut	30	Sealing plate
15	Special washer	31	Spring
16	Coupling sleeve	32	Split pin

H·5658

19.3 Distributor drive gear and thrust washer

19.4 Distributor drive gear on front of camshaft

20.3A Unscrewing flywheel bolts

20.3B Removing flywheel

Fig. 1.15. Crankshaft thrust washers (Sec. 21)

21.5 Removing socket headed screw from crankshaft rear oil seal

bolts.

2   Note the corresponding numbers stamped on the caps and on the bottom face of the crankcase. The caps must be correctly identified if they are not marked.

3   Undo the bolts and remove the main bearing caps. If a main bearing shell does not come away with its cap, remove it from the crankshaft and keep it with its cap.

4   Note the thrust washers fitted in the recess at each side of the centre main bearing cap.

5   Detach the bottom of the crankshaft rear oil seal cover by removing the two Allen securing screws (photo). Note that the two halves are located by hollow dowels.

6   The crankshaft can now be lifted away from the crankcase.

7   Collect the remaining halves of the main bearing shells and, if they are to be refitted, identify them with the position from which they were removed using tape or a spirit pen.

22 Lubrication system - description

A force feed system of lubrication is employed with oil being circulated round the engine from the sump below the cylinder block. The level of the oil in the sump is indicated by the dipstick located on the left-hand rear side of the engine. High and Low level of oil is indicated by marks on the dipstick and ideally the level of oil should not be above the high mark and should never be allowed to fall below the low mark. Oil is replenished via the filler cap in the left-hand camshaft cover. The oil is circulated round the engine by an eccentric rotor type oil pump which consists of five main parts: the body, the driving spindle with the inner rotor pinned to it the outer rotor and the cover which is secured to the main body by four bolts.

Oil is drawn from the sump and is then passed under pressure by the pump to the filter on the right-hand exterior of the crankcase and thence through drillings to the big-end and main bearings; the camshaft bearings are fed via an external oil pipe. A longitudinal drilling through the connecting rod feeds the small end and the gudgeon pin with oil and a small hole in each connecting rod throws a small jet of oil to the cylinder wall with each revolution. The oil filter is of the full flow type with a replaceable element. The filter base incorporates a removable oil pressure relief valve and a balance valve which provides a safeguard against the possibility of the filter element becoming so choked as to prevent oil reaching the bearings. Oil which passes the oil pressure relief valve is returned to the engine sump by an external rubber hose.

23 Crankcase ventilation system

1   Extraction of crankcase fumes and blow-by gases is accomplished by means of a breather on the front of the engine and a connecting hose to the air filter attached to the carburettor.

2   Periodically, unbolt the breather and withdraw the flame trap (gauze) and disconnect the hose. Clean the gauze and hose, renew the breather gaskets and refit it to the engine.

24 Crankshaft and main bearings - examination and renovation

1   Examine the surfaces of the crankshaft journals, if there is evidence of scoring then the crankshaft will have to be reground. If the bearing surfaces are in good condition, always take the opportunity of renewing the bearing shells (photo).

2   Using a micrometer, check the journals for ovality by measuring the journal diameter at several different points. If the journal is oval or worn in excess of 0.003 in (0.8 mm), again the crankshaft will have to be reground.

3   Provided the original crankshaft is suitable for reconditioning, it can be exchanged for a factory reconditioned one at a Leyland agent. Undersize bearings are available in steps of 0.010 in (0.25 mm), 0.020 in (0.51 mm), 0.030 in (0.76 mm) and 0.040 in (1.02 mm). If the crankshaft has already been exchanged for one with undersize main bearings, the undersize will usually be found stamped on the crankshaft webs (Fig. 1.16).

4   If the original crankshaft is re-ground at an engineering works then the undersize bearings will be supplied to be compatible with the reground diameter of the main bearing journals.

5   Examine the pilot bush which is installed in the flywheel mounting

24.1 Typical scored crankshaft journal

H.5660

Fig. 1.16. Location of crankshaft regrind undersize (Sec. 24)

flange at the rear end of the crankshaft. If it is worn, it must be renewed. To do this, either tap a thread into it and screw in a bolt to extract the bush or fill the bush with grease and drive in a close fitting mandrel. The hydraulic pressure created by the latter method will eject the bush. The new bush should be soaked in engine oil for 24 hours before pressing it into position.

6 To ensure that the crankshaft oil passages are clear, remove the socket screws from the crankshaft webs and clean out the passages with wire or compressed air.

7 Refit the screws and stake them securely in position.
8 The thrust washers which fit either side of the centre main bearing should normally be renewed at the time of major overhaul. However, when the crankshaft is installed, its endfloat must be checked, as described in Section 41, and new thrust washers of different thicknesses may be required to bring the endfloat within the specified tolerance.

25 Big-end bearings and connecting rods - examination and renovation

1 Examine and check the crankshaft crankpins in a similar manner to that described for the journals in the preceding Section.
2 If the crankshaft is renewed on an exchange basis or if it is reground, then undersize big-end shell bearings will be supplied.
3 If the crankpins are in good condition, take the opportunity of renewing the big-end bearing shells in any event.
4 Any wear in the connecting rod small end bush can be overcome by pressing out the worn bush and pressing in a new one but as the bush will then have to be reamed to the specified diameter this is a job best left to your dealer.
5 Should a connecting rod have to be renewed because of damage or distortion, make sure that its weight does not vary by more than 3.5 grammes when compared with the other rods.
6 It is recommended that new big-end bolts and nuts are used on reassembly.

26 Crankshaft pulley and damper - examination and renovation

1 Check that the rubber of the damper has not deteriorated; if it has, renew the damper.
2 The drivebelt should not bottom in the Vee of the pulley; if it does, try renewing the belt but if this new belt still bottoms, then the pulley will have to be renewed as well.

27 Cylinder bores - examination and renovation

1 The cylinder bores must be examined for taper, ovality, scoring and scratches. Start by carefully examining the top of the cylinder bores. If they are at all worn a very slight ridge will be found on the thrust side. This marks the top of the piston ring travel. The owner will have a good indication of the bore wear prior to dismantling the engine, or removing the cylinder head. Excessive oil consumption accompanied by blue smoke from the exhaust is a sure sign of worn cylinder bores and piston rings.

2 Measure the bore diameter just under the ridge with a micrometer and compare it with the diameter at the bottom of the bore, which is not subject to wear. If the difference between the two measurements is more than 0.006 in (0.15 mm) then it will be necessary to fit special pistons and rings or to have the cylinders rebored and fit oversize pistons. If no micrometer is available remove the rings from a piston and place the piston in each bore in turn about 1 in (25.4 mm) below the top of the bore. If an 0.0012 in (0.0254 mm) feeler gauge slid between the piston and the cylinder wall requires more than a pull of between 1.1 and 3.3 lbs (0.5 and 1.5 kg) to withdraw it, using a spring balance then remedial action must be taken. Oversize pistons are available as listed in Specifications.

3 These are accurately machined to just below the indicated measurements so as to provide correct running clearances in bores bored out to the exact oversize dimensions.
4 If the bores are slightly worn but not so badly worn as to justify reboring them, then special oil control rings and pistons can be fitted which will restore compression and stop the engine burning oil. Several different types are available and the manufacturer's instructions concerning their fitting must be followed closely.
5 If new pistons are being fitted and the bores have not been reground, it is essential to slightly roughen the hard glaze on the sides of the bores with fine glass paper so the new piston rings will have a chance to bed in properly.
6 Reboring beyond 0.030 in (0.76 mm) should not be carried out and when this stage is reached, the only remedy is to have liners fitted with standard pistons.
7 Series 2 engines are originally fitted with dry liners and these will have to be pressed out so that they emerge from the top of the block and new ones fitted.

28 Pistons, piston rings and gudgeon pins - examination and renovation

1 The method of removing the gudgeon pin and piston rings has already been described in Section 16.

2 Clean carbon from the head of the piston using worn emery cloth and paraffin. Do not use a scraper or any tool that may score the head.

3 Do not use an abrasive to clean the outside of the piston despite the discolouration that may be present; a wipe with a cloth and paraffin will suffice.

4 Examine the lands for burrs as these may prevent freedom of movement of the ring, rectify as necessary using fine emery cloth.

5 Clean all dirt out of the grooves especially in the corners. A broken piston ring is a handy tool for this job but be careful not to dig in or remove metal.

6 Examine the skirt for fractures at the extremity of the split.

7 When a new piston ring is brought into use its gap, when sprung out in the cylinder bore, must be measured and adjusted as necessary. If the gap is too small seizure will result when the ring expands, if the gap is too great compression pressure will be lost.

8 Push the new ring down the bore as far as possible using a piston; this will ensure that the ring is square in the bore.

9 Measure the piston ring end-gap which should be in accordance with the tolerance listed in Specifications for the appropriate ring and engine type.

10 Repeat the check on each ring in turn in its respective bore.

11 Check the ring to groove clearance again using a feeler gauge. The clearance should be as specified. If the ring is tight, it can be eased by rubbing it on a sheet of emery cloth held on a piece of plate glass. If the ring is excessively tight then the groove will have to be machined out.

12 Check the gudgeon pin for wear in the piston and the connecting rod small end bush. Any slackness can only be overcome by renewal of the components concerned.

29 Flywheel and starter ring gear - examination and renovation

1 If the starter ring gear is worn or the teeth are chipped, then the flywheel should be renewed complete.

2 If the surface of the flywheel is badly scored or small cracks are visible, it should be renewed; machining or surface grinding is not recommended (photo).

3 The flywheel and clutch are balanced and if a new flywheel is fitted, then before installation, have the components re-balanced by your Jaguar dealer.

4 *On cars equipped with automatic transmission,* examine the bolt holes of the driveplate for cracks and the starter ring gear for wear. If these conditions are evident, renew the driveplate complete.

30 Camshaft and camshaft bearings - examination and renovation

1 The camshafts and bearings normally give a very long life but there are always exceptions to the rule. The photograph shows a camshaft which has failed due to a breakdown in the surface hardening of the cam lobe; it is estimated that the engine from which this shaft was removed had done well over 100,000 miles (160,000 km). This type of fault is not so common as general wear on the lobes, this point can be checked by making a comparison with a new shaft although a good estimate of their condition can be obtained by comparing one lobe with another and with those on the other camshaft (photo).

2 Scoring on the bearing surfaces is a more likely fault to be found. It may be possible to remove slight score marks by gently rubbing down with fine emery cloth or an oilstone but this must not be overdone as undersize bearings are not supplied. Therefore, if the scoring cannot be rectified, or if wear on the lobes is found, the shaft should be scrapped.

3 Examine the shell bearings for scoring, pitting and general signs of wear. It is advisable to fit new bearings if there is any doubt as to their condition.

31 Valves and seats - examination and renovation

1 Examine the heads of the valves for pitting and burning, especially the exhaust valves.

2 If the valves appear serviceable re-use after grinding to their seats in the cylinder head, scrape all the carbon away and carefully clean the stem of the valve. Clean the valve guide in the cylinder head and fit the valve to its guide.

3 With the valve about threequarters of its way in the guide, check it for sideways movement. If the movement appears to be excessive, remove the valve and measure the diameter of the stem, this should be not less than specified. If the stem diameter is satisfactory it means that the valve guide is worn and remedial action as indicated in Section 33 will have to be taken.

4 If no wear is present, check the valve stem for distortion by moving the valve up and down in its guide and at the same time rotating it, no restriction to movement should be felt.

5 Grinding the valves to their seats is easily carried out. First place the cylinder head upside down on the bench resting on a block of wood at each end to give clearance for the valve stems.

6 Smear a trace of coarse carburundum (photo) on the seat face and apply a suction grinding tool to the head of the valve. With a semi-rotary action, grind the valve to its seat (photo), lifting the valve occasionally to re-distribute the paste. When a continuous ring of dull matt even finish is produced on both the valve seat and the valve, then wipe off the coarse paste and repeat the process with a fine paste, lifting and turning the valve as before. A light spring placed under the head of the valve will assist in the lifting operation. When a smooth unbroken ring of light grey matt is produced on both valve and valve seat faces, the grinding operation is complete. Be very careful during the grinding operation not to get the abrasive paste on the stem of the valve, do not handle the valve stem once you have started to use the paste because it will be transferred from the fingers to the stem and the result will be rapid wear of the valve guide. Trouble is often experienced with the suction tool not gripping the valve head, this can be overcome if the valve head and the tool are kept free of oil and grease at all times

7 When grinding is completed, thoroughly clean the cylinder head to remove any trace of carburundum as this can cause a lot of damage

Fig. 1.17. Checking piston ring end-gap (Sec. 28)

29.2 Typical scored flywheel

30.1 Typical pitted camshaft lobe

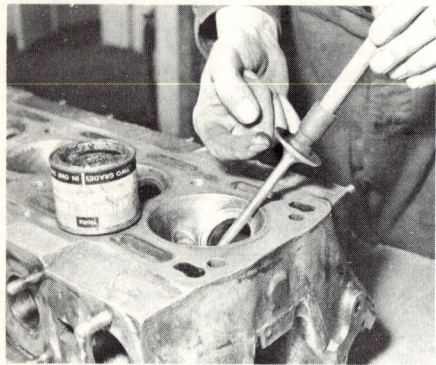

31.6A Applying grinding paste to a valve

31.6B Grinding in a valve

INLET   EXHAUST

Fig. 1.18. Valve guide fitting diagram (Sec. 33)

after first start up of the engine.
8 If a valve seat is too badly burned to be renovated by grinding, it should be re-cut or renewed by your Jaguar dealer.

32 Valve springs - examination and renewal

1 The valve springs should be renewed as a matter of course if they have been in use for 25,000 miles (40,000 km) or more.
2 If they have been in use for a shorter period, check their free lengths against Specification. If they have been compressed excessively when compared with a new spring, renew them.

33 Valve guides - renewal

1 The valve guides are of cast-iron construction differing in length between inlet and exhaust types. The guides are secured by circlips and those for the inlet valves incorporate valve stem oil seals.
2 If the guides are found to be worn as a result of testing, as described in Section 31, renew them in the following way.
3 Immerse the cylinder head in boiling water for thirty minutes and then using a suitable drift drive out the old guide from the combustion chamber end of the head.
4 The old valve guide must now be examined to establish its size which represents external diameter.
  No external groove - 0.501 to 0.502 in (12.70 to 12.725 mm)
  One external groove - 0.503 to 0.504 in (12.776 to 12.801 mm)
  Two external grooves - 0.506 to 0.507 in (12.852 to 12.877 mm)
  Three external grooves - 0.511 to 0.512 in (12.979 to 13.005 mm)
The new valve guide should be an oversize. Where the original guide did not have a groove, install a new guide with one groove. If the old guide had one groove, install a new guide with two grooves and if it had two grooves previously, install a new guide with three grooves. When installing a new guide which has one groove, no reaming will be necessary. If installing a new valve guide with two grooves which previously had one groove, ream the cylinder head to 0.505 in (12.83 mm) diameter to accept (interference fit) the new valve guide. If installing a new guide with three grooves which previously had two grooves, ream the cylinder head to 0.510 in (12.95 mm) to accept (interference fit) the new valve guide.
5 To fit the new guide, keep the cylinder head at high temperature in boiling water and then smear the guide with graphite grease and drive in the guide from the top face of the cylinder head until the guide circlip registers.

34 Tappets and shims - examination and renovation

1 Examine the bearing surface of the tappet on which the camshaft bears. Any indentation on this surface or any cracks indicate serious wear and the tappet must be renewed.
2 It is unlikely that the sides of the tappet will be worn, but if the tappet can be rocked in its guide in the cylinder head it should be established by measurement which item is at fault; details of dimensions are given under Specifications at the beginning of this

Chapter.
3 The tappet should also be checked to see that it moves freely in its guide, the most likely cause of restriction is dirt but rectify as necessary.
4 Clean and examine the valve adjusting shims. After a considerable mileage the valve stem will probably have made an indentation on its face. In this case the shim should be renewed but where the valves have been ground in, shims of alternative thickness will probably be required (refer to Section 48).

35 Timing gear and chains - examination and renovation

1 Clean the sprockets and chains in a paraffin bath and dry them on a non-fluffy rag.
2 Examine the teeth of the sprockets for wear. Each tooth forms an inverted 'V' with the periphery of the sprocket and, if worn, the side of the tooth under tension will be slightly concave in shape when compared with the other side of the tooth. If any wear is present the sprocket should be renewed.
3 Examine the links of the chain for side slackness and renew the chain if any slackness is noticeable when compared to a new chain. It is sensible to replace the chain if the engine is stripped for overhaul and when the cylinder head is removed for decarbonisation or some other purpose, if it is known that the chain has been in use for a considerable time.
4 The chain tension slipper and the rubbing surfaces of the guides should be examined for grooves or deterioration and renewed, if necessary.

36 Cylinder head - decarbonising and examination

1 With the cylinder head removed, use a blunt scraper to remove all trace of carbon and deposits from the combustion spaces and ports. Remember that the cylinder head is aluminium alloy and can be damaged easily during the decarbonising operations. Scrape the cylinder head free from scale or old pieces of gasket or jointing compound. Clean the cylinder head by washing it in paraffin and take particular care to pull a piece of rag through the ports and cylinder head bolt holes. Any dirt remaining in these recesses may well drop onto the gasket or cylinder block mating surface as the cylinder head is lowered into position and could lead to a gasket leak after reassembly is complete.
2 With the cylinder head clean, test for distortion if a history of coolant leakage has been apparent. Carry out this test using a straight edge and feeler gauges or a piece of plate glass. If the surface shows any warping in excess of 0.039 in (0.1015 mm) then the cylinder head will have to be resurfaced which is a job for a specialist engineering company.
3 Clean the pistons and top of the cylinder bores. If the pistons are still in the block then it is essential that great care is taken to ensure that no carbon gets into the cylinder bores as this could scratch the cylinder walls or cause damage to the piston and rings. To ensure this does not happen, first turn the crankshaft so that two of the pistons are at the top of their bores. Stuff rag into the other four bores or seal them off with paper and masking tape to prevent particles of carbon entering the cooling system and damaging the water pump.
4 Rotate the crankshaft and repeat the carbon removal operations

on the remaining pistons and cylinder bores.
5   Thoroughly clean all particles of carbon from the bores and then inject a little light oil round the edges of the pistons to lubricate the piston rings.

37 Oil pump - examination and renovation

1   With the oil pump removed, as described in Section 14, remove the bottom cover (four bolts) from the pump body.
2   Withdraw the rotors from the pump body but do not attempt to separate the inner rotor from the driveshaft.
3   If the rotors or body show signs of scoring or wear it will probably be best to renew the oil pump complete. The need for individual replacement parts can be determined by checking for wear in the following manner.
4   Using a feeler blade, check the clearance between the inner and outer rotors. This should not exceed 0.006 in (0.15 mm).
5   Check the clearance between the outer rotor and the oil pump body. This should not exceed 0.010 in (0.25 mm).
6   Check the rotor endfloat by measuring the gap between the rotor endfaces and a straight-edge placed across the body.
7   Reassembly is a reversal of dismantling.

38 Oil seals - renewal

1   At time of major overhaul always renew engine oil seals even if they appear in good condition.
2   Renew the crankshaft front and rear oil seals and the 'O' rings on the oil pump suction and return pipes.

39 Engine - preparation for reassembly

1   To ensure maximum life with reliability from a rebuilt engine, not only must everything be correctly assembled but all components must be spotlessly clean and the correct spring or plain washers used where originally located. Always lubricate bearing and working surfaces with clean engine oil during reassembly of engine parts.
2   Before reassembly commences, renew any bolts or studs the threads of which are damaged or corroded.
3   As well as your normal tool kit, gather together clean rags, oil can, a torque wrench and a complete (overhaul) set of gaskets and oil seals.

40 Engine reassembly sequence

1   If the engine has been complete dismantled then the following reassembly sequence is recommended:

   Crankshaft and main bearings.
   Flywheel (or driveplate - automatic transmission).
   Distributor drive.
   Piston/connecting rods.
   Timing chains and gear.
   Oil pump and sump.
   Camshaft and valve clearance adjustment.
   Cylinder head.

41 Crankshaft and main bearings - installation

1   Fit the top half of the rear oil seal cover assembly and then fit the top half of the oil seal. First prepare the new oil seal by carefully tapping it on its side face to narrow the section. Now fit the seal to the housing and press into the groove, using a hammer handle, until the seal does not protrude from the ends of the housing. **Do not** cut the ends off the seal if they do protrude but continue pressing into the groove until both ends are flush. Using a knife or similar tool, press all loose ends of asbestos into the ends of the groove so that they will not be trapped between the two halves of the housing when assembled. Fit the asbestos seal to the bottom half of the cover assembly in the same manner as described above (Fig. 1.22).
2   Clean the locations for the half main bearing shells in the crankcase and fit the half bearing shells. Lubricate the shells liberally.

Fig. 1.19. Checking oil pump rotor tip clearance (Sec. 37)

Fig. 1.20. Checking oil pump outer rotor to body clearance (Sec. 37)

Fig. 1.21. Checking oil pump rotor endfloat (Sec. 37)

Fig. 1.22. Crankshaft rear oil seal assembly (Sec. 41)

41.5 Checking crankshaft endfloat

Fig. 1.23. Crankshaft main bearing numbers (Sec. 41)

3   Lay the crankshaft in the bearing shells.
4   Fit the bottom half of the oil seal cover to the top half which was previously bolted to the cylinder block behind the rear main bearing.
5   Fit the centre main bearing cap with a new thrust washer, white metal side outwards, in the recess at each side of the cap. Tighten down on the cap and check the crankshaft endfloat (photo), this should be 0.004 in to 0.006 in (0.10 to 0.15 mm). The thrust washers are supplied in two thicknesses, standard and 0.004 in (0.10 mm) oversize and should be selected to bring the endfloat within permissible limits. There is no objection to the use of a standard and an oversize washer on the same shaft. The oversize washers are stamped +0.004 (0.010) on the steel face.
6   Fit the main bearing caps and shells to the crankshaft. But do make sure that the numbers stamped on the caps correspond with those stamped on the crankcase.
7   Fit the main bearing cap bolts and tab washers and tighten down to specified torque. The tab washers for the rear main bearing bolts are longer than the remainder and the plain ends should be tapped down round the bolt hole bosses.
8   Test the crankshaft for freedom of rotation. If there is no undue restriction to movement of the crankshaft, knock up the tab washers to secure the bolts.

42 Flywheel (or driveplate - auto. transmission) - refitting

1   Install the flywheel to the crankshaft mounting flange so that the alignment marks are correctly mated.
2   Fit a new lockplate and screw in the bolts and tighten to the specified torque.

43 Distributor drive - refitting

1   If the drive gear on the front of the crankshaft was removed, drive it into position using a suitable piece of tubing so that the thicker boss is to the rear.
2   Install the distributor driveshaft, gear and thrust washer and then drive the distributor driveshaft downwards into the driven gear.
3   Refit the nut, special washer and lockplate, tighten the nut fully and then bend up the tab of the lockplate.

44 Piston/connecting rod - installation

1   If the piston was removed from the connecting rod by pushing out the gudgeon pin, reassemble the piston to the connecting rod so that with the word 'FRONT' on the piston crown towards the crankshaft pulley, the mating numbers on the connecting rod and cap will be in alignment and on the left-hand side when looking towards the crankshaft pulley from the rear of the engine. Fit new circlips to the ends of the gudgeon pin.
2   The piston ring gaps will have been checked as described in Section 28, now fit them to the pistons. The top and second compression rings are tapered and must be fitted so that the word 'TOP' is uppermost. Do not remove any red coating from these rings.
3   The oil control ring is of three section type incorporating two rails and an expander. The assembly is usually supplied, held together with adhesive for ease of installation. Make sure that the expander has its ends butted together when installed and not overlapping.
4   Wipe the cylinder bores clean with a non-fluffy rag, and then liberally lubricate the walls of each.
5   The pistons, complete with connecting rods must be fitted to their respective bores, from the top of the cylinder block. As each piston is inserted in the bore, make sure that it is the correct assembly for that bore by checking the number stamped on the connecting rod (no. 1 cylinder is at the rear of the engine).
6   Ensure that the pistons are the correct way round in the cylinder, the piston crown is marked 'Front' to aid correct assembly.
7   Check that the piston ring gaps are not in alignment to cause gas blow-by.
8   Compress the piston rings in a clamp. Guide the piston into the bore until it reaches the ring compressor. Gently tap the piston into the bore with a wood or hide faced hammer.
9   Do not try to fit the pistons without a ring compressor as the chance of breaking a ring and scoring the bore is very high.

10 Wipe the connecting rod half of the big-end bearing location and the underside of the shell bearing clean. Fit the shell bearing in position with its locating tongue engaged with the corresponding groove in the connecting rod.

11 Wipe clean and then generously lubricate the crankpin journals with engine oil. Turn the crankshaft to a handy position for the connecting rod to be drawn onto it and for the connecting rod cap to be fitted.

12 Fit the bearing shell to the connecting rod cap in the same manner as with the connecting rod itself.

13 Generously lubricate the shell bearing and offer up the cap to the connecting rod, ensure that the numbers are mating.

14 Fit the connecting rod bolts (it is advisable to use new bolts), fit the nuts and tighten down to the specified torque.

45 Timing gear - reassembly and installation

1 To the front of the crankshaft fit the sprocket with Woodruff key, the oil thrower and distance piece (photo).

2 Fit the eccentric shaft to the hole in the front mounting bracket.

3 Insert the spring and locking plunger for the serrated plate to the hole in the front mounting bracket.

4 Fit the serrated plate and secure it with the lockwasher and nut.

5 Fit the idler sprocket (21 teeth) to the eccentric shaft.

6 Fit the intermediate sprocket assembly (20 to 28 teeth) to their shaft so that the larger sprocket is to the front of the engine, then press the shaft through the lower central hole in the rear mounting bracket and locate the tension pin of the shaft in the groove which is machined in the rear bracket. Secure the assembly by fitting the circlip at the rear of the bracket.

7 Fit the upper timing chain (the longer one) to the small intermediate sprocket and the lower chain (the shorter one) to the larger of the two intermediate sprockets.

8 Loop the upper timing chain under the idler sprocket and assemble the front mounting bracket to the rear bracket with the two chain dampers and distance pieces interposed between them.

9 Position the lugs of the top timing chain retainer on the front mounting bracket and pass the four securing bolts through the retainer lugs, the dampers and the distance pieces.

10 Secure the two mounting brackets together with the four studs and nuts.

11 Engage the lower chain with the crankshaft sprocket and attach the timing gear to the cylinder block with four bolts.

12 Engage the upper chain with the camshaft sprockets.

13 Bolt the lower chain damper to the cylinder block.

14 Insert the conical shaped filter into the oil feed hole in the cylinder block. Install shims, as necessary, between the backing plate of the chain tensioner and the cylinder block so that the timing chain runs in the centre of the tensioner slipper. Install the tensioner and bolt it into position and bend up the tabs of the lockplate.

15 Insert the Allen key into the chain tensioner and turn the key clockwise until the slipper moves forward against the chain. Install the plug to the hole in the tensioner body and secure with the tabwasher.

16 The intermediate damper (A) should now be adjusted within the limit of travel of its elongated holes until the slipper of the chain tensioner projects 1/8 in (3.2 mm) (B) from its body. If a badly worn or stretched chain is being refitted then it will not be possible to achieve this projection but a greater figure will have to be accepted. Set damper (C) in light contact with chain (Fig. 1.24).

17 With a new seal in position, refit the timing cover using gasket cement on the joint faces.

18 Refit the crankshaft damper assembly by reversing the removal operations (Section 17).

46 Oil pump and sump - refitting

1 Fit the coupling shaft between the squared end of the distributor drive shaft and the driving gear of the pump.

2 Secure the oil pump to the front main bearing cap by the three dowel bolts and tab washers. Check that there is appreciable endfloat of the short coupling shaft.

3 Fit the oil delivery pipe from the oil pump to the bottom face of the crankcase with a new 'O' ring and gasket.

4 Fit the suction pipe with a new 'O' ring at the oil pump end and secure to its clip on the main bracket cap.

45.1 Refitting crankshaft sprocket

Fig. 1.24. Timing chain tensioning diagram (Sec. 45)

5 The oil sump may be refitted at this stage or, if it desired to use the base of the cylinder block on which to rest the engine for further assembly work, it may be left until later. However, to refit the sump:

6 Clean the mating faces of the sump and the crankcase. Although not really necessary, they may be treated with jointing compound if desired.

7 Fit a new sump gasket to the bottom face of the crankcase.

8 Fit the oil seal to the recess in the rear main bearing cap.

9 Fit the sump to the crankcase and secure with the twenty-six set screws and the four nuts and washers. Remember that the short set screw goes at the right-hand front corner of the sump.

10 Fit the sump strainer in position using new gaskets.

47 Cylinder head - reassembly and refitting

1   With the cylinder head standing on the bench, oil the first two valve stems and then insert the valves into their guide making sure that each valve is returned to its original location, or if new valves have been fitted, to the seats into which they have been ground.

2   Install a small wooden block into the combustion chamber so that when the cylinder head is placed face down on the bench, the two valves will not drop out.

3   When looking down on the head from the crankshaft pulley and the inlet valves are on the left and the exhaust valves are on the right. Remember that oil seals must be fitted to the inlet valve stems.

4   To the first valve fit the valve spring seat, the double valve springs (close coils nearer cylinder head) and the valve spring collar. Compress the valve springs, using either a conventional compressor or a tube made up to a design similar to the one shown with a cut-out for inserting the split collets (photo).

5   Insert the split collets, retaining them in position if required, with a dab of thick grease. Release the compressor.

6   Repeat the operations on the remaining 11 valves.

7   Install the shim and tappet to each valve. If the valves have been ground in or new valves have been installed, the valve clearances must be checked and adjusted, as described in Section 48.

48 Camshaft installation and valve clearance adjustment

1   Clean the location in the cylinder head for the camshaft bearing shells. Fit the half bearing shells to the head.

2   Clean the bearing location in the camshaft bearing caps and fit the half shell bearings.

3   Fit one camshaft to the cylinder head making sure that the correct shaft is being offered to the correct set of valves. Check the numbers on the caps to that shaft and the corresponding numbers on the cylinder head and fit the caps in their correct position. Fit the nuts and 'D' washers to the bearing studs (photo).

4   Tighten down on the nuts to a torque of 9 lb/ft (12 Nm).

5   Rotate the camshaft to bring the back of a cam to the valve tappet. Measure, and record, the clearance between the cam and the tappet. Repeat for all the valves in that bank. The clearances should be between 0.012 and 0.014 in (0.304 and 0.355 mm) for all valves (photo).

6   Adjusting pads are available rising in 0.001 in (0.03 mm) sizes from 0.85 in to 0.110 in (2.16 to 2.79 mm) and are etched on the surface with the letter 'A' to 'Z', each letter indicating an increase in size of 0.001 in (0.03 mm).

7   Should any valve clearance require adjustment, remove the camshaft, the tappet and adjusting pad.

8   Observe the letter stamped on the adjusting pad and should the recorded clearance for this valve have shown, say, 0.002 in (0.05 mm) in excess of the correct value, select a new adjusting pad bearing a letter two lower than the original pad.

9   After all the adjusting pads have been changed as may be required, reassemble the camshaft and carry out a final check to ensure that the clearances are indeed correct. Remove the camshaft or slacken all the nuts to relieve all pressure on the valves.

When checking the valve clearances the camshafts must be fitted one at a time as, if one camshaft is rotated when the other shaft is in position, fouling is likely to take place between the inlet and exhaust valves. When checking of the clearances of one set of valves is completed, the shaft must either be removed or the bearing cap bolts must be slackened to the extent of relieving all pressure on the valves.

10 Repeat the foregoing to check the valve clearances for the other set of valves. When satisfied that the clearances are correct, check the security of the nuts and turn the camshaft so that the square slot in the shaft at the rear of the front bearing is at 90° to the camshaft cover face.

11 Fit the other camshaft and position it so that its slot is also at 90° to the camshaft cover face. Fit the nuts to the studs and tighten them down to a torque of 9 lb/ft (12 Nm).

12 From now on, the camshafts must not be rotated independently of each other, otherwise the valves may impinge on each other and bend.

49 Cylinder head - installation

1   Turn the crankshaft so that no. 6 piston (the one nearest the crankshaft pulley) is at TDC. This can be ascertained by checking that the 'O' mark on the crankshaft damper is opposite the pointer on the crankcase.

2   Make sure that the mating surfaces of cylinder head and block are absolutely clean and position a new gasket on the cylinder block so that the word 'TOP' on the gasket is visible.

3   On no account move the camshafts from their previously set position (see Section 48).

4   Lower the cylinder head carefully into position complete with inlet manifold assembly.

5   Fit the spark plug lead carrier to some of the studs on the right-hand side and the 'D' washers to the remaining ones.

6   Tighten the cylinder head dome nuts, half a turn each at a time to the specified torques in the sequence shown in Fig. 1.26. Tighten the six nuts at the front of the cylinder head.

7   If the cylinder head was removed while the engine was still in the car, reverse all the operations described in paragraphs 1 to 21, of Section 11.

50 Valve timing

1   Check that no. 6 piston is at TDC ('O' mark on crankshaft damper opposite pointer on crankcase).

2   Check that the notches in the camshaft sprocket flanges are at 90° to a line touching the two rocker cover mating surfaces. A gauge can be made up as shown in Fig. 1.28 to set the camshaft position.

3   Withdraw the circlips which retain the adjusting plates to the camshaft sprockets. Pull the adjusting plates forward until the serrations disengage.

4   Fit the sprockets to the camshaft flanges and then align the bolt holes. If these holes are not in exact alignment, turn the adjuster plates through 180° On no account attempt to force a bolt in otherwise the camshaft position will be altered.

5   Fit the circlips to the sprocket and insert one bolt into its hole in

47.4 Refitting split cotters after compressing valve spring with tubular tool

48.3 Fitting a camshaft 'D' washer

48.5 Checking a valve clearance

each of the adjuster plates. Turn the crankshaft until the two other bolt holes are accessible and insert the two remaining bolts.

6 Now tension the timing chain by pressing the stop peg (plunger) inwards and rotating the serrated plate anticlockwise. A special tool will be needed to carry out this operation (tool no. JD 2B) or one can be made up to the dimensions shown in Fig. 1.29 (photo).

Fig. 1.25. Camshaft alignment (Sec. 48)

7 When correctly tensioned, there should be slight flexibility of the chain below the camshaft sprockets. The chain must not be absolutely taut. Release the locking plunger and securely tighten the locknut on the idler shaft.

8 Turn the engine until the 'O' mark on the crankshaft damper is again opposite the pointer and use the gauge to check the setting of both camshafts. If all is correct, lock the camshaft sprocket bolts head with new wire (Fig. 1.30).

9 Use new gaskets and refit the camshaft covers.

10 Refit the breather housing to the front of the cylinder head.

11 Refit the water pump (Chapter 2).

51 Engine ancillaries - refitting

1 Refit the alternator and drivebelt (Chapter 10).

2 Refit the clutch having centralised it, as described in Chapter 5.

3 Refit the distributor as described in Chapter 4.

4 Refit the starter motor (Chapter 10).

52 Engine to transmission - reconnection

1 This is a reversal of operations described in Sections 7 or 8.

2 Where the car is equipped with automatic transmission, make sure

Fig. 1.26. Cylinder head nut tightening sequence (Sec. 49)

Fig. 1.27. Ignition timing marks on crankshaft damper (Sec. 50)

Fig. 1.28. Camshaft setting gauge (Sec. 50)

50.6 Tool for tensioning upper timing chain

Fig. 1.29. Timing chain adjusting tool diagram (Sec. 50)

that the torque converter is fully engaged with the tangs of the oil pump before offering up the transmission to the engine.

53 Engine/transmission - installation

1   Refer to Section 5 or 6, and reverse the removal operations.

Fig. 1.30. Camshaft sprocket showing bolts locked with wire (Sec. 50)

2   Make sure that wires and controls are well out of the way before the engine/transmission is lowered into position.
3   With the engine installed, check that all drain plugs have been refitted and tightened and that the oil filter has been renewed and that drivebelts have been correctly adjusted.
4   Refill the cooling system (with antifreeze mixture), the engine sump and check and top-up the transmission oil level.

54 Initial start-up after major overhaul

1   Refer to Chapter 3 and follow the instructions for initial setting of the carburettors, and follow the instructions in Chapter 4 for timing of the ignition.
2   Make sure that the battery is fully charged and that all lubricants and fuels are replenished.
3   Switch on the ignition and allow the petrol pump time to fill the carburettor float chambers.
4   Start the engine, as soon as it fires and runs, keep it going at a fast tickover only (no faster). Watch the oil pressure gauge, after a very short wait, whilst the oil filter is being filled, it should register around 40 lbs per sq. in. If, after about 30 seconds, no oil pressure is registered, switch off the engine and investigate the cause; it may be that you have not fully tightened a union or the filter canister is not correctly seated on the rubber sealing ring in the head of the filter.
5   Bring the engine up to its normal working temperature, as it warms up there will be odd smells and some smoke from parts getting hot and burning off oil deposits. Look round carefully for water and oil leaks.
6   When the engine running temperature has been reached adjust the carburettors as described in Chapter 3.
7   Stop the engine and wait a few minutes to see if there are any water or oil leaks.
8   Before road testing the car it is advisable to have an assistant listening to the brake servo, run the engine for a few minutes and then operate the foot brake. If the brake servo connections are satisfactory the exhaust from the servo will be plainly heard.
9   Road test the car to check that the timing is correct and is giving the necessary smoothness and power. Do not race the engine. If new bearings or pistons or rings have been fitted, it should be treated as a new engine and run in at reduced revolutions for the first 500 miles (800 km).

55 Fault diagnosis - engine

Symptom	Reason/s
Engine fails to turn over when starter switch operated	Flat or defective battery. Loose battery leads. Defective starter solenoid or switch or broken wiring. Engine earth strap disconnected. Defective starter motor.
Engine turns over but will not start	Ignition system damp or wet. Ignition leads to spark plugs loose. Shorted or disconnected low tension leads. Dirty, incorrectly set, or pitted contact breaker points. Faulty condenser. Defective ignition switch. Ignition leads connected wrong way round. Faulty coil. Contact breaker point spring earthed or broken. No petrol in petrol tank. Vapour lock in fuel line (in hot conditions or at high altitude). Blocked float chamber needle valve. Fuel pump filter blocked. Faulty fuel pump. Too much choke allowing too rich a mixture to wet plugs. Float damaged or leaking or needle not seating. Float lever incorrectly adjusted.
Engine stalls and will not start	Ignition failure - sudden. Ignition failure - misfiring precludes total stoppage. Ignition failure - in severe rain or after traversing water splash No petrol in petrol tank. Petrol tank breather choked. Sudden obstruction in carburettor(s). Water in fuel system. Ignition leads loose. Battery leads loose on terminals. Battery earth strap loose on body of attachment point.
Engine misfires or idles unevenly	Engine earth lead loose. Low tension leads to SW and CB terminals on coil loose. Low tension lead from CB terminal side to distributor loose. Dirty, or incorrectly gapped plugs. Dirty, incorrectly set, or pitted contact breaker points. Tracking across inside of distributor cover. Ignition too retarded. Faulty coil. Mixture too weak. Air leak in carburettor. Air leak at inlet manifold to cylinder. Incorrect valve clearances. Burnt out exhaust valves. Sticking or leaking valves. Weak or broken valve springs. Worn valve guides or stems. Worn pistons and piston rings.
Lack of power and poor compression	Burnt out exhaust valves. Sticking or leaking valves. Worn valve guides and stems. Weak or broken valve springs. Blown cylinder head gasket (accompanied by increase in noise). Worn pistons and piston rings. Worn or scored cylinder bores. Ignition timing wrongly set. Too advanced or retarded. Contact breaker points incorrectly gapped. Incorrect valve clearances. Incorrectly set spark plugs. Carburation too rich or too weak. Dirty contact breaker points. Fuel filters blocked causing fuel starvation. Distributor automatic balance weights or vacuum advance and retard mechanisms not functioning correctly. Faulty fuel pump giving top end fuel starvation.

Symptom	Reason/s
Excessive oil consumption	Badly worn, perished or missing inlet valve stem oil seals.
	Excessively worn valve stems and valve guides.
	Worn piston rings.
	Worn pistons and cylinder bores.
	Excessive piston ring gap allowing blow-up.
	Piston oil return holes choked.
	Leaking oil filter gasket.
	Leaking camshaft cover gasket.
	Leaking timing case gasket.
	Leaking sump gasket.
	Loose sump plug.
Unusual noises from engine	Worn valve gear (noisy tapping from top cover).
	Worn big-end bearing (regular heavy knocking).
	Worn main bearings.
	Worn camshaft chains.

Chapter 2 Cooling system

Contents

Specifications

System	Thermo-syphon with radiator and water pump. Belt driven fan with fluid coupling
Fan	12 blades
Fluid coupling slip commences	1500 to 1900 rev/min
Pressure cap rating	13 lb/sq in (0.9140 kg/sq cm)

Thermostat

Standard	Opens 159°F (70.5°C); Fully open 165°F (74°C)
Special (extreme cold)	Opens 174°F (78.8°C); Fully open 179°F (82°C)

Coolant capacity

2.8 litre engine	30 Imp pints (17 litres/36 US pints)
3.4 litre engine	30 Imp Pints (17 litres/36 US pints)
4.2 litre engine	32 Imp pints (18 litres/38.5 US pints)

Torque wrench settings

	lb/ft	Nm
Radiator mounting bolts	26	36
Retainer to radiator crossmember	18	25
Expansion tank to wing valance	18	25
Fan cowl upper bracket to body	7	10

1 General description

1 The cooling system incorporates a crossflow radiator with a header tank which is pressurised and thermostatically flow controlled.
2 The header tank on smaller engined cars is mounted above the radiator matrix while on larger cars it is attached to the inlet manifold. With larger engined models, an expansion tank is mounted on the left-hand wing valance.
3 Coolant circulation is assisted by an impeller type pump driven by a belt from the crankshaft pulley.
4 The cooling fan is driven through a fluid coupling which slips at a pre-determined speed.
5 A pressure type cap is fitted to the header tank on smaller engined cars also to the expansion tank of larger models while a plain cap is fitted to the header tank of the larger engined models (Figs. 2.1 and 2.2).

2 Cooling system - draining

1 The engine cooling system is provided with two drain taps, one located in the base of the radiator block and the other positioned on the rear left-hand side of the cylinder block below the exhaust manifold. A drain plug is located in the bottom water pipe.

Fig. 2.1. Header tank filler cap on smaller capacity engines (Sec. 1)

Fig. 2.2. Expansion tank cap (A) and header tank cap (B) on larger capacity engines (Sec. 1)

Fig. 2.3. Radiator drain tap remote control rod (Sec. 2)

Fig. 2.4. Cylinder block drain tap (Sec. 2)

Fig. 2.5. Drain plug in bottom water pipe (Sec. 2)

2   Place the car on level ground.

3   If possible, wait until the engine is cold. Unscrew and remove the header tank/expansion chamber filler cap. **Remember** the system is pressurised so **do not** remove the cap whilst the engine is hot without taking precautions to prevent injury to yourself by the hot liquid which will be thrown out when the pressure is released. If any liquid containing anti-freeze mixture comes into contact with painted surfaces remove it immediately by washing with clean water otherwise the surface will be damaged.

4   Place the heater control at 'HOT'.

5   Open the radiator drain tap. It sometimes happens that this tap becomes blocked with sludge accumulated in the bottom of the radiator and it may be possible to clear the tap by poking with a piece of wire but if this is not successful, the tap will have to be removed. To do this, first disconnect the tap remote control rod by extracting the split pin from the forked end of the rod.

6   Open the cylinder block drain tap. This tap may also be blocked by scale and sludge in the cylinder block passages; if poking with wire fails to clear it, remove it by unscrewing with a spanner. Again take precautions if the engine is hot.

7   Unscrew and remove the plug from the bottom water pipe.

3   Cooling system - flushing

1   After prolonged use it is possible that the cooling system will gradually deteriorate in efficiency as the radiator becomes choked with rust scale, deposits from the water and other sediment. The symptom of deterioration is boiling of the engine or high operating temperatures which cannot be accounted for by fuel, ignition and other faults. These conditions are unlikely to arise if the coolant is renewed regularly as specified in 'Routine Maintenance.'

2   To flush the cooling system, remove the filler caps and open the radiator and cylinder block drain taps and remove the plug from the bottom water pipe. Place a cold water hose in the filler neck of the radiator header tank and let the water run until it is clear in appearance.

3   In severe cases of contamination, place the hose in the lower of the two radiator matrix hose connections and reverse flush the matrix until the water runs clear from the neck of the header tank.

4   Remove the hose, reconnect any hoses which were disconnected and close the two drain taps and refit the plug to the bottom water pipe.

4   Cooling system - filling

1   Check that all drain plugs and taps are closed.

2   Place the heater control in the 'HOT' position.

3   Pour in two or three pints of water (preferably rain water or softened water) and then pour in the specified quantity of antifreeze product. Continue to pour in more water until the coolant level reaches the filler neck of the header tank. Fit the cap to the header tank.

4   Where an expansion tank is fitted, pour in coolant (mixed in similar proportions to the main quantity of coolant) until the tank is half filled and then fit the cap.

5   Always fill the cooling system slowly and when filled, run the engine for a few minutes and then check the coolant level again when the engine has had a chance to cool down.

On cars without an expansion tank, the coolant level should be at the bottom of the header tank filler neck.

On cars with expansion tank, top-up the coolant level to half way up the expansion tank - do not remove the header tank cap.

5   Antifreeze mixture

1   Plain water should never be used in the cooling system as apart from not providing protection against adverse climatic conditions, the internal metal surfaces of the water passages will also corrode. The inhibitors found in good quality antifreeze mixtures protect iron and aluminium against corrosion for periods not exceeding twelve months.

2   In conditions where antifreeze is not required make sure that a

suitable corrosion inhibitor is used in the coolant.

3   The following table gives a guide to the proportion of antifreeze required for various levels of protection:

Antifreeze volume	Protection to
25%	$-15^{o}F$ $(-26^{o}C)$
35%	$-38^{o}F$ $(-39^{o}C)$
40%	$-42^{o}F$ $(-41^{o}C)$
50%	$-53^{o}F$ $(-47^{o}C)$

4   When carrying out routine topping-up of the cooling system, always use coolant which has been mixed in the same proportion as the original coolant.

6   Radiator - removal and installation

1   Drain the cooling system as previously described, retaining the coolant if required for further use.
2   Disconnect the coolant hoses from the radiator (photos).
3   Remove the two setscrews with their plain and lock washers which secure the top half of the fan cowl to the body upper cross panel (photo).
4   Remove the two setscrews and their washers which secure the upper cowl to the lower cowl and detach the upper cowl.
5   Remove the eight setscrews with their washers and withdraw the body upper cross panel complete with header tank.

6.2A Removing radiator upper hose clip

6.2B Releasing header tank hose clip

6.3 Removing radiator upper shroud bolt

Fig. 2.6. Radiator components (Sec. 6)

1	Matrix	6	Bottom water pipe (manual gearbox)	
2	Header tank (smaller engine)	7	Hose clip	
3	Header tank (larger engine)	8	Radiator	
4	Expansion tank (larger engine)	9	Radiator top hose	
5	Radiator hose			

10	Hose clip
11	Radiator cowl (top section)
12	Radiator cowl (bottom section)
13	Bottom water pipe (automatic transmission)
14	Upper cross panel

15	Sealing strip
16	Mounting rubber
17	Stud
18	Distance piece
19	Fibre washer
20	Drain tap
21	Tap remote control

H.5532

Fig. 2.7. Radiator upper mounting points (Sec. 6)

Fig. 2.8. Radiator lower mounting points (Sec. 6)

Fig. 2.9. Location of thermostat (Sec. 9)

Fig. 2.10. Fan/steering pump jockey pulley (Sec. 10)

6　The header tank can be detached from the panel by the removal of two setscrews.

7　Extract the split pin and withdraw the radiator drain tap remote control rod.

8　Remove the radiator lower mounting setscrews and extract the mounting rubbers.

9　If the car is equipped with air-conditioning equipment, the setscrews must be withdrawn from the condenser mounting brackets at this stage. The condenser must then be supported away from the radiator **but on no account must any pipe be disconnected within the air-conditioning system circuit.**

10　Lift the radiator matrix clear from its side mounting cradle and collect the foam insulator.

11　Installation is a reversal of removal.

7　Bottom water pipe - removal and refitting

1　The rigid section of water pipe which is located below the radiator need normally only be removed if the flexible coolant hoses are being renewed.

2　The water pipe is fitted with a drain plug and acts as a cooler for the automatic transmission fluid on cars equipped with this type of transmission.

3　To remove the pipe, drain the cooling system and disconnect the flexible hoses from the radiator.

4　On cars with automatic transmission, disconnect the fluid pipe

unions from the water pipe and plug them to prevent loss of fluid or entry of dirt.

5　Installation is a reversal of removal but with automatic transmission, check the fluid level in the transmission after the car has been driven a few miles and top-up as necessary.

8　Radiator - inspection and cleaning

1　Examine the top and bottom tanks for damage and leaking especially at the seams. Any leaks or possible weakness can be repaired with a proprietary compound. The application of heat to the radiator, soldering for instance, is not recommended for the home enthusiast as this may result in breaking other soldered seams.

2　Examine the core for damage and corrosion. It may be possible to repair leaks from physical damage temporarily but if leaks are present due to corrosion it is best to renew the radiator as any repair that is made will only effect a temporary remedy. A replacement radiator can be obtained from your Jaguar agent on an exchange basis.

3　When the radiator is out of the car it is advantageous to reverse flush it in the manner described in Section 3. Clean the outside of the radiator by hosing down the matrix with a strong jet of water to clean away road dirt, dead flies etc.

4　Inspect the radiator hoses for cracks, internal and external perishing and cuts on the exterior from the hose clips. Change the **hose** if its condition is at all doubtful. Examine the hose clips for rust and damage and renew as necessary.

Fig. 2.11. Dismantling fan and fluid coupling (A) early cars (B) later cars (Sec. 11)

11.3 Removing fan/fluid coupling

9 Thermostat - removal, testing and refitting

1   The thermostat is located on the right-hand side at the front of the cylinder head above the steering pump.
2   To remove the thermostat first partially drain the system, approx: 8 Imp. pints (4.5 litres) will be sufficient, collect the coolant in a suitable container if it is desired to re-use it.
3   Slacken the clip securing the hose to the thermostat housing and remove the hose.
4   Remove the three nuts securing the elbow pipe to the housing and remove the pipe and gasket. The thermostat will now be visible in its housing.
5   Remove the thermostat from its housing, it is possible that it will be securely held in place by scale in which case careful levering with a small screwdriver will be necessary but do not lever on the circular valve which will be seen on the top face of the thermostat.
6   Clean the thermostat and ensure that the small hole on the valve is clear. If the valve is open it indicates that the thermostat is unserviceable and should be renewed with one of similar operating temperature, this figure will be seen on the top side of the thermostat.
7   If correct operation of the thermostat is in doubt test it by immersing it together with a 0 to 212°F (0 - 100°C) thermometer in a container of cold water. Heat the water, keeping it stirred, and observe if the operation of the valve is in close agreement to the temperature marked on the body of the thermostat. Allow the water to cool down and check that the valve closes correctly.
8   If the operation is satisfactory, the thermostat may be refitted in the reverse order to the above. A new gasket should be fitted between the elbow pipe and the thermostat housing.

10 Fan belt - removal and refitting

1   Release the bolt on the power steering pump adjustment strap and press the pump in towards the engine.
2   Press against the spring of the jockey pulley and ease the fan belt from the pulley and over the tips of the fan blades.
3   Refitting the belt is a reversal of removal.

11 Fan unit - removal and refitting

1   *On early cars,* slacken the steering pump adjustment link and disconnect the drive belt. Unscrew and remove the four nuts which secure the fan to the fluid coupling.
2   Slide the fan up the hub of the pulley to expose the four nuts which secure the fluid coupling to the pulley.
3   Withdraw the fan and fluid coupling (photo).
4   *On later cars,* remove the top section of the fan cowl then the four nuts which secure the fan to the fluid coupling. Allow the fan to rest in the cowl.
5   Remove the centre bolt and special washer from the fluid coupling and tap the coupling off the pulley spigot. Remove the coupling and the fan.

6 The fluid coupling is a sealed unit and it should be renwed if faulty, not dismantled.

7 Refitting is a reversal of removal.

12 Water pump - removal and refitting

1 Drain the cooling system by opening the radiator and cylinder block taps.

2 Remove the radiator header tank, fan, fluid coupling and the drivebelt and pulley (use an extractor for the latter).

3 Remove the power steering pump adjuster bolt.

4 If the car is equipped with air-conditioning, remove the compressor front mounting bracket.

5 Disconnect all heater hoses.

6 Remove the nuts and screws which secure the water pump to the engine front cover and withdraw the pump.

7 Clean away all traces of the old gasket.

8 Refitting is a reversal of removal but use a new gasket to which either grease or jointing compound has been applied.

13 Water pump - overhaul

1 In the event of a water pump leaking or becoming noisy in operation, undoubtedly the best way to overcome the problem is to install a new or factory reconditioned pump.

2 However, where a repair kit can be obtained, the unit can be overhauled in the following way.

3 Remove the pump and withdraw the pulley as described in the preceding Section.

4 Slacken the locknut (4) and remove the screw (3) (Fig. 2.12).

5 Press the spindle/impeller assembly from the pump. To do this, apply pressure by placing a piece of tubing against the bearing. On no account apply pressure to the end of the spindle or the bearing will be ruined.

6 The impeller must then be supported and the spindle pressed from it.

7 Remove the seal and thrower.

8 The components cannot be further dismantled and any which are worn must be renewed as assemblies.

9 Commence reassembly by installing the spindle/bearing assembly into the pump body from the rear making sure to align the hole in the bearing with the tapped hole in the pump body. Insert the lock screw and locknut.

10 Place the rubber thrower in its groove on the spindle and in front of the seal.

11 Apply jointing compound to the outside of the brass seal housing and install the seal into the recess in the pump body.

12 Support the end of the spindle and press on the impeller to its opposite end until the gap between the impeller and the body is as shown, when measured with a feeler blade (Fig. 2.13).

13 Refit the pump pulley.

14 Water temperature gauge and transmitter

1 The water temperature gauge operates on the thermal principle using a bi-metal strip surrounded by a heater winding.

2 The transmitter unit is mounted in the inlet manifold water jacket adjacent to the thermostat.

3 Failure of the gauge to register correctly may be due to a loose connection or faulty wiring insulation.

4 Testing of the gauge or transmitter cannot be undertaken without special equipment.

5 Removal of the gauge can be carried out, as described in Chapter 10.

6 If the fuel contents gauge and the water temperature gauge both become faulty at the same time, then the instrument voltage stabilizer may be the cause.

Fig. 2.12. Water pump and fan components (Sec. 13)

1	Pump body	5	Thrower	9	Copper washer	13	Fan
2	Spindle	6	Seal	10	Fan pulley	14	Fluid coupling
3	Lockscrew	7	Impeller	11	Stud	15	Belt
4	Locknut	8	Adaptor	12	Gasket		

.015 ± .003"
(.381 ± .07 mm)

Fig. 2.13. Water pump impeller clearance setting diagram (Sec. 13)

H.5539

15 Fault diagnosis - cooling system

Symptom	Reason/s
Overheating	Insufficient water in cooling system. Fan belt slipping. Radiator core blocked or radiator grille obstructed. Thermostat not opening properly. Ignition advance and retard incorrectly set (accompanied by loss of power and perhaps misfiring). Incorrect fuel/air mixture. Exhaust system partially blocked. Oil level in sump too low. Blown cylinder head gasket (water/steam being forced down the radiator overflow pipe under pressure). Engine not yet 'run-in'. Brakes binding.
Engine running 'cold'	Thermostat jammed open. Incorrect grade of thermostat fitted. Thermostat missing.
Leaks in system	Loose clips on water hoses. Top or bottom water hoses perished. Radiator leaking. Thermostat gasket leaking. Pressure cap spring worn or seal ineffective. Cylinder wall or head cracked. Core plug corroded.

Chapter 3 Carburation; fuel, exhaust and emission control systems

Contents

Specifications

| System ... ... | Dual rear mounted fuel tanks, twin electric fuel pumps and twin carburettors |

Fuel capacity (each tank)
All models except Series 2:

Except N. America	12 Imp. gals. (54.6 litres)
N. America	11 Imp. gals. (50.0 litres/13.2 US gals.)
Series 2 (each tank)	10.5 Imp. gals. (47.75 litres/12.6 US gals.)

Carburettors (application)
Except N. America:

Early cars	Twin SU HD8
Later cars	Twin SU HS8
N. America	Twin Stromberg 175 CD2SE (in conjunction with emission control system)

Carburettor specification (SU HD8)

Size	2 in (5.08 cm)
Needle	UM (4.2 litre), UVV (2.8 litre)
Jet	0.125 in (3.17 mm)
Auxiliary carburettor needle	425/8

Carburettor specification (SU HS8)

Needle *	BAW (4.2 litre); BCX (3.4 litre); BAU (2.8 litre)

Later cars with air intake temperature control BBK or BCC

Carburettor specifications (Stromberg 175 CD2SE)

Needle **	B1BT (early cars)

** *Later cars B1CG (fixed orifice EGR); B2AZ (variable orifice EGR)*

C.O. content (Stromberg carburettors with air pump delivery hose disconnected, ...   Not exceeding 4½%

Idling speeds

		lb ft	Nm
SU HD8 carburettors:			
Manual gearbox (in neutral)	700 rev/min		
Automatic transmission (in N or P)	600 rev/min		
SU HS8 carburettors:			
Manual gearbox (in neutral)	750 rev/min		
Automatic transmission (in N or P)	650 rev/min		
Stromberg 175 CD2SE carburettors:			
Manual gearbox (in neutral)	750 rev/min		
Automatic transmission (in N or P)	650 rev/min		

Torque wrench settings

	lb ft	Nm
Fuel tank drain plug:		
Large	28	39
Small	25	35
Fuel pipe banjo union bolts	25	35
Exhaust downpipes to manifold	25	35
Exhaust mounting to crossmember	18	25

1 General description

1 The fuel system incorporates two rear mounted fuel tanks, dual electrically-operated fuel pumps and twin carburettors.

2 Emission control equipment is fitted to later cars but only the most comprehensive systems are installed on cars destined for operation in North America.

3 The make and type of carburettors depends upon the date of production of the car and the type of emission control system with which it is equipped.

2 Air cleaner - renewal of element

Non-emission control type

1 Raise the toggle type clips, detach the front cover of the air cleaner and withdraw the disposable paper element (photo).

2 Wipe out the air cleaner casing and check the condition of the rubber sealing gaskets. Renew them if they are deformed or have perished.

3 If for any reason the air cleaner backplate must be removed, it can be unbolted from the carburettor flanges. Always renew the backplate gaskets before refitting.

4 Insert the new element, refit the air cleaner front cover making sure that the bottom edge of the cover engages with the lip on the backplate before locking the toggle clips.

Emission control type

5 Slacken the nut which secures the inner end of the stay to the mounting bracket (Fig. 3.2).

6 Remove the nut and bolt which secure the outer end of the stay to the mounting bracket and swing the outer end of the stay away from the air cleaner.

7 Slacken the clip and disconnect the flexible inlet pipe.

8 Slacken the clip and disconnect the air duct flexible pipe.

9 Disconnect the vacuum pipe from the vacuum capsule.

10 Release the toggle clips and withdraw the air cleaner cover.

11 Lift out and discard the filter element, wipe out the interior of the casing and refit the new element by reversing the removal operations.

12 If the air cleaner backplate must be removed for any reason, first withdraw the element as just described and then prise the gulp valve hose from the backplate. Unbolt the backplate, withdraw it from the carburettor flanges and disconnect the vacuum pipe from the thermal sensing switch.

13 Refit by reversing the removal process using new flange gaskets.

2.1 Air cleaner element

Fig. 3.1. Air cleaner (non-emission control type) (Sec. 2)

Fig. 3.2. Air cleaner (emission control type) (Sec. 2)

1   Inner end of stay
2   Outer end of stay
3   Flexible inlet pipe
4   Air duct
5   Vacuum pipe
6   Toggle clips
7   Filter element
8   Gulp valve

3   Fuel line filter (up to 1973) - renewal of element

1   On cars built up until 1973, a disposable element glass bowl type filter is located on the wing valance within the engine compartment.
2   At the specified maintenance intervals, close the fuel tap on top pf the filter by turning it fully clockwise.
3   Slacken the locknut and swing the retaining clip to one side so that the filter bowl can be removed.
4   Discard the element and wipe out the bowl (photo).
5   Check that the sealing washers are in good condition, otherwise renew them.
6   Insert the new filter element and refit the bowl and turn the fuel tap anticlockwise.

4   Fuel line filter (1973 on) - renewal of element

1   The filter is located on one side of the spare wheel recess.
2   In the interest of safety, disconnect the lead from the battery negative terminal.
3   Remove the spare wheel.
4   Fit a clamp on the fuel inlet pipe. A pair of self-locking grips will serve this purpose provided that the pipe is protected by wrapping something round it first.
5   Place a suitable container underneath the filter and then unscrew the centre bolt which retains the filter bowl.
6   Discard the filter element and wipe out the bowl and then check that the seals are in good condition.
7   Install the new element and refit the filter bowl but do not overtighten the centre bolt.
8   Remove the container and pipe clamp, reconnect the battery and start the engine and check for leaks from the filter.
9   Refit the spare wheel into its recess.

5   Carburettor fuel filters - cleaning

1   On cars with SU carburettors, a small gauze filter is located in the fuel inlet union on each of the carburettor float chambers.
2   At the specified maintenance intervals, remove the hollow bolts from the banjo unions and extract the filter and spring.
3   Clean the filter gauze using a small brush and some clean fuel and then refit by reversing the dismantling operation. Make sure that a fibre washer is located each side of the banjo union.

3.4 Fuel filter element

Fig. 3.3. Fuel line filter (up to 1973) (Sec. 3)

Fig. 3.4. Fuel line filter (1973 onwards) (Sec. 4)

3   Fuel pipe temporary clamp   7   Filter centre bolt

6.1 Location of electric fuel pumps

Fig. 3.5. S.U. fuel inlet filter (Sec. 5)

Fig. 3.6. Location of fuel pumps (Sec. 6)

6   Fuel pumps - removal and refitting

1   The dual fuel pumps are located in the spare wheel recess below the luggage compartment floor panel (photo).
2   Remove the floor panel and the spare wheel.
3   Remove the pump protective covers.
4   Either drain the fuel tank or clamp the inlet hose to prevent loss of fuel when the pump which is to be removed is disconnected.
5   Disconnect the lead from the battery negative terminal.
6   Disconnect the leads from the pump which is going to be removed.
7   Disconnect the fuel pipes and the pump mounting clamp and lift the fuel pump from its location.
8   Refitting is a reversal of removal but make sure that the rubber insulated mounting studs have not deteriorated otherwise excessive pump noise can occur.

7   Fuel pump - overhaul

1   With the pump removed from the car unwind the tape and remove the band.
2   Remove the insulating sleeve, nut, connector and washer and lift off the end cap.
3   Mark the relationship of the pump body to the coil housing and then extract the coil housing screws and lift off the housing.
4   Unscrew and remove (anticlockwise) the diaphragm and spindle. Do not try to dismantle the diaphragm/spindle.
5   Extract the contact blade securing screw and the pedestal securing

screws and lift off the condenser.
6   Remove the washer, terminal nut, contact and terminal tag.
7   Lift off the pedestal complete with rocker assembly.
8   Extract the pin and detach the rocker assembly.
9   Extract the two crosshead screws and lift off the clamp plate, valve caps, valves, sealing washers and filter.
10 Extract the screws which secure the flow smoothing device cover and lift off the cover, 'O' ring, diaphragm and support ring.
11 Remove the inlet air bottle cover and gasket.
12 Renew any worn components and all gaskets and seals.
13 Commence reassembly by fitting the rocker assembly to the pedestal.
14 Fit the terminal stud, spring washer, terminal, terminal tag, nut and seal.
15 Install pedestal and condenser.
16 Fit impact washer and the spring to the diaphragm spindle.
17 Fit the diaphragm and then screw the spindle into the trunnion until the rocker will not throw over.
18 Fit the plastic armature guide (flat face towards diaphragm) and then unscrew the diaphragm spindle until the rocker will just throw over then unscrew it to its nearest hole plus a further 2/3rds of a turn. This is the correct diaphragm setting.
19 Refit the valves into the body, fit the clamp plate but do not overtighten the screws.
20 Fit the flow smoothing diaphragm, the 'O' ring and the cover.
21 Fit the air bottle cover and the gasket, making sure not to overtighten the centre screw.
22 Connect the coil housing to the pump body making sure that they are in their original relative positions, insert the screws and tighten

Fig. 3.8. Fuel pump contact setting diagram (Sec. 7)

A   *0.030 to 0.040 in (0.77 to 1.03 mm)*
B   *0.065 to 0.075 in (1.67 to 1.93 mm)*

diagonally.
23 Fit the contact blade.
24 Now using a feeler blade, check the two gaps shown in Fig. 3.8. If necessary, bend the stop finger to achieve the specified clearances.
25 Install the end cap, seal and cover joint. Tape the joint with fresh tape.

---

8   Fuel tanks - removal, servicing and installation

1   A fuel tank is located in each of the rear wings. Each tank has its own filler cap and level transmitter.
2   Certain models have a fuel evaporative emission control device (see Section 28) but the following operations still apply except that additional pipework is connected to the tank.
3   Disconnect the rear number plate lamp and remove the rear bumper.
4   Remove the fuel tank cover panel (fifteen screws).
5   Remove the drain plug and drain the fuel into a clean container.
6   Remove the exhaust tail pipe.
7   Unscrew and remove the four setscrews and detach the fuel filler assembly from the body.
8   Disconnect the flexible hose from the overflow pipe.
9   Disconnect the fuel pump feed pipe from the union at the base of the tank.
10 Remove the cover plate from the rear of the wheel arch and disconnect the two electrical leads from the tank transmitter unit. Mark the leads so that they can be correctly reconnected.
11 Unscrew and remove the tank securing bolts. These are accessible in the following positions:
    Wheel arch.
    Side panel within luggage compartment.
    Lower rear edge of fuel tank accessible through aperture from which exhaust tail pipe has been removed.
    Self-locking nut on support rod at the front lower edge of tank.
12 Carefully lower the tank and remove it.
13 If the tank contains sediment, remove the transmitter unit (Section 9) and shake the tank vigorously using several changes of fuel.
14 If the tank has a leak, never be tempted to repair it by soldering or welding but leave it to professional repairers. A fuel tank must be steamed out for several hours before risk of explosion can be eliminated. A temporary repair can be made using a proprietary compound.
15 Installation is a reversal of removal.

---

9   Fuel tank transmitter and level gauge

1   A fuel contents transmitter unit is installed in each fuel tank.
2   In the event of a fault developing, first check all the connecting wires and terminals for security.
3   Refer to Chapter 2, Section 14.
4   Removal of a tank transmitter unit can be carried out using two levers to rotate the securing ring.
5   Always use a new rubber sealing ring when installing the transmitter unit.

Fig. 3.7. Exploded view of a fuel pump (Sec. 7)

1	*Seal*	*8*	*Terminal nut*
2	*Sleeve, nut*	*9*	*Pedestal/rocker assembly*
3	*Washer and connector*	*10*	*Rocker assembly pin*
4	*Coil housing*	*11*	*Clamp plate, valves and filter*
5	*Diaphragm and spindle*	*12*	*Screw*
6	*Contact blade screw*	*13*	*Flow smoothing device*
7	*Pedestal screws and condenser*	*14*	*Inlet air bottle*

Fig. 3.9. Fuel tank and mounting components (one side) (Sec. 8)

Fig. 3.10. Fuel tank transmitter (Sec. 9)

10 Carburettors - description and maintenance

1   A twin carburettor arrangement is fitted to all models but the carburettors, although of variable choke design, differ in type and make according to engine size and operating territory.

2   The only regular maintenance required is to clean the fuel filter gauze on SU carburettors and to check and top-up the oil in the dampers on all models.

3   To top-up the damper, unscrew the piston cap and withdraw the piston assembly. Inject SAE 20 engine oil into the hollow piston and then refit the piston. When sufficient oil has been injected, the piston should require a firm downward pressure to install it.

11 SU carburettor (HD8) - adjustment and tuning

1   It is useless to attempt carburettor tuning until the cylinder compressions, valve clearances, spark plug gaps and contact breaker gaps have been tested, checked and adjusted as necessary. The distributor centrifugal advance mechanism and vacuum advance

Fig. 3.11. Topping up a carburettor damper (Sec. 10)

Fig. 3.12. SU - HD8 carburettor adjustment screws (Sec. 11)

A   Slow-running volume screws

B   Mixture adjusting screws

Fig. 3.13. Piston lifting pin (SU carburettor) (Sec. 11)

Fig. 3.14. Synchronising SU carburettors (Sec. 11)

operation should be checked and ignition timing set to the correct figure. The ignition timing is important since if retarded or advanced too far the setting of the carburettors will be affected. Check that petrol filters are clean.

2 Run the engine to normal operating temperature and then remove the air cleaner.

3 Slacken one of the pinch bolts on the coupling which is located between the throttle spindles.

4 Make sure that both butterfly valve plates are fully closed by rotating the throttle spindles clockwise when viewed from the front of the car.

5 Tighten the coupling pinch bolt.

6 Screw in each of the slow-running volume screws (A) until they are fully seated then unscrew each screw exactly two turns (Fig. 3.12.)

7 Remove the piston and suction chambers and unscrew each of the mixture adjusting screws (B) until each jet is flush with the bridge of its carburettor.

8 Refit the pistons and suction chambers and then check that each piston falls freely by pressing the small lifting pin upwards and letting the pistons fall onto their bridges. A distinct 'clunk' should be heard.

9 Turn each of the screws (B) down 2½ turns and then top-up the piston dampers with SAE 20 oil.

10 Start the engine and adjust each of the volume screws (A) by an equal amount until the engine idling speed is 600 rev/min for cars equipped with automatic transmission or 700 rev/min for cars with manual transmission. To make sure that both carburettors are synchronised, use a length of tubing placed between the carburettor intake and the ear and adjust screws (A) fractionally until the hiss from both units is similar. Alternatively, use a balancing device (flowmeter) in accordance with its manufacturer's instructions.

11 When the carburettors have been correctly synchronised, screw the mixture screws (B) up or down by a similar amount until the fastest idling speed is obtained consistent with even firing. If necessary, readjust the volume screws (A) until the specified idling speeds are again obtained.

12 Now check the mixture strength. With the engine idling raise the piston on the front carburettor by about 1/32 in (0.8 mm) using the lifting pin. One of the following conditions will occur:

The engine speed increases and continues at this higher speed indicating a rich mixture.

The engine speed drops and may even stall indicating a weak mixture.

The engine speed momentarily increases slightly then resumes its previous level. This indicates that the mixture is correct.

13 Repeat the mixture strength tests on the rear carburettor and then recheck the front one again as the carburettors are interdependent.

---

12 SU carburettors (HD8) - removal and installation

1 Remove the air cleaner, including the backplate and filter element (see Section 2).

2 Close the tap on the fuel filter and disconnect the fuel line banjo unions from the carburettor float chambers.

3 Remove the distributor vacuum advance pipe.

4 Disconnect the fuel feed pipe from the auxiliary starting carburettor.

5 Disconnect the throttle cables and the leads from the choke solenoid.

6 On cars equipped with automatic transmission, remove the spring clip which secures the kick-down link at the rear of the rear carburettor.

7 Disconnect the throttle return springs.

8 Remove the four nuts which secure each carburettor to the inlet manifold and lift the carburettors away.

9 Installation is a reversal of removal but always renew the gaskets or 'O' rings located on the flanges whichever type of sealing device is used.

---

13 SU carburettor (HD8) - examination, overhaul and adjustment

1 The SU carburettor, generally speaking is most reliable and it is very rarely that you would have to completely dismantle it. However, after a long period of use some deterioration must be expected, therefore when the time arrives for a major overhaul of the engine, serious

consideration should be given to replacing the carburettors with factory reconditioned items.

2 Thoroughly clean the outside of the carburettor.

3 Clean down the top of the bench, it is advisable to lay out a sheet of paper on which all parts can be placed as they are removed.

4 Unscrew the damper and remove it together with its washer.

5 Using a small file or scriber, mark the suction chamber so that it can be refitted in its original position.

6 Remove the three suction chamber securing screws and remove the chamber from the body leaving the piston in position. Be careful when lifting off the suction chamber not to apply side loads to the piston otherwise the piston needle may be bent.

7 Lift the piston spring from the piston noting which way round it is fitted.

8 Remove the piston and invert it over a container to allow the oil in the damper bore to drain out. Place the piston in a safe place so that the needle will not be damaged or that the piston will not roll onto the floor. It is suggested that the piston is placed in a suitably sized jar with the needle inside, so acting as a stand.

9 It is recommended that, unless absolutely necessary, the needle is not separated from the piston. However, if the needle must be removed, slacken the retaining screw in the side of the body and remove the needle.

10 Mark the position of the float chamber lid in relation to the body. Undo the cap nut and remove it together with the washer. Lift off the float chamber lid.

11 Withdraw the pin from the float chamber lever and remove the lever. You will find that the pin is serrated and can be removed in one direction only.

12 Using the correct sized spanner, unscrew the brass valve body and remove it together with the float needle.

13 Lift the float out of the float chamber and place it in a position where it will not be damaged.

14 Remove the four setscrews securing the float chamber to the body.

15 Separate the float chamber from the body and this will free the jet spring, the jet and diaphragm and the jet housing which may now be lifted out of the body.

16 Unscrew the jet bearing nut and lift out the jet bearing.

17 Unscrew the slow running control valve from the body and collect the spring and the gland washers. Note the position of the gland washers for reassembly.

18 No further dismantling of the carburettor is necessary, indeed, it is rarely that dismantling beyond the stage decided in paragraph 13 will ever be required.

19 Reassembly is the reverse of the above. Fit new washers throughout and, if you removed the jet needle, install it in the piston so that the shoulder of the needle is flush with the base of the piston.

20 The jet will almost certainly require centring in the following way.

21 Using a ring spanner, slacken the jet locking nut approximately half a turn.

22 Refer to Fig. 3.17. Replace the jet and diaphragm assembly. Push

Fig. 3.15. Jet needle setting diagram (SU carburettor) (Sec. 13)

Fig. 3.16. Exploded view of SU carburettor (Sec. 13)

1	Screw	28	Cap nut
2	Body	29	Serrated washer
3	Throttle spindle	30	Aluminium washer
4	Bush	31	Filter gauze
5	Circlip	32	Banjo bolt
6	Circlip	33	Fibre washer
7	Butterfly valve plate	34	Auxiliary (starter) carburettor
8	Adaptor		body
9	Gasket	35	Acceleration needle assembly
10	Distributor vacuum pipe	36	Spring
	connection	37	Jet
11	Suction chamber	38	Spring plate
12	Damper	39	Dust shield
13	Washer	40	Screw
14	Spring	41	Lockwasher
15	Needle	42	Solenoid
16	Jet assembly	43	Bracket
17	Jet bearing	44	Connecting arm
18	Nut	45	Banjo bolt
19	Spring	46	Washer
20	Jet housing	47	Washer
21	Float chamber	48	Banjo bolt
22	Float chamber lid	49	Fibre washer
23	Float	50	Aluminium washer
24	Fuel inlet needle and seat	51	Valve
25	Float arm	52	Spring
26	Float pivot pin	53	Gland washer
27	Gasket	54	Dished washer

Fig. 3.17. Centring the jet (SU carburettor) (Sec. 13)

the jet and diaphragm assembly as high as possible with hand pressure and at the same time press the piston down onto the jet bridge, using a pencil or a piece of rod for this. Centralisation will be helped by lightly tapping on the side of the carburettor body.

23 Tighten the jet locking nut.

24 The actual centring must be carried out with the setscrew holes in the jet diaphragm and carburettor in alignment. After tightening the jet locking nut the jet diaphragm must be kept in the same position relative to the carburettor body and to do this it is advisable to mark one of the corresponding jet diaphragm and carburettor setscrew holes with a soft pencil. Centring will be upset if the diaphragm is moved radically after tightening the jet nut.

25 The jet is correctly centred when the piston falls freely and hits the jet 'bridge' with a metallic click. Check if there is any difference in the sound of the piston hitting the bridge with the jet in its highest and lowest positions. If there is any difference in the sound, the procedure for centralising the jet will have to be repeated.

26 The float level should be checked, particularly if flooding of the carburettor has been encountered during operating conditions. To do this, invert the float chamber lid and check that a bar 7/16 in (11.1 mm) in diameter will just slide between the float lever fork and the lid as shown. Any correction must be carried out by bending at the junction of the curved and straight sections of the lever (Fig. 3.18).

27 Finally, and before fitting the suction chamber, fill the piston damper bore to within ¼ in (6.35 mm) of its top with SAE 20 engine oil, wipe any spillage off the outside of the piston. After fitting the

suction chamber, raise the piston by means of the lifting pin and check that it falls back smartly on to the upper face of the body. Any sluggishness, assuming all other factors to be correct, will probably be due to oil on the outside of the piston.

28 Whenever a carburettor has been overhauled and refitted to the engine, carry out the adjustments described in Section 11.

14 SU carburettor (HD8) - auxiliary starting carburettor - adjustment

1 Run the engine to normal operating temperature.

2 Adjust the stop screw until the mixture has a tendency towards richness. This stage should be evident by the emission of black gases from the exhaust when lower temperature engine running is artificially created by energising the solenoid by short circuiting the terminal of the thermostatic switch directly to earth with a screwdriver and flicking open the throttles. Actuation of the auxiliary starting carburettor will be evident by a pronounced hissing noise (photo).

3 The stop screw should be turned in an anticlockwise direction to enrich the mixture. Ideally turn the screw to the point where any further movement would cause the engine to idle roughly under conditions where the thermostatic switch is being short circuited.

4 If for any reason the thermostatic switch must be removed, loss of water from the cooling system will be minimised if the radiator filler cap is kept securely tightened.

Fig. 3.18. Float lever setting diagram (SU carburettor) (Sec. 13)

A Coned end of needle valve

Fig. 3.20. Thermostatic switch - SU auxiliary starting carburettor (Sec. 14)

Fig. 3.19. Sectional view of auxiliary starting carburettor (SU) (Sec. 14)

1	*Body*	*8*	*Connecting passage*
2	*Valve seating*	*9*	*Jet*
3	*Valve*	*10*	*Needle*
4	*Iron core (solenoid)*	*11*	*Spring*
5	*Solenoid winding*	*12*	*Disc*
6	*Solenoid terminals*	*13*	*Adjustable stop*
7	*Air intake*	*14*	*Connecting passage*

(Refer also to Fig. 3.16).

14.2 Auxiliary starting carburettor (SU HD8)

15 SU carburettor (HS8) - adjustment and tuning

1   The twin carburettor installation of this type incorporates an automatic enrichment device (A.E.D.) which is essentially an auxiliary carburettor which increases the fuel/air mixture ratio when the engine is below normal operating temperature.

Slow-running adjustment
2   Make sure that ignition and all other engine adjustments are correct.
3   Run the engine to normal operating temperature and check that the mixture delivery pipe is warm.
4   Screw both the throttle speed adjusting screws back until they no longer contact the throttle levers. **On no account disturb the mixture screws,** these are preset in production (Fig. 3.21.)
5   Check that the throttle butterfly valve in each carburettor is fully closed.
6   Screw the throttle speed screws in until they just make contact with the throttle levers and then turn them a further 1½ turns inwards.
7   Remove the air cleaner cover and the element.

8   Balance the carburettors by one of the methods and in a similar way to that described in Section 11, paragraph 10. The correct idling speed is:
650 rev/min cars with manual gearbox
750 rev/min cars with automatic transmission
9   It is recommended that a final check is made using an exhaust gas analyser to ensure that the level of CO emission is within the specified limit (under 4½%).

Fig. 3.21. Adjustment screws (SU - HS8 carburettor) (Sec. 15)
1   *Slow-running screws*   2   *Pre-set mixture screws*

Fig. 3.22. Automatic enrichment device (A.E.D.) filter (Sec. 16)

Fig. 3.23. Hot air pick-up unit filter (SU - HS8 carburettor) (Sec. 17)

1   *Clip*   2   *Filter*   3   *Filter mesh*

16 SU carburettors (HS8) - servicing of automatic enrichment device (A.E.D.)

1   At the recommended internals specified in 'Routine Maintenance',

Fig. 3.24. Hot air pick-up unit air delivery pipe (SU - HS8 carburettor) (Sec. 17)

1   *Clip*   2   *Support*   3   *Pipe to A.E.D.*

Fig. 3.25. Automatic enrichment device (A.E.D.) connections (Sec. 18)

2   *Fuel inlet pipe*   4   *Air delivery pipe*
3   *Fuel overflow pipe*   5   *Mixture delivery pipe*

Fig. 3.26. Automatic enrichment device (A.E.D.) mounting components (Sec. 18)

remove the plug and aluminium washer from the float chamber of the automatic enrichment device.

2 Withdraw the filter gauge, clean with fuel and dry with air from a tyre pump and refit.

17 SU carburettors (HS8) - hot air pick-up unit, servicing and removal and refitting

1 At the intervals specified in 'Routine maintenance' slacken the clamp, move the filter towards the cylinder block and withdraw it.
2 Clean the filter in fuel, dry it and then lightly apply engine oil to the filter gauze.
3 If required, the hot air unit can be removed from the exhaust manifold after disconnecting the air delivery tube and withdrawing the two securing bolts.
4 Refitting is a reversal of removal.

18 SU carburettor (HS8) - removal and refitting of automatic enrichment device (A.E.D.)

1 Disconnect the lead from the battery negative terminal.
2 Disconnect the fuel inlet pipe.
3 Disconnect the fuel overflow pipe.
4 Disconnect the air delivery pipe.
5 Disconnect the mixture delivery pipe.
6 Unbolt and remove the securing bolts and lift off the automatic enrichment device.
7 Refitting is a reversal of removal.

19 SU carburettors (HS8) - removal and refitting

1 Remove the automatic enrichment device as described in the preceding Section.
2 Disconnect the crankcase breather pipe from the carburettors.
3 Disconnect the fuel inlet and the overflow pipes from the carburettor float chambers.
4 Disconnect the mixture delivery pipes.
5 Disconnect the vacuum pipe from the rear carburettor.
6 Slacken the slow-running adjustment screws until they are no longer contacting the throttle levers.
7 Mark the relative position of the throttle rod to the clamping bracket.
8 Slacken the clamping bracket pinch bolt and slide the bracket along the throttle rod until it is disengaged from the carburettor linkage.
9 Withdraw the throttle rod from the hollow nut by pressing the rod towards the engine compartment rear bulkhead.
10 Remove the carburettor securing nuts and lift the carburettor assembly from the inlet manifold complete with throttle lever return springs and brackets.
11 Peel off the flange gaskets and discard them.
12 Slacken the clamp pinch bolt and withdraw the front carburettor from the throttle link rod.
13 Commence installation by placing new flange gaskets on the inlet manifolds.
14 Fit the carburettors and tighten the flange nuts in diagonal sequence.
15 Make sure that both throttle butterfly valve plates are closed and then tighten the clamp pinch bolt.
16 Locate the throttle rod in the hollow nut and engage the clamp

Fig. 3.27. Carburettor connections (SU - HS8) (Sec. 19)

1 A.E.D. unit	5 Vacuum pipe connection from distributor	9 Hollow nut
2 Crankcase breather pipes	6 Slow-running screws	10 Flange nuts
3 Fuel inlet and overflow pipes	7 Clamp	11 Gasket
4 Mixture delivery pipes	8 Throttle rod	12 Clamp bolt

Fig. 3.28. Exploded view of SU - HS8 carburettor (Sec. 20)

1	Damper piston	5	Body	9	Fuel inlet needle valve	13	Hollow nut
2	Suction chamber	6	Float chamber lid	10	Float chamber	14	Jet assembly
3	Spring	7	Float	11	Throttle valve spindle	15	Flexible pipe
4	Piston/needle	8	Fuel inlet valve seat	12	Throttle butterfly valve plate	16	Jet fork

bracket with the carburettor linkage.

17 Place a spanner on the hollow nut and so keep the throttle butterfly valve plates closed. Now rotate the throttle rod until the reference marks on the rod and clamping bracket are in alignment. Tighten the clamp pinch bolt.

18 Reconnect all pipes to the carburettors and then refit the automatic enrichment device.

19 Adjust the carburettor slow-running, as described in Section 15.

20 SU carburettor (HS8) - examination, overhaul and adjustment

1 With the carburettors removed from the engine as described in the preceding Section, clean all dirt from their external surfaces.
2 Unscrew and remove the damper and washer.
3 Mark the relationship of the suction chamber and the carburettor body, extract the suction chamber screws and lift the chamber from the body.
4 Remove the piston spring and withdraw the piston and needle assembly.
5 Unscrew and remove the needle locking screw and then withdraw the needle from the piston complete with bias sleeve and spring.
6 Extract the split pins which retain the jet spring anchor pin and the jet fork pivot pin. Withdraw the pins and spring.
7 Withdraw the jet fork from its bracket.
8 Remove the bolt, washer and bush which secure the link arm to the carburettor body.
9 Unscrew the nut which secures the flexi-pipe to the float chamber, withdraw the pipe and the washer and the gland.
10 Withdraw the jet assembly together with the bi-metal sensor, washer and spacer.
11 Remove the bolts, washer and spacers which secure the fork bracket to the carburettor body.
12 Withdraw the jet bearing together with spacer and concave washers.
13 Bend back the tabs and unscrew the throttle lever securing nut, withdraw the lever and plain washer.
14 Only dismantle the throttle butterfly valve plate from its spindle if essential. To dismantle, extract the securing screws and discard them.
15 Mark the relationship of the float chamber lid to the float chamber and then extract the screws and lift off the lid and gasket.
16 Remove the fuel inlet needle from the lid and using a close fitting spanner, unscrew the fuel inlet valve seating.
17 Extract the float hinge pin. The pin is serrated at one end and should be driven out by applying a drift to the serrated end. Remove the float.
18 Remove the bolt which secures the float chamber to the carburettor body. Detach the float chamber and remove the flexible coupling and steel backing washer.
19 Clean all components in fuel and examine for wear or damage. Obtain a repair kit which will contain all the necessary gaskets and other renewable items.
20 If the throttle valve and spindle were dismantled, commence reassembly by inserting the spindle into the carburettor body.
21 Insert the butterfly valve plate into the slot in the spindle and insert two new securing screws but tighten them only finger tight at this stage. Note that the 'pip' on the valve plate should be below and on the same side as the countersunk screw holes in the throttle spindle.
22 Adjust the valve plate until it closes smoothly and fully and then

tighten the two screws fully and spread their split ends to lock them.
23 Screw in the fuel inlet valve seating, insert needle valve so that the coned end enters first.
24 Refit the float and pivot pin and then invert the float chamber lid and check the float level. The gap between the closest point of the float and the lid should be between 1/8 and 3/16 in (3.2 and 4.7 mm) (A in Fig. 3.29). If this is not so, a new float or needle valve will be required as there is no provision for adjustment.
25 Fit a new gasket to the float chamber lid.
26 Refit the lid and gasket to the float chamber in the original relative position and tighten the securing screws in diagonal sequence.
27 Insert the float chamber bolt into the carburettor body, refit the flexible coupling, washer and float chamber.
28 Install the bias sleeve and spring to the needle in the position shown. Screw in the needle securing screw and check that the needle is free to move (Fig. 3.30).
29 Check that the suction piston key is securely fitted, lightly oil the piston and install it into the carburettor body.
30 Fit the piston spring.
31 Install the suction chamber, aligning the marks made before dismantling and insert and tighten the securing screws in diagonal sequence.
32 Fit the jet bearing with concave washers and spacers.
33 Install the fork bracket, spacers and bolts.
34 Locate the jet fork in the bracket, insert the pivot pin and lock with a new split pin.
35 Locate the bush in the link arm, securing with bolt and double spring washer.
36 Locate the bi-metal sensor, copper washer and spacer on the jet assembly and slide the assembly into the jet bearing. The spacer must be positioned as shown in the diagram (Fig. 3.31).
37 Fit the jet spring, insert the anchor pin and secure it with a new split pin.
38 Slide the nut onto the flexi-pipe followed by the steel washer and a new gland.
39 Locate the flexi-tube in the bottom of the float-chamber and fit the nut but do not overtighten it.
40 Fit the plain washer, throttle lever, a new tab washer and nut to the throttle butterfly valve spindle. Hold the valve plate closed while tightening the nut and then secure the nut by bending over the lock tabs.
41 After installing the carburettors, top-up the dampers and tune them as described in Section 15.

21 Throttle kick-down switch (auto. transmission with SU-HS8 carburettor) - testing and adjustment

1 Any fault occurring in the kick-down function such as delay or too early an actuation may be due to the switch being out of adjustment.
2 Disconnect the red/black lead from the switch.
3 Connect a test lamp between the switch terminal and earth.
4 Switch on the ignition and depress accelerator pedal to the kick-down position when the test lamp should illuminate. If it does not, gently raise the spring steel lever on the switch until a 'click' is heard. The test lamp should now illuminate. If it does, adjust the position of the switch by releasing the securing screws. If it does not, the switch is faulty and must be renewed.

Fig. 3.29. Float level checking diagram (SU - HS8 carburettor) (Sec. 20)

Fig. 3.30. Piston and needle components (SU - H.S.8 carburettor) (Sec. 20)

Fig. 3.31. Jet assembly (SU - HS8 carburettor) (Sec. 20)

Fig. 3.32. Jet spring and anchor pin arrangement (SU - HS8 carburettor) (Sec. 20)

Fig. 3.33. Automatic transmission kick-down switch test (Sec. 21)

1 *Red/black lead*	5 *Spring steel lever*
2 *Test lamp*	6 *Switch adjustment travel*
4 *Accelerator pedal rod*	

22 Stromberg 175CD2SE carburettors - adjustment and tuning

1   This carburettor has been specially developed to meet the most exacting emission control requirements and operations should therefore be limited to those described.

2   Make sure that ignition and engine adjustments are correctly set.

3   Run the engine until normal operating temperature is reached. Switch off the engine and remove the air cleaner cover and element.

4   Check and top-up if necessary, the oil in the carburettor dampers.

5   Slacken each of the two idle speed screws until they no longer contact the throttle levers.

6   Slacken the choke inner cable clamp bolts, check that the choke valve plates are fully open and then retighten the bolts.

7   Slacken the throttle spindle clamp bolts, check that the throttle valve plates are are fully closed and then retighten the clamp bolts.

8   Screw in the idle speed screw on the rear carburettor until it just

contacts the throttle lever.

9   Start the engine and adjust the idle speed screw on the rear carburettor until the engine idling speed is as follows:

750 rev/min - cars with manual gearbox (in neutral)
650 rev/min - cars with automatic transmission (in 'N' or 'P')

10   On some carburettors an idle trim screw is fitted adjacent to the temperature compensator cover. This screw is normally only adjusted to compensate for engine stiffness which is apparent at start-up of a new engine. When the initial stiffness wears off, the screw may be screwed in slightly to offset the weak mixture necessary in stiff engines.

11   On some carburettors, a throttle bypass valve is installed. This is a vacuum-operated valve actuated by manifold depression which during periods of engine overrun when the throttle is closed, allows fuel to feed to the downstream side of the primary throttle. This arrangement causes the gases in the engine combustion chambers to become enriched to a combustible level.

12   The throttle bypass valve is preset and normally requires no adjustment but it is possible for particles of dirt to become trapped under the valve seating. In the event of this happening and the valve action becoming unsatisfactory, remove the valve cover and carefully clean the valve and its seat.

13   The fast idle setting does not normally require altering. With the choke fully released (control knob fully in) the gap between the head of the fast idle screw and the cam should be 0.067 in (1.6 mm). If necessary, release the screw locknut and turn the screw in or out to obtain the correct gap.

14   A 'Summer' and 'Winter' position can be selected for the choke. If the pin on the knurled brass plunger is lying horizontally in its slot, this is the 'Winter' setting. To move it to 'Summer' position, depress the plunger and turn it through 90°.

15   Check the CO emission level is below 4½% using an exhaust gas analyser to prove that your adjustments have been carried out correctly.

23 Stromberg 175CD2SE carburettors - removal and installation

1   Remove the air cleaner as described in Section 2.

2   Disconnect the crankcase breather pipe from each carburettor.

3   Disconnect the vacuum pipe from each bypass valve.

4   Slacken the clip and disconnect the fuel inlet pipe from the Tee-piece.

Fig. 3.34. Stromberg carburettor adjustment screws (Sec. 22)

4 *Idle speed screw*	6 *Throttle spindle clamp bolts*
5 *Choke cable clamp bolts*	*Inset - fast idle SUMMER position*

Fig. 3.35. Exploded view of Stromberg carburettor (jet cover arrangement may differ according to date of production)
Inset - Location of idle trim screw (arrowed) and throttle by-pass valve (A)

1 Damper
2 Seal
3 Cover
4 Diaphragm retaining ring
5 Piston return spring
6 Needle securing screw
7 Butterfly valve plate
8 Bush
9 Pick-up lever
10 Floating lever
11 Washer
12 Lockwasher
13 Nut
14 Diaphragm
15 Idle trim screw
16 Gasket
17 By-pass valve
18 Gasket
19 Spring
20 Cover
21 Seal
22 Seal
23 Gasket
24 Temperature compensator
25 Tapered plug
26 Bi-metallic strip
27 Cover
28 Jet assembly
29 Float
30 Float chamber
31 Float pivot
32 'O' ring
33 Fuel inlet needle valve
34 Washer
35 Choke assembly
36 Needle
37 Spring
38 Throttle stop screw
39 Throttle spindle
40 Piston
41 Diaphragm

5 Slacken the clamp bolts and withdraw the choke inner cables. Disconnect the choke outer cables from their clips.
6 Prise off the spring clip which secures the front throttle lever to its connecting link. Do not disconnect the lever from the link at this stage.
7 Prise off the spring clip which secures the rear throttle lever by following the same procedure.
8 *On cars equipped with automatic transmission,* release the spring clip and disconnect the kick-down rod from the throttle lever.
9 Remove the nuts and spring washers which secure the carburettor assembly to the secondary throttle housing.
10 Withdraw the carburettors enough to be able to disconnect the front and rear throttle levers from their connecting links. Remove the carburettors completely.
11 Peel off and discard the flange gaskets.
12 Mark the relative position of the throttle spindles to the connecting rod and then slacken one bolt on each connecting clamp.
13 Remove the clips which secure the T-piece to the carburettors and separate the carburettors.
14 Installation is a reversal of removal but always use new flange gaskets and once installed, adjust them as described in Section 22.

24 Stromberg 175CD2SE carburettor - examination and overhaul

1 Dismantle one unit at a time so that components will not become interchanged between the carburettors as many parts are individually matched during production.
2 With the carburettors removed from the engine as described in the preceding Section, clean away all external dirt.
3 Prise out the soft plug from one of the cover screws.
4 Mark the relationship of the cover to the carburettor body, remove the four cover screws, lift off the cover and withdraw the spring.
5 Carefully withdraw the piston/diaphragm assembly. If the diaphragm is split or has hardened, remove the screws which secure the diaphragm retaining ring to the piston. Lift off the ring and discard the diaphragm.
6 *Do not remove needle locking screw or needle.* This is selected and positioned during manufacture. If the needle must be renewed because it has become worn or distorted, then it can only be renewed complete with piston as an assembly. The needle size is B1BT and it should appear biased to one side - this is correct.
7 Remove the float chamber screws and lift the float chamber from the carburettor body.
8 Do not remove the jet cover unless absolutely essential in which case bend back the retaining lugs and withdraw the cover and 'O' ring. On reassembly, renew the jet cover, 'O' ring and float chamber gasket.
9 Disconnect the float pivot pin and detach the float.
10 Unscrew the fuel inlet needle valve.
11 Remove the nut, serrated and plain washers which secure the throttle lever to the throttle spindle. Withdraw the throttle lever, bush and actuating link.
12 Do not dismantle throttle valve plate unless essential in which case mark its relative position to the spindle, remove the securing screws and slide the plate from the slot in the spindle.
13 Withdraw the spindle having noted the position of the spindle return spring.
14 Remove the screws and lockwashers which secure the bypass valve and cover to the carburettor body, discard the joint gasket. Do not separate the bypass valve cover from the body or its adjustment will be lost.
15 Prise the throttle spindle seals from the carburettor body and discard them.
16 Remove the screws which secure the temperature compensator to the carburettor body, withdraw the compensator and discard the seals. If a countersunk brass screw is observed adjacent to the compensator, make sure that this is fully tightened otherwise an air leak can occur at this point.
17 Clean and examine all components, renewing any that are worn or damaged. Obtain a repair kit for each carburettor - part no. JS478.
18 Reassembly is a reversal of dismantling but observe the following points.
19 Check that the tapered plug is free to move in the temperature compensator housing. If it sticks, renew the assembly.
20 Fit all new seals and gaskets supplied in the kit.
21 Do not tighten the throttle valve plate screws until smooth and positive closure of the valve plate has been checked.

22 Once the float has been reassembled, invert the carburettor body so that the float arm closes the needle valve and then check the distance between the face of the carburettor body and the highest point on the visible surface of the float. This should be between 0.650 and 0.670 in (16.5 and 17.0 mm). Any adjustment should be carried out by bending the float arm. Make sure both floats are equal in height.
23 When reassembly is complete and the carburettors are installed to the engine, tune and adjust them, as described in Section 22.

25 Secondary throttle housing (in conjunction with Stromberg carburettor). - removal, overhaul and refitting

1 Remove the cap from the radiator header tank.
2 Open the radiator drain tap and drain off about one (US) gallon of coolant. Retain the coolant for replenishment.
3 Remove the carburettors, as described in Section 23.
4 Disconnect the inlet manifold hose from the gulp valve.
5 Slacken the clip and disconnect the water inlet hose.
6 Detach the secondary throttle return springs having first noted into which anchor bracket holes they are secured.
7 Slacken the clip and disconnect the water outlet hose.
8 Remove the nuts which secure the secondary throttle housing and spring anchor brackets to the inlet manifold and withdraw the housing and gulp valve. Discard all gaskets.
9 To dismantle the secondary throttle housing, remove the nut and

Fig. 3.36. Secondary throttle housing (with Stromberg carburettor) (Sec. 25)

4 Inlet manifold hose from gulp valve	7 Water outlet hose
5 Inlet water hose	8 Housing and anchor bracket securing nuts
6 Spring anchor brackets	9 Secondary throttle housing

Fig. 3.37. Secondary throttle housing components (Sec. 25)

2 Bellcrank (front)	4 Throttle valve plate
3 Bellcrank (rear)	5 Screws
	6 Spindle

washer which secure the bellcrank to the front secondary throttle spindle, withdraw the bellcrank.
10 Repeat these operations to remove the rear bellcrank.
11 If the throttle plates are to be removed from their spindles then mark the relationship of the valve plates to the spindles and the spindles to the housing.
12 Remove the valve plate screws, withdraw the spindles and prise out the spindle seals.
13 Reassembly is a reversal of dismantling, use new spindle seals.
14 Refitting is a reversal of removal, use new joint gaskets.

26 Manifolds and exhaust system

1 The inlet and exhaust manifolds fitted to all cars with SU carburettors are secured in a straightforward way with studs and nuts. Always use new joint gaskets when refitting a manifold.
2 The inlet manifold fitted to cars which have Stromberg carburettors is much more complicated and the following removal procedure should be followed.
3 Remove the cap from the radiator header tank, open the radiator drain tap and drain about one (US) gallon of coolant. Retain the coolant for replenishment purposes.
4 Remove the secondary throttle housing, as described in Section 25.
5 Remove the air duct which runs across the top of the camshaft covers.
6 Disconnect the water outlet hose.
7 Detach the crankcase breather pipe from its retaining clips and withdraw the pipe from the elbow.
8 Disengage the HT leads from their retaining clip.
9 Disconnect the radiator upper hose.
10 Disconnect the hoses from the radiator header tank filler neck.
11 Slacken the clip that secures the water pump hose to the header tank.
12 Withdraw throttle linkage and support in its frame (three nuts).
13 Disconnect pipes and water temperature transmitter lead from the underside of the inlet manifold.

14 Disconnect the pipes from the thermostatic switch.
15 Note the position of the two pipe clips and then remove the nuts which secure the inlet manifold to the cylinder head.
16 Withdraw the inlet manifold far enough to be able to disconnect the water pump hose from the underside of the radiator header tank. Lift away the inlet manifold and discard the old gaskets.
17 Installation is a reversal of removal, always use new gaskets.
18 The exhaust system is of dual type having twin downpipes and then left and right-hand intermediate rear silencer and tailpipe assemblies. The flexible sections of the exhaust pipes may be renewed

Fig. 3.38. Inlet manifold connections (Stromberg carburettors) (Sec. 26)

5 Water outlet hose	13 Thermostatic switch pipes
11 Throttle linkage	14 Pipe clips
12 Pipes and cables on underside	15 Water pump hose
	16 Gaskets

A Water temperature sensor unit cable
B Thermostatic vacuum switch pipe
C Brake servo hose
D Air cleaner vacuum pipe
E Heater vacuum reservoir pipe
F Gulp valve vacuum pipe
G Vacuum servo pipe (automatic transmission)

Fig. 3.39. Exhaust system (typical) (Sec. 26)

independently by cutting and brazing.

19 Depending upon the date of car production, the design of the exhaust system may vary slightly.

20 Examination of the exhaust pipe and silencers at regular intervals is worthwhile as small defects may be repairable when, if left, they will almost certainly require renewal of one of the sections of the system. Also, any leaks, apart from the noise factor, may cause poisonous exhaust gases to get inside the car which can be unpleasant, to say the least, even in mild concentrations. Prolonged inhalation could cause sickness and giddiness.

21 As the sleeve connections and clamps are usually very difficult to separate it is quicker and easier in the long run to remove the complete system from the car when renewing a section. It can be expensive if another section is damaged when trying to separate a bad section from it.

22 Refitting should be carried out after connecting the sections together. De-burr and grease the connecting socket and make sure that the clamp is in good condition and slipped over the front pipe but do not tighten it at this stage.

23 Connect the system to the manifold and connect the rear support. Now adjust the attitude of the silencers, so that they are properly aligned and will not knock against any part of the bodyframe when deflected to the limit of travel on their flexible mountings. When alignment is correct, tighten the pipe clamps.

24 The tailpipe trims are retained by socket-headed grub screws.

27 Emission control systems - description

1 The emission control systems are designed to reduce (i) the emission of fumes from the engine crankcase which are generated by blow-by past the piston rings, (ii) fumes which are the result of evaporation of fuel stored in the fuel tank and the carburettor float chambers and (iii) noxious gases which are emitted from the exhaust pipes and which are the result of the normal combustion cycle within the engine.

2 The crankcase ventilation system is described in Chapter 1, Section 23.

3 The exhaust emission control systems are undoubtedly the most complex and a very comprehensive layout is employed in conjunction with Stromberg carburettors on cars destined for operation in North America.

4 It must be emphasised that the condition and adjustment of the engine components (valve clearances, air filter etc.) and the setting of the ignition and carburettors are all essential factors in meeting the requirements of emission regulations quite apart from the function of the emission control equipment itself.

28 Fuel evaporative control system - description and maintenance

1 The system is designed to store vapour from the fuel tank and carburettor float chambers in a charcoal-filled canister during periods when the engine is not running. When the engine is running, the vapour is drawn from the charcoal canister into the engine crankcase emission control system and burned in the engine combustion chambers.

2 At the intervals specified in 'Routine Maintenance' the charcoal canister should be renewed. The canister design and connections vary according to the date of production of the car and particular care should be taken to identify the pipe connection on later models.

29 Anti-run on valve - description, testing and renewal

1 This valve is fitted to later cars to prevent any tendency to run-on when the engine is switched off. The system comprises a solenoid valve, an extra oil pressure switch and an additional contact in the ignition switch. When the ignition switch is turned off, voltage is applied to a solenoid valve in the evaporative control canister purge line, closing the line to atmosphere. The valve is connected electrically to an oil pressure switch which is closed while oil pressure exists. The solenoid valve at the same time applies manifold depression through the medium of the canister to the interior of the float chambers to equalise pressure on both sides of the carburettor jet and so prevents any fuel flowing past the metering needle. The foregoing action is applied only momentarily while the oil pressure still exists after the engine is switched off. Once the oil pressure drops, the pressure switch opens to de-actuate the solenoid valve and the canister purge line is re-opened to atmosphere.

2 If the system is suspected of being faulty, first check the fuse below the fascia panel on the driver's side.

3 If the fuse is sound, check the vacuum pipe between the inlet manifold and the solenoid valve which is located on the wing valance within the engine compartment.

4 Remove the air cleaner filter element and then pull the lead from the oil pressure switch which is located to the left-hand side of the oil filter. Start the engine and short the oil pressure switch lead to the engine block. Switch off the engine, if the engine does not run on, renew the oil pressure switch.

5 If the engine does run on, the switch is satisfactory and continue with the final test.

6 Check the security of all electrical connections making sure that 12 volt is present at the solenoid valve when the ignition switch is off. If it is then the solenoid must have an internal fault and should be renewed.

Fig. 3.40. Fuel evaporative control system (earlier cars) - charcoal canister attachments and under-bonnet location (Sec. 28)

1 *Outlet hoses*   3 *Canister securing bolt*
2 *Inlet hose*   4 *Canister*

Fig. 3.41. Fuel evaporative control system (later cars) - charcoal canister attachments and under front wing location (Sec. 28)

1 *Front roadwheel*   3 *Securing clamp*
2 *Pipes*   4 *Canister*

30 Air injection system - description and maintenance

1   This system was fitted to earlier cars in order to reduce the level of noxious gases from the exhaust pipes. It is a method of injecting air to the exhaust ports in order to dilute the combustion gases before they are emitted from the exhaust system. Clean air is drawn through a small filter, compressed by a belt-driven pump and injected through a system of pipes and a non-return valve.

2   Periodically check the tension of the air pump drivebelt. The centre point of the upper run of the belt should have a deflection of ½ in (12.7 mm). If adjustment is required, slacken the pump mounting bolts and adjust the effective length of the rod by releasing the locknuts.

31 Exhaust gas recirculation (E.G.R) system - description and maintenance

1   This system is fitted to later cars as a substitute for the air injection system. It operates by tapping off a predetermined volume of exhaust gas and injecting it into the carburettor inlet. The admission of this exhaust gas reduces the combustion temperature and so helps to minimise the level of noxious gases produced during the normal engine combustion cycles.

Fig. 3.42. Air injection system pipework (Sec. 30)

2   *Non-return valve hose*
3   *Air delivery pipe brackets*
4   *Air injection pipe cylinder head union*
5   *Non-return valve*

Fig. 3.43. Air injection system air pump (Sec. 30)

1   *Air pump delivery pipe*
2   *Pipe clip*
3   *Pump outlet elbow*
4   *Pump elbow*
5   *Adjustment rod*
6   *Pump lower mounting*
7   *Air pump*
8   *Drivebelt*

All cars except series 2 models

2   At the intervals specified in 'Routine maintenance' remove the blanking screw from the top of the left-hand carburettor mounting flange.

3   Hold the throttle fully open and then remove any carbon deposits from the inlet drilling using a piece of mild steel rod 8 in long x 1/8 in diameter (203 mm x 3.2 mm). Refit the blanking plug.

4   Repeat the operations on the second carburettor.

5   The connecting 'Y' piece and restrictor should also be decarbonised. To do this, unscrew the union nut which secures the outlet pipe to the adaptor. Remove the carburettors and withdraw the restrictor from the adaptor.

6   Clean the 'Y' piece and restrictor with a wire brush and then blow through with air from a tyre pump.

7   Refit all components using new gaskets.

Series 2 cars

8   A variable orifice E.G.R. system is used on these cars which incorporates a diaphragm type recirculation valve.

Fig. 3.44. Removing inlet drilling carbon deposits (E.G.R. system) (Sec. 31)

1   *Blanking screw*
3   *Mild steel rod*

Fig. 3.45. Location of E.G.R. valve and unit securing nuts (Sec. 31)

2   *Alignment marks*
3   *Adjuster screw and locknut*
4   *Valve delivery port*
6   *Secondary throttle housing cover screw*
7   *Secondary throttle housing cover*
8   *Pillar nut*
9   *E.G.R. valve*
10 *Valve bracket*
11 *Vacuum pipe*
12 *Securing nuts*

9   At regular intervals, mark the relationship of the diaphragm unit to the valve body by scribing a mark across the flange joint. Remove the three securing nuts and separate the diaphragm unit from the valve body. On no account disturb the adjuster screw and locknut on the top of the diaphragm unit.

10 Clean all components free from carbon deposits using a wire brush and air from a tyre pump and check the condition of the valve head, shaft and seat, also the diaphragm for wear. If the components are faulty, the complete valve/diaphragm assembly must be renewed.

32 Fuel cut-off inertia switch

1   In the interest of safety, this device is fitted to most Series 2 cars. It is located below the fascia panel on the passenger side and is secured in spring clips.

2   To remove the switch, disconnect the leads and pull it from the clips. Refit by reversing the removal procedure, the leads can be connected to either terminal. When installed, depress the plunger and fit the cover.

33 Accelerator pedal linkage

1   This comprises an 'organ' type pedal and a mixed system of rods and cables.

2   Dismantling and reassembly is quite straightforward, the cable and rods being disconnected after removal of circlips or split pins and clevis pins.

3   There are minor differences in design of components used in the various models and whether left or right-hand steering.

4   When a new cable is fitted always check that the throttle valve plates are closed when the pedal is released and that an almost imperceptible amount of slack exists in the cable to allow for engine rocking.

5   Check that the throttle valve plates are fully open with the pedal depressed, but do not allow the cable to be strained by over-depression of the pedal. A floor-mounted stop bolt is provided to limit the downward travel of the pedal.

6   On cars equipped with automatic transmission, refer to Section 21.

Fig. 3.46. Fuel line heat exchanger (cars equipped with air conditioning) (Sec. 34)

A   *Refrigerant pipes (do not disconnect)*
B   *Fuel lines*

34 Fuel feed line heat exchanger (cars with air-conditioning)

1   On cars equipped with an air-conditioning system, a small heat exchanger is mounted in the fuel supply line above a heat shield on the induction side of the engine. Its purpose is to prevent a fuel vapour lock occurring in exceptionally hot operating conditions and the design utilises some of the cooling action which takes place as fuel passes through a jacket which surrounds the air-conditioning system suction pipe.

2   **On no account disconnect the refrigerant pipes from the heat exchanger unless the air-conditioning system has first been discharged.** This is a job for your Jaguar dealer or a professional refrigeration engineer.

35 Fault diagnosis - carburation and fuel systems

Symptom	Reason/s
Excessive fuel consumption	Air filter choked. Leakage from pump, carburettor or fuel lines or fuel tank. Float chamber flooding. Distributor capacitor faulty. Distributor weights or vacuum capsule faulty. Mixture too rich. Contact breaker gap too wide. Incorrect valve clearances. Incorrect spark plug gaps. Tyres under inflated. Dragging brakes.
Insufficient fuel delivery or weak mixture	Fuel tank air vent or pipe blocked or flattened. Clogged fuel filter. Float chamber needle valve clogged. Faulty fuel pump valves. Fuel pump faulty. Fuel pipe unions loose. Inlet manifold gasket or carburettor flange gasket leaking. Incorrect adjustment of carburettor.
Rough idling	Sticking piston. Split diaphragm (Stromberg). Faulty temperature compensator (Stromberg). Perforated vacuum pipes.

36 Fault diagnosis - automatic enrichment device (AED)

Symptom	Reason/s
Engine fails to fire when cold	Lack of fuel to AED. Lack of fuel from AED to inlet manifold.
Engine fires when cold but fails to keep running	Sticking or faulty needle valve or float. Faulty air flap valve on AED air inlet elbow. Inadequate fuel supply.
Engine warm or hot; fails to start or keep running	Leaks in system pipes. Sticking or faulty needle valve or float. Faulty AED unit.

37 Fault diagnosis - emission control systems

Symptom	Reason/s
Fault in air injection system	Slack pump drivebelt. Perforated or loose connecting hoses. Choked air pump air filter.
Fault in EGR system	Choked inlet drilling, restrictor or 'Y' piece Clogged EGR valve (cause of backfire).

Chapter 4 Ignition system

Contents

Specifications

System ... ... 12 volt, negative earth, battery coil and crankshaft driven distributor

Distributor
Type:

2.8 litre	Lucas 25D6 - 41275
3.4 litre	Lucas 45D6
4.2 litre	Lucas 22D6 - 41060A (later models - Lucas 45D6)
Rotation	Anticlockwise
Contact breaker gap	0.014 to 0.016 in (0.36 to 0.41 mm)
Dwell angle	$35^o \pm 3^o$
Firing order	1 — 5 — 3 — 6 — 2 — 4

Ignition timing

	2.8 litre	3.4 litre	4.2 litre
Static:			
7.8 : 1 compression ratio	—	8° BTDC	—
8 : 1 compression ratio	12° BTDC	—	8° BTDC
8.4 : 1 compression ratio	—	8° BTDC	8° BTDC
9 : 1 compression ratio	12° BTDC	—	8° BTDC
9 : 1 compression ratio (N. America)	—	—	10° BTDC
Dynamic (with stroboscope) Vacuum pipe disconnected, where applicable:			
7.8 : 1 compression ratio	—	18° BTDC @ 1500 rev/min	—
8 : 1 compression ratio	22° BTDC @ 1000 rev/min	—	20° BTDC @ 1700 rev/min
8.4 : 1 compression ratio	—	18° BTDC @ 1500 rev/min	20° BTDC @ 1700 rev/min
9 : 1 compression ratio	22° BTDC @ 1000 rev/min	—	20° BTDC @ 1700 rev/min
9 : 1 compression ratio (N. America)	—	—	TDC @ 650 rev/min

Spark plugs
Type:

2.8 litre	Champion N7Y
3.4 litre	Champion N12Y
4.2 litre	Champion N11Y
Gap	0.025 in (0.64 mm)

Torque wrench settings

	lb ft	Nm
Spark plugs	18	25

1 General description

The ignition system is based on the supply of low tension voltage from the battery to the ignition coil where it is converted into high tension voltage. The high tension voltage is powerful enough to jump the spark plug gap in the cylinders under high compression pressures - provided that the ignition system is in good working order and that all adjustments are correct.

The ignition system comprises two individual circuits known as the low tension (LT) and the high tension (HT) circuits. The LT circuit which is sometimes referred to as the primary circuit, comprises the battery, the lead to the control box, the lead to the ignition switch and from there to the low tension or primary coil windings of the coil (terminal SW), and the lead from the low tension coil windings (terminal CB) to the contact breaker points and condenser in the distributor.

The HT circuit consists of the high tension or secondary coil windings, the heavy ignition lead from the centre of the coil to the centre position in the distributor cap and thence via a carbon brush to the rotor arm and then through the spark plug leads to the spark plugs.

The system functions as follows. Low tension voltage is changed in the coil into high tension voltage by the opening and closing of the contact breaker points in the low tension circuit. HT voltage is then fed

Measuring plug gap. A feeler gauge of the correct size (see ignition system specifications) should have a slight 'drag' when slid between the electrodes. Adjust gap if necessary

Adjusting plug gap. The plug gap is adjusted by bending the earth electrode inwards, or outwards, as necessary until the correct clearance is obtained. Note the use of the correct tool

Normal. Grey-brown deposits lightly coated core nose. Gap increasing by around 0.001 in (0.025 mm) per 1000 miles (1600 km). Plugs ideally suited to engine and engine in good condition

Carbon fouling. Dry, black, sooty deposits. Will cause weak spark and eventually misfire. Fault: over-rich fuel mixture. Check: carburettor mixture settings, float level and jet sizes; choke operation and cleanliness of air filter. Plugs can be re-used after cleaning

Oil fouling. Wet, oily deposits. Will cause weak spark and eventually misfire. Fault: worn bores/piston rings or valve guides; sometimes occurs (temporarily) during running-in period. Plugs can be re-used after thorough cleaning

Overheating. Electrodes have glazed appearance, core nose very white - few deposits. Fault: plug overheating. Check: plug value, ignition timing, fuel octane rating (too low) and fuel mixture (too weak). Discard plugs and cure fault immediately

Electrode damage. Electrodes burned away; core nose has burned, glazed appearance. Fault: initial pre-ignition. Check: as for 'Overheating' but may be more severe. Discard plugs and remedy fault before piston or valve damage occurs

Split core nose (may appear initially as a crack). Damage is self-evident, but cracks will only show after cleaning. Fault: pre-ignition or wrong gap-setting technique. Check: ignition timing, cooling system, fuel octane rating (too low) and fuel mixture (too weak). Discard plugs, rectify fault immediately via the carbon brush in the centre of the distributor cap to the rotor arm of the distributor. The rotor arm revolves inside the distributor cap and each time it comes into line with one of the six metal segments in the cap, which are connected to the spark plug leads, the opening and closing of the contact breaker points causes the HT voltage to build up, jump the gap from the rotor arm to the appropriate metal segment and so via the lead to the spark plug, where it finally jumps the spark plug gap before going to earth. The contact breaker points consist of one fixed and one free point. The free point bears on the shaft which carries the rotor arm and movement of this point is governed by the shape of the shaft which is hexagonal at the position where the point bears. As the shaft revolves the free contact breaker point moves over one of the humps of the hexagon and is so brought out of contact with the fixed point.

The ignition is advanced and retarded automatically to ensure that the spark occurs at the right moment for the particular load at the prevailing engine speed.

The ignition advance is controlled both mechanically and by a vacuum operated system. The mechanical system comprises two lead weights, which act in the same manner as a governor, and which due to centrifugal force, move out from the distributor shaft as the engine speed rises. As they move outwards they rotate a cam relative to the distributor shaft and so advance the spark. The weights are held in position by two light springs and it is the tension of the springs which is largely responsible for correct spark advancement.

The vacuum control consists of a diaphragm, one side of which is connected via a small bore tube to the inlet manifold and the other side to the contact breaker plate. Depression in the inlet manifold, which varies with engine speed and throttle opening, causes the diaphragm to move carrying with it the contact breaker plate and thus advancing or retarding the spark. A fine degree of control is achieved by a spring in the vacuum assembly. It will be seen from the specification at the beginning of the Chapter that the type of distributor used varies with the model of the car. There is little or no outward difference in either of them and the above description and the following sections apply to each.

2 Contact breaker points - adjustment

1 At intervals of 6000 miles (9600 km) check the contact breaker gap in the following way. This check should also be carried out at the end of the first 1000 miles (1600 km) after new points have been fitted as the plastic heel of the movable contact arm will probably have bedded in and the gap will have been decreased.

2 Slip back the spring clips from the distributor cap, remove the cap and pull off the rotor arm. Later models have a waterproof cover which can be removed after the condenser securing screw and the contact arm terminal nut have been removed.

3 Turn the crankshaft until the plastic heel of the movable contact arm is in one of the high points of the cam. The crankshaft can be turned by applying a spanner to the crankshaft damper bolt or on cars with a manual gearbox, by engaging top gear and pushing the car. It will be found easier with either method if the spark plugs are first removed.

4 Check the points gap with a feeler blade, it should be between 0.014 and 0.016 in (0.36 and 0.41 mm).

5 If the gap requires adjusting, release the screw which secures the fixed contact breaker plate and turn the breaker plate by inserting a screwdriver in the two small slots which are provided for the purpose in contact plate and baseplate.

6 Retighten the contact breaker plate screw.

7 It is emphasised that if the points are pitted or one of them has a 'pip' on it which is the result of extended service, then a false reading will be obtained using the feeler blades. In this case, the points should either be renewed or removed and dressed as described in the following Section.

8 Check the dwell angle (see Section 4).

3 Contact breaker points - removal and refitting

1 If on examination, the contact breaker points are seen to be pitted or eroded, or one of the points has a 'pip' on it, then the contact breaker arms must be removed.

2 Unscrew and remove the small nut from the anchor post to which

Fig. 4.1. Waterproof cover fitted to some distributors (Sec. 2)

4 Condenser securing screw   6 Waterproof cover
5 Contact terminal nut

Fig. 4.2. Adjusting distributor contact points (Sec. 2)

1 Feeler blade   3 Adjustment leverage
2 Fixed breaker arm screw   notch

the spring arm of the movable contact is attached, extract the insulating bush and the low tension wire terminal tag and the condenser lead tag.

3 Prise up the spring arm and lift the movable contact from its pivot post.

4 Unscrew and remove the screw from the fixed contact breaker arm and lift the arm from the distributor baseplate.

5 If the points are only lightly pitted, dress them smooth on an oilstone, keeping their faces quite square. If they are deeply pitted,

then they should be renewed.

6   Clean the faces of the points, before installing them, with solvent or methylated spirit.

7   Refit the contact breaker arms and adjust the gap as described in the preceding Section.

8   Apply lubricant to the distributor at the points indicated, refit the rotor arm and distributor cap (Fig. 4.3.)

9   Check the dwell angle (Section 4) and the ignition timing (Section 8).

4   Dwell angle - description and checking

1   The setting of the contact breaker points gap using a feeler blade must be regarded as an initial adjustment only and wherever possible the dwell angle must be checked as soon as possible thereafter. This is particularly important with engines which are equipped with full emission control systems.

2   The dwell angle is the number of degrees through which the distributor cam turns during the period between the instants of closure and opening of the contact points. It can only be checked with a dwell meter. If the dwell angle is found to be too large, increase the points gap, if the dwell angle is too small, reduce the size of the points gap.

5   Condenser (capacitor) - removal, testing and refitting

1   The condenser ensures that with the contact breaker points open, the sparking between them is not excessive to cause severe pitting. The condenser is fitted in parallel and its failure will automatically cause failure of the ignition system as the points will be prevented from interrupting the low tension circuit.

2   Testing for an unserviceable condenser may be effected by switching on the ignition and separating the contact points by hand. If this action is accompanied by a blue flash then condenser failure is indicated. Difficult starting, missing of the engine after several miles running or badly pitted points are other indications of a faulty condenser.

3   The surest test is by substitution of a new unit.

4   The condenser is secured to the distributor baseplate by a single screw and its head is attached to the top of the contact breaker spring arm anchor post.

6   Distributor - removal and installation

1   The distributor is driven by a shaft which is an upper extension of the oil pump driveshaft, both of which are gear driven from the crankshaft.

2   To remove the distributor, pull off the low tension wire from the terminal block on the side of the distributor body.

3   Prise back the spring clips and remove the distributor cap. Extract the condenser screw and contact breaker terminal nut and remove the waterproof cover (later models only).

4   Pull off the vacuum tube from the distributor vacuum capsule.

5   Mark the position of the distributor body in relation to the clamp plate, release the pinch bolt on the clamp plate and pull the distributor straight upwards from its recess.

6   The distributor is driven by an offset dog (large and small segments) and if no further dismantling of the distributor drive is carried out then the distributor can be installed simply by pushing it back into its recess so that the offset dog mates with its slot. Set the distributor in its original relative position to the clamp plate and tighten the pinch bolt.

7   If the engine has been dismantled to the extent where the distributor drive has been disturbed, then the following installation procedure must be followed.

8   Turn the crankshaft until nos. 1 and 6 pistons are at TDC. This can be checked by observing that the 'O' mark on the crankshaft damper is opposite the crankcase pointer (photo).

9   Hold the distributor driveshaft over the recess in the cylinder block so that the offset slot in the end of the shaft is in the position shown in Fig. 4.4. Withdraw the shaft (keeping the slot in the same attitude) enough to be able to fit the thrust washer and drivegear to the end of the shaft. Press the shaft into the gear, making sure that the key engages correctly.

10 Fit the pegged tab washer so that the peg is in the keyway of the

Fig. 4.3. Distributor lubrication points (Sec. 3)

1   *Pivot post (engine oil)*
2   *Baseplate cut-out (engine oil)*
3   *Cam high points (grease or petroleum jelly)*
4   *Centre screw (engine oil)*

6.8 Crankshaft damper timing marks and timing cover pointer

Fig. 4.4. Distributor driveshaft installation diagram (Sec. 6)

drive gear (see Fig. 1.14 Chapter 1).

11 Fully tighten the nut and secure with the tab washer. The endfloat of the shaft should be between 0.004 and 0.006 in (0.10 and 0.15 mm).

12 Install the distributor and bolt the clamp plate to the cylinder block so that the vacuum capsule is towards the rear of the engine.

13 Turn the distributor until the contact breaker points are just about to open and tighten the pinch bolt.

14 Time the ignition, as described in Section 8, whenever the distributor has been removed and installed.

7   Distributor - overhaul

1   Remove the distributor from the car as described in Section 6.

2   Refer to Fig. 4.5. which shows an exploded view of the distributor.

3   Remove the contact breaker points as described in Section 2 and remove the condenser as described in Section 5.

4   Remove the two screws securing the baseplate and earth lead. Disconnect the link to the vacuum control unit and lift off the baseplate.

5   Before proceeding any further, take careful note of the relative positions of the rotor arm slot located above the cam and of the offset driving dog. It is possible to assemble these items 180° out on reassembly, which means that the distributor would have to be rotated 180° in order to obtain correct timing of the engine and connections cannot be made with the distributor so located.

6   Remove the cam retaining screw and remove the cam.

7   Lift out the automatic timing control weights and their springs. Note how these are fitted.

8   Remove the circlip securing the knurled advance and retard adjustment nut. Remove the adjusting nut and spring. The vacuum unit can now be withdrawn.

9   Remove the clamp plate by undoing the pinch bolt and sliding the plate off the base of the distributor.

10 To remove the driving dog, knock out the taper pin and lift off the dog and thrust washer. The shaft may now be lifted upwards.

11 Thoroughly wash all mechanical parts in petrol and wipe dry using a clean non-fluffy rag.

12 Check the contact breaker points as described in Section 2.

13 Check the distributor cap for signs of 'tracking' which will be indicated by a thin black line between the segments. Renew the cap if this defect is noted.

14 Ensure that the carbon brush in the cap is free to move in its holder and is not worn down. Do not remove the brush needlessly as the spring is usually a tight fit in the holder and will be badly stretched as you pull the brush out.

15 If the metal portion of the rotor arm is badly burned or is loose, renew the arm. Slight burning can be rectified with a piece of fine 'wet-and-dry' paper but maintain the face square.

16 Examine the fit of the contact breaker plate on the baseplate and check the breaker arm pivot for looseness or wear. Renew the plate if necessary.

17 Examine the centrifugal weights and pivot pins for wear and renew the weights or cam assembly if a degree of wear is found.

18 Examine the shaft and the fit of the cam assembly on the shaft. If the clearance appears to be excessive, compare with new items and renew either or both if they show excessive wear.

19 If the shaft is a loose fit in a distributor bush and can be 'rocked', we suggest that a reconditioned distributor is obtained.

20 Reassembly is a straightforward reversal of the dismantling process. Note in addition:

21 Lubricate the centrifugal weights and other parts of the mechanical advance mechanism with thin machine oil. Lubricate the distributor shaft with clean engine oil and smear the cam face with engine oil or petroleum jelly. Do not be too lavish with the oil.

22 Check the action of the weights in the fully advanced and retarded positions, make sure they are not binding.

23 Adjust the micrometer advance and retard adjusting nut to bring the mechanism to the mid position of the timing scale.

24 Finally set the contact breaker points as described in Section 2.

8   Ignition timing

1   It is recommended that the static ignition timing is set initially

Fig. 4.5. Exploded view of type 22D6 distributor (Sec. 7)

1	Rotor	10	Contact points
2	LT terminal	11	Moving baseplate
3	Fixed contact securing screw	12	Cam
4	Baseplate	13	Action plate
5	Centrifugal counterweights	14	Collar
6	Vacuum capsule	15	Vernier adjuster knurled
7	Thrust washer		nut
8	Earth bond	16	'O' ring
9	Condenser	17	Offset dog and pin

using a test bulb and then checked with a stroboscope with the engine running.

2   Set the vernier adjuster to the centre of its scale.

3   Remove the no. 6 (front) spark plug and turn the crankshaft until compression can be felt being generated when the finger is placed over the plug hole.

4   Continue turning the crankshaft until the appropriate BTDC mark (see Specifications) is exactly opposite the pointer on the crankcase (Fig. 4.6).

5   Connect a 12v test lamp between the CB terminal of the coil and a good earth.

6   Slacken the distributor clamp plate pinch bolt until the distributor will turn stiffly.

7   Switch on the ignition and turn the distributor one way or the other, until the test lamp just lights up which indicates that the contact points are just open.

8   Switch off the ignition and tighten the pinch bolt without disturbing the setting of the distributor.

9   Fine adjustment may be carried out from this setting to accommodate

Fig. 4.6. Ignition timing marks on crankshaft damper (Sec. 8)

variations in fuel and operating conditions by turning the vernier
adjuster screw not more than six 'clicks' in either direction.
10 The ignition timing should now be checked with a stroboscope in
the following manner.
11 Run the engine to normal operating temperature then switch off
the ignition and disconnect the vacuum pipe from the distributor and
plug the pipe.
12 Connect a stroboscope in accordance with the manufacturer's
instructions (usually between no. 6 spark plug and the end of no. 6
spark plug lead).
13 Start the engine and let it idle at the specified speed shown in
Specification Section. Point the stroboscope at the crankshaft damper,
the appropriate degree mark should then appear stationary opposite
the crankcase pointer. If it is not opposite, adjust the distributor until
the mark and pointer coincide. This can usually be achieved by using
the vernier adjuster provided the static setting was carried out correctly.
14 If the timing mark and pointer are difficult to see, paint them with
a dab of white paint.
15 Remove the stroboscope, reconnect the spark plug lead and
reconnect the vacuum pipe to the distributor.

9 The coil

1 High tension current should be negative at the spark plug terminals.
To ensure this, check the LT connections to the coil are correctly made.
2 The LT wire from the distributor must connect with the (−)
negative terminal on the coil.
3 The coil (+) positive terminal is connected to the ignition/start
switch.
4 An incorrect connection can cause as much as a 60% loss of spark
efficiency and can cause rough idling and misfiring at speed.
5 Earlier models were fitted with a standard 12 volt ignition coil
while later models have a ballast resistor ignition system. The coils are
not interchangeable between systems.
6 The purpose of the ballast resistor is to ensure maximum efficiency
at high engine speeds and to facilitate engine starting at low ambient
temperature conditions. The ballast resistor prevents the voltage applied
to the coil from falling during the period when the starter motor is
cranking the engine. This is normally the case in systems without this
device, due to the starter motor load conditions.
7 The ballast resistor is mounted on early cars in conjunction with the
coil on the right-hand wing valance at the front of the engine compartment. On later cars, the coil and ballast resistor are mounted on a plate
on the right-hand side of the engine.

10 Spark plugs and high tension (HT) leads

1 At intervals of 2000 miles (3200 km), the spark plugs should be
removed, cleaned and the gaps checked and adjusted. Always adjust by
bending the side electrode.
2 At intervals of 10000 miles (16000 km) the plugs should be
renewed even if they appear in good condition, as they will almost

Fig. 4.7. Ballast ignition system circuit diagram (Sec. 9)

1	Starter motor	9	Solenoid terminal
2	Field windings	10	Relay coil
3	Armature	11	LT lead
4	Solenoid terminal 'STA'	12	Ignition supply lead
5	Battery supply terminal	13	Coil
6	Solenoid core	14	Ballast resistor
7	Solenoid shunt winding	15	Ignition/starter switch
8	Solenoid series winding	16	Relay

Fig. 4.8. Coil and ballast resistor (later cars) (Sec. 9)

certainly have a low efficiency when sparking under compression in
combustion chamber conditions after this length of service. Renew
with plugs of currently specified type.
3 The appearance of a spark plug will tell much about the overall
condition of the engine, for example, if the insulator nose of the spark
plug is clean and white, with no deposits, this is indicative of a weak
mixture, or too hot a plug. (A hot plug transfers heat away from the
electrode slowly - a cold plug transfers it away quickly).
4 If the top and insulator nose is covered with hard black looking
deposits, then this is indicative that the mixture is too rich. Should the
plug be black and oily, then it is likely that the engine is fairly worn, as
well as the mixture being too rich.

Fig. 4.11. Spark plug lead connection diagram (Sec. 10)

5 If the insulator nose is covered with light tan to greyish brown deposits, then the mixture is correct and it is likely that the engine is in good condition.

6 If there are any traces of long brown tapering stains on the outside of the white portion of the plug, then the plug will have to be renewed, as this shows that there is a faulty joint between the plug body and the insulator, and compression is being allowed to leak away.

7 Plugs should be cleaned by a sand blasting machine, which will free them from carbon more thoroughly than cleaning by hand. The machine will also test the condition of the plugs under compression. Any plug that fails to spark at the recommended pressure should be renewed.

8 The spark plug gap is of considerable importance, as, if it is too large or too small the size of the spark and its efficiency will be seriously impaired. The spark plug gap should be set to 0.025 in (0.64 mm) for the best results.

9 To set it, measure the gap with a feeler gauge, and then bend open, or close, the outer plug electrode until the correct gap is achieved. The centre electrode should never be bent as this may crack the insulation and cause plug failure, if nothing worse.

10 When replacing the plugs, remember to use new plug washers and replace the leads from the distributor in the correct firing order which is 1–5–3–6–2–4. Number 1 cylinder being at the rear of the engine and number 6 being nearest the radiator (Fig. 4.11).

11 Occassionally wipe the plug leads free from dirt and grease.

11 Ignition system - fault diagnosis

Failures of the ignition system will either be due to faults in the HT or LT circuits. Initial checks should be made by observing the security of spark plug terminals, Lucar type terminals, coil and battery connection. More detailed investigation and the explanation and remedial action in respect of symptoms of ignition malfunction are described in the following sub-Sections.

Engine fails to start

1 If the engine fails to start and the car was running normally when it was last used, first check there is fuel in the fuel tank. If the engine turns over normally on the starter motor and the battery is evidently well charged, then the fault may be in either the high or low tension circuits. First check the HT circuit. **Note:** If the battery is known to be fully charged; the ignition light comes on, and the starter motor fails to turn the engine **check the tightness of the leads on the battery terminals** and also the secureness of the earth lead to its **connection to the body.** It is quite common for the leads to have worked loose, even if they look and feel secure. If one of the battery terminal posts gets very hot when trying to work the starter motor this is a sure indication of a faulty connection to that terminal.

2 One of the commonest reasons for bad starting is wet or damp spark plug leads and distributor. Remove the distributor cap. If condensation is visible internally, dry the cap with a rag and also wipe over the leads. Replace the cap.

3 If the engine still fails to start, check that current is reaching the plugs, by disconnecting each plug lead in turn at the spark plug end, and hold the end of the cable about 3/16th inch (5.0 mm) away from the cylinder block. Spin the engine on the starter motor.

4 Sparking between the end of the cable and the block should be fairly strong with a regular blue spark. (Hold the lead with rubber to avoid electric shocks). If current is reaching the plugs, then remove them and clean and regap them. The engine should now start.

5 If there is no spark at the plug leads take off the HT lead from the centre of the distributor cap and hold it to the block as before. Spin the engine on the starter once more. A rapid succession of blue sparks between the end of the lead and the block indicate that the coil is in order and that the distributor cap is cracked, the rotor arm faulty, or the carbon brush in the top of the distributor cap is not making good contact with the spring on the rotor arm. Possibly the points are in bad condition. Clean and reset them as described in this Chapter.

6 If there are no sparks from the end of the lead from the coil, check the connections at the coil end of the lead. If it is in order start checking the low tension circuit.

7 Use a 12v voltmeter or a 12v bulb and two lengths of wire. With the ignition switch on and the points open test between the low tension wire to the coil (it is marked (+) and earth. No reading indicates a break in the supply from the ignition switch. Check the connections at the switch to see if any are loose. Refit them and the engine should run. A reading shows a faulty coil or condenser, or broken lead between the coil and the distributor.

8 Take the condenser wire off the points assembly and with the points open, test between the moving point and earth. If there now is a reading, then the fault is in the condenser. Fit a new one and the fault is cleared.

9 With no reading from the moving point to earth, take a reading between earth and the (–) terminal of the coil. A reading here shows a broken wire which will need to be replaced between the coil and distributor. No reading confirms that the coil has failed and must be replaced, after which the engine will run once more. Remember to refit the condenser wire to the points assembly. For these tests it is sufficient to separate the points with a piece of dry paper while testing with the points open.

Engine misfires

10 If the engine misfires regularly run it at a fast idling speed. Pull off each of the plug caps in turn and listen to the note of the engine. Hold the plug cap in a dry cloth or with a rubber glove as additional protection against a shock from the HT supply.

11 No difference in engine running will be noticed when the lead from the defective circuit is removed. Removing the lead from one of the good cylinders will accentuate the misfire.

12 Remove the plug lead from the end of the defective plug and hold it about 3/16 inch (5 mm) away from the block. Restart the engine. If the sparking is fairly strong and regular the fault must lie in the spark plug.

13 The plug may be loose, the insulation may be cracked, or the points may have burnt away giving too wide a gap for the spark to jump. Worse still, one of the points may have broken off. Either renew the plug, or clean it, reset the gap, and then test it.

14 If there is no spark at the end of the plug lead, or if it is weak and intermittent, check the ignition lead from the distributor to the plug. If the insulation is cracked or perished, renew the lead. Check the connections at the distributor cap.

15 If there is still no spark, examine the distributor cap carefully for tracking. This can be recognised by a very thin black line running between two or more electrodes, or between an electrode and some other part of the distributor. These lines are paths which now conduct electricity across the cap thus letting it run to earth. The only answer is a new distributor cap.

16 Apart from the ignition timing being incorrect, other causes of misfiring have already been dealt with under the section dealing with the failure of the engine to start. To recap - these are that:

    a) *The coil may be faulty giving an intermittent misfire*
    b) *There may be a damaged wire or loose connection in the low tension circuit.*
    c) *The condenser may be short circuiting*
    d) *There may be a mechanical fault in the distributor (broken driving spindle or contact breaker spring).*

17 If the ignition timing is too far retarded, it should be noted that the engine will tend to overheat, and there will be a quite noticeable drop in power. If the engine is overheating and the power is down, and the ignition timing is correct, then the carburettor should be checked, as it is likely that this is where the fault lies.

Chapter 5 Clutch

Contents

Specifications

Type	Diaphragm spring with hydraulic actuation
Make	Borg and Beck 9.5 in
Release bearing	Graphite
Free-movement at withdrawal lever	
Except Series 2	1/16 in (1.5 mm) at pedal ¼ in (6.35 mm)
Series 2	0.125 in (3.2 mm)

Torque wrench settings	lb ft	Nm
Clutch cover bolts	20	28
Clutch bellhousing to gearbox bolts	42	58
Clutch bellhousing to engine bolts	35	48
Slave cylinder bolts	25	35

1 General description

1   The clutch fitted to all models is of Borg and Beck diaphragm spring type.

2   The diaphragm spring is riveted inside the pressure plate cover and has two fulcrum rings interposed between the shoulders of the rivets and the cover. The diaphragm spring pivots on these rings and depression of the clutch pedal actuates the release bearing causing the diaphragm spring to deflect and pull the pressure plate from the driven plate (friction disc) thus freeing the clutch.

3   Clutch actuation is hydraulic.

2 Clutch - adjustment

1   The clutch is virtually self-adjusting and the correct free-movement will normally be maintained throughout the life of the clutch driven plate.

2   However, after overhaul or renewal of any of the actuating components, check that there is specified free-movement at the point of connection of the operating rod and withdrawal lever. This can be felt more easily if the return spring is first unhooked.

3   Any adjustment can be carried out by releasing the locknut on the operating rod and rotating the rod.

3 Master cylinder - removal, overhaul and refitting

1   Disconnect the fluid outlet pipe from the master cylinder.

2   Remove the four setscrews which secure the clutch pedal box to the engine compartment rear bulkhead. These screws are accessible from within the car (Fig. 5.2).

3   Remove the pedal box and master cylinder as an assembly.

4   Extract the lockscrew and withdraw the pedal pivot pin. Pull the

1/16" (1.5 mm)

Fig. 5.1. Clutch free movement diagram (Sec. 2)

pedal back so that the split pin can be withdrawn.

5   Extract the split pin and clevis pin from the pushrod fork end.

6   Remove the two setscrews and detach the master cylinder from the pedal box.

7   Clean external dirt from the master cylinder and pull off the rubber boot from the master cylinder body rim.

8   Depress the pushrod slightly and extract the circlip (10). The pushrod (9), piston (7) and the other internal components will now be ejected from the cylinder body (Fig. 5.3.)

9   At this stage wash all components in clean hydraulic fluid or methylated spirit (nothing else) and examine the surfaces of piston and cylinder for scoring or 'bright' wear areas. If these are evident then the master cylinder should be renewed complete.

10 If the components are found to be in good condition, discard the

Fig. 5.3. Exploded view of the clutch master cylinder (Sec. 3)

1	Cylinder/reservoir	7	Piston
2	Filler/vent cap	8	Secondary cup seal
3	Piston return spring	9	Push-rod
4	Spring retainer	10	Circlip
5	Cup seal	11	Rubber boot
6	Washer		

Fig. 5.2. Clutch pedal and master cylinder mounting box (Sec. 3)

rubber seals and obtain a repair kit which will contain all the necessary new seals and other items.

11 Fit the seals using the fingers only to manipulate them into position and making sure that the lips are correctly positioned.

12 Dip the internal components in clean hydraulic fluid before installing them in the master cylinder body.

13 When reassembly is complete, refit the master cylinder by reversing the removal process and fill it with clean fluid.

14 Bleed the clutch hydraulic system (Section 5) and check the free-movement (Section 2).

4 Clutch slave cylinder - removal, overhaul and refitting

1 Disconnect the fluid inlet pipe from the slave cylinder and plug the pipe or let the fluid drain into a clean container.
2 Peel back the rubber boot which surrounds the pushrod and then disconnect the return spring.
3 Unbolt and remove the cylinder leaving the pushrod attached to the withdrawal lever.
4 Clean external dirt from the cylinder and then extract the circlip.
5 Apply air pressure from a tyre foot pump to the fluid inlet hole and expel the internal components.
6 Wash the internal parts in clean hydraulic fluid or methylated spirit (nothing else) and examine the surfaces of piston and cylinder bore for scoring or 'bright' wear areas. If these are evident, renew the slave cylinder complete.
7 Where the components are in good order, discard the seals and obtain a repair kit which will contain all the necessary new seals and other renewable items.
8 Fit the new seals using the fingers only to manipulate them into position ensuring the lips face the correct way.
9 Dip the internal components in clean hydraulic fluid and insert

them into the slave cylinder taking care not to trap the seal lips.
10 Fit the circlip and the rubber boot.
11 Refit the slave cylinder by first entering the pushrod into it and then bolting the cylinder to the clutch housing. Reconnect the return spring and check the free-movement.
12 Fill the clutch master cylinder reservoir and then bleed the clutch hydraulic system as described in the next Section.

5 Clutch hydraulic system - bleeding

1 Bleeding the clutch hydraulic system (expelling air) is not a routine maintenance operation and should only be necessary when some portion of the hydraulic system has been disconnected or where, due to a leak, the level of fluid in the hydraulic reservoir has been allowed to drop too low. The presence of air in the system will result in poor clutch operation as, unlike fluid, the bubbles of air can be compressed.
2 Thoroughly clean the top of the clutch fluid reservoir and fill the reservoir with hydraulic fluid.
3 The bleed nipple for the system is located on the slave cylinder on the right-hand side of the clutch housing. Thoroughly clean the exterior of the nipple.
4 Attach a length of rubber tube to the nipple and allow it to hang in a clean glass jar, partly filled with hydraulic fluid. The open end of the tube must be submerged.
5 Unscrew the screw nipple one complete turn.
6 Have an assistant in the car to depress the clutch pedal slowly to the full extent of its travel. Tighten the screw nipple whilst the clutch pedal is held depressed.
7 Release pressure on the clutch pedal and repeat operations 5 and 6 until the fluid issuing from the tube is entirely free of air. Take care to replenish the reservoir frequently during these operations because if the fluid level is allowed to drop more than halfway, air will enter the system.
8 When you are satisfied that the system is clear of air, top up the master cylinder reservoir to the 'fluid level' mark.
9 Do not use the fluid which has been bled through the system as this will be aerated. Always use fresh fluid straight from a sealed container which has remained unshaken for the preceding 24 hours.

6 Clutch - removal

1 Access to the clutch is obtained by removing the engine/gearbox, as described in Chapter 1, and then unbolting the gearbox and withdrawing it from the engine.
2 Unscrew and remove the bolts which secure the clutch assembly to

Fig. 5.4. Exploded view of the clutch slave cylinder (Sec. 4)

1 Piston return spring
2 Cup seal former
3 Cup seal
4 Body
5 Piston
6 Circlip
7 Rubber boot

Fig. 5.5. Exploded view of the clutch assembly

1 Driven plate
2 Pressure plate
3 Rivet
4 Centre sleeve
5 Belleville washer
6 Fulcrum ring
7 Diaphragm spring
8 Cover pressing
9 Release plate
10 Retainer
11 Tab washer
12 Setscrew
13 Retainer
14 Release bearing

the flywheel. The position of any balance weights fitted must be noted and the weights retained for refitting in their original positions.

3   Withdraw the clutch assembly taking care to catch the driven plate as it falls from the face of the flywheel.

7   Clutch - inspection and renovation

1   Examine the friction facings. They will probably be highly polished, through which the grain of the material can be clearly seen, and mid-brown in colour. The facings are satisfactory if in this condition but if there are dark, highly glazed, patches which hide the grain or if there is a resinous deposit on the facings or if they have a black soaked appearance the indication is that they are contaminated with oil and the driven plate assembly should be renewed.

2   Examine the rivets of the driven plate. They should be well below the surface of the friction material and should be secure. Renew the driven plate if the facings are worn or if any rivets are loose.

3   Check the driven plate springs for fracture and security. Check the condition of the splines in the centre hub; excessive wear, which results from faulty alignment will mean renewing the plate.

4   Inspect the diaphragm spring for cracks or distortion.

5   The face of the pressure plate should not be ridged or pitted and this also applies to the face of the flywheel in the bearing area of the driven plate.

6   Check that the flange of the cover is not distorted.

7   If any of the faults just described are evident, renew the pressure plate assembly or the driven plate on a factory reconditioned exchange basis - do not waste your time trying to repair, overhaul or re-line them.

8   Before fitting new components always rectify oil leaks. These are probably due to a faulty crankshaft rear oil seal or a gearbox front oil seal.

8   Clutch release bearing and withdrawal mechanism - overhaul

1   With the gearbox separated from the engine, take the opportunity to inspect the withdrawal lever and release fork within the clutch bellhousing. Any wear in the pivot will necessitate renewal of the pin and bushes in the bellhousing and if wear has taken place in the fork as well then a new fork will be required.

2   If the clutch release bearing has been in use for 20,000 miles (32,000 km) or more it should be renewed as a matter of routine. The bearing is of graphite type.

3   To remove the bearing, disconnect the small coil spring clip at each side of the release fork and lift the bearing from the fork. Use new spring clips when installing.

9   Clutch - installation

1   With fingers free from grease, hold the driven plate against the flywheel so that the greater projecting side of the hub is towards the gearbox.

2   Place the pressure plate assembly on the flywheel so that the 'B' stamped close to one of the dowel holes coincides with the 'B' stamped on the flywheel.

3   Insert the clutch retaining bolts finger-tight.

4   Now centralise the driven plate by pushing a suitable guide tool through the splined hub of the driven plate to engage in the pilot bush of the flywheel. This tool may be an old gearbox primary shaft or a suitably stepped mandrel.

5   When the tool is a smooth sliding fit (having centralised the driven plate) then tighten the clutch securing bolts evenly to specified torque in diametrically opposite sequence.

6   Withdraw the guide tool.

7   Install the gearbox to the engine, supporting the weight of the

Fig. 5.6. Clutch bellhousing and release fork (Sec. 8)

1 Pushrod return spring	5 Release fork
2 Bellhousing	6 Clutch bellhousing to
3 Release fork pivot bushes	engine bolts
4 Release fork pivot pin	7 Bellhousing lower cover plate

Fig. 5.7. Centralising the clutch driven plate (Sec. 9)

gearbox so that it does not hang upon the primary shaft while the latter is engaged in the splined hub of the driven plate.

8   Insert the bolts which secure the clutch bellhousing to the engine and tighten them to specified torque.

10 Fault diagnosis - clutch

Symptom	Reason/s
Judder when taking up drive (snatch)	Loose engine or gearbox mountings. Badly worn friction surfaces or contaminated with oil. Worn splines on gearbox input shaft or driven plate hub. Worn input shaft spigot bush in flywheel.
Clutch spin (failure to disengage) so that gears cannot be meshed	Incorrect release bearing to diaphragm spring finger clearance. Driven plate sticking on input shaft splines due to rust. May occur after vehicle standing idle for long period. Damage or misaligned pressure plate assembly.
Clutch slip (increase in engine speed does not result in increase in vehicle road speed - particularly on gradients)	Incorrect release bearing to diaphragm spring finger clearance. Friction surfaces worn out or oil contaminated.
Noise evident on depressing clutch pedal	Cracked, worn or damaged release bearing. Insufficient pedal free travel. Weak or broken pedal return spring. Weak or broken clutch release lever return spring. Excessive play between driven plate hub splines and input shaft splines.
Noise evident as clutch pedal released	Distorted driven plate. Broken or weak driven plate cushion coil springs. Insufficient pedal free travel. Weak or broken clutch pedal return spring. Weak or broken release lever return spring. Distorted or worn input shaft. Graphite bearing loose in retainer.

Chapter 6 Part I: Manual gearbox

Contents

Specifications

Type	Four forward and one reverse speed. Synchromesh on all forward gears

Ratios

1st gear	2.933 : 1
2nd gear	1.905 : 1
3rd gear	1.389 : 1
4th gear	1.00 : 1
Reverse gear	3.378 : 1

Endfloat tolerances

1st gear on mainshaft	0.005 to 0.007 in (0.13 to 0.18 mm)
2nd gear on mainshaft	0.005 to 0.008 in (0.13 to 0.20 mm)
3rd gear on mainshaft	0.005 to 0.008 in (0.13 to 0.20 mm)
Countergear endfloat	0.004 to 0.006 in (0.10 to 0.15 mm)

Oil capacity

Gearbox without overdrive (early cars)	2½ Imp. pints (1.5 litres/3 US pints)
Gearbox with overdrive (early cars)	4 Imp. pints (2.25 litres/4¾ US pints)
Gearbox without overdrive (later cars)	3 Imp. pints (1.6 litres/3¼ US pints)
Gearbox with overdrive (later cars)	4½ Imp. pints (2.4 litres/5 US pints)

Overdrive

Type	Laycock de Normanville
Clutch movement from direct to overdrive	0.080 to 0.120 in (2.0 to 3.0 mm)
Hydraulic pressure:	
2.8 litre cars	400/420 lb/sq in (28.1 to 20.5 kg/sq cm)
4.2 litre cars	490/510 lb/sq in (34.5 to 35.8 kg/sq cm)

Torque wrench settings
Manual gearbox and overdrive

	lb ft	Nm
Clutch bellhousing to engine bolts	35	48
Gearbox output coupling flange nut	100	138
Overdrive unit output coupling flange nut	100	138
Gearbox mainshaft front nut	120	166
Top cover bolts	14	19
Rear cover bolts	14	19
Clutch bellhousing to gearbox bolts	42	58
Oil filler plug	25	35
Oil drain plug	25	35
Propeller shaft flange nuts	34	47
Reverse lever setscrew	25	35

1 General description

The gearbox is of four forward speed and one reverse type. Synchromesh is fitted to all forward speeds. Except for reverse gear, the detents for the gears are incorporated in the synchromesh assemblies.

The reverse gear detent is conventional with a spring-loaded ball engaging in a groove in the selector rod.

Two interlock balls and a pin prevent the engagement of more than one gear at a time.

An oil pump, driven from the rear end of the mainshaft, pressure feeds the gears on standard gearboxes. Where an overdrive unit is

Fig. 6.1. Gear casing and top cover detail

1	Casing	20b	3rd/4th shift fork	38	Plunger	54	Pivot pin
2	Drain plug	21	Reverse shift fork	39	Spring	55	Nut
3	Filler/level plug	22	Locating arm	40	Welch plug	56	Gearshift lever (not with overdrive)
4	Fibre washer	23	Plunger	41	Welch plug		
5	Rear bearing	24	Spring	42	Breather	56a	Gearshift lever (with overdrive)
6	Circlip	25	Ball	43	Locknut		
7	Front bearing	26	Spring	44	Pivot	56b	Locknut
8	Circlip	27	Screw	45	Bush	56c	Overdrive switch lead
9	Collar	28	Nut	46	Washer	57	Knob
10	Fibre blanking disc	29	Dowel bolt	47	Nut	57a	Overdrive switch and knob
11	Gasket	30	Roller	48	Spring washer	58	Locking cone (not with overdrive)
12	Gasket	31	Detent balls	49	'D' washer		
14	1st/2nd selector rod	32	Top cover	50	Selector lever	58a	Locking cone (with overdrive)
15	3rd/4th selector rod	33	Switches for reversing lamps and overdrive isolation	50a	Remote control rod		
16	Reverse selector rod			50b	Remote control finger	59	Upper bush
17	'O' ring	34	Gasket	50c	Screw	60	Washer
18	Stop	35	Gasket	51	Bush	61	Lower bush
19	Stop	36	Dowel	52	Washer	62	Washer
20a	1st/2nd shift fork	37	Ball	53	Spring washer	63	Nut

installed, the overdrive oil pump provides the pressurised lubrication for the gearbox as well.

2   Lubrication and maintenance

1   At the intervals specified in 'Routine maintenance' at the beginning of this manual, place the car on level ground and remove the combined level/filler plug from the left-hand side of the gearbox (early cars) or the right-hand side (later cars). The oil should be at the bottom of the hole.
2   Where overdrive is fitted, the same oil from the gearbox feeds the overdrive therefore checking the gearbox oil level automatically checks the overdrive oil level as well.
3   The gearbox and (where fitted) the overdrive should be drained and refilled at the intervals specified in 'Routine maintenance'. Although the two units use common oil, they must be drained separately.
4   The drain plugs are located at the bases of the gearbox and the overdrive unit and whenever the overdrive is drained, also remove the filter plug from the side of the overdrive casing and thoroughly clean the filter and magnetic washers before refitting them.
5   Always observe strict cleanliness when refilling the overdrive unit or gearbox, or topping up.

Fig. 6.2. Gearbox drain plug (A) overdrive drain plug (B) and overdrive filter plug (C). Gearbox combined filler/level plug (early cars) arrowed. Later cars have filler/level plug on opposite side of casing (Sec. 2)

3   Gearbox - removal and installation

1   Remove the engine, gearbox and overdrive (where fitted) as a combined unit and as described in Chapter 1, Section 5.
2   Separate the engine and gearbox as described in Chapter 1, Section 7.
3   Installation is a reversal of removal again as described in Chapter 1, Sections 52 and 53, but after installation in the car, run the car on the road in top gear as soon as possible in order that the mainshaft speed will be high enough to prime the oil pump.

4   Gearbox - dismantling into major assemblies

1   If an overdrive is fitted, remove it as described in Section 11. Remove the clutch release bearing and fork (Chapter 5, Section 8) and unbolt and remove the clutch bellhousing from the gear casing.
2   Place the gear lever in neutral, unscrew and remove the eight setscrews and two nuts and lift off the top cover (early cars). On later cars, ten setscrews are used to retain the top cover. These setscrews are of varying lengths and must be refitted in their original positions. A good way of ensuring this is to make a template of the top cover with holes punched in it corresponding to the bolt holes in the top cover and then place the bolts in their respective holes in the template as each one is withdrawn.
3   **To remove the rear extension (gearbox without overdrive),** flatten the locking tab on the output coupling flange nut. Engage 1st and reverse gears together to lock the mainshaft.
4   Unscrew and remove the flange nut and withdraw the flange complete with thrust washer and four coupling flange bolts.
5   Unscrew and remove the speedometer pinion lockbolt and then withdraw the pinion and bush from the rear extension.
6   Unscrew and remove the setscrews which retain the rear extension to the main gearbox casing and withdraw the extension at the same time collecting the distance piece, the oil pump driving pin and oil filter from the output shaft.
7   Working within the rear extension, relieve the staking of the three countersunk screws which secure the oil pump gear housing. Withdraw the housing by screwing in two of the retaining screws into the tapped holes provided in the housing. It is important that the oil pump gears are marked with spirit pen or masking tape to ensure that they are meshed the same way up on reassembly. Renew the rear extension housing oil seal and the bearing if the latter is worn or noisy when turned.
8   *To remove the countershaft* from the main gear casing, extract the fibre plug from the front of the shaft.
9   Drive out the countershaft so that it emerges from the front of the casing. Make sure that the countershaft rear thrust washer drops down as shown in the illustration otherwise it may be trapped by reverse gear when removing the mainshaft (Fig. 6.4).

Fig. 6.3. Gearbox rear extension detail (Sec. 4)

Fig. 6.4. Position of countergear thrust washer after withdrawal of countershaft (Sec. 4)

Fig. 6.5. Removing constant pinion shaft (Sec. 4)

Fig. 6.6. Setting 3rd/4th synchro. hub prior to removal of mainshaft (Sec. 4)

10 *To remove the constant pinion shaft,* rotate the shaft until the cut-away parts of the driving gear are facing the top and bottom of the casing. Ease the constant pinion shaft and front bearing from the gear casing using two screwdrivers as levers.

11 *To remove the mainshaft,* rotate it until one of the cut-away parts in the 3rd/4th synchro. hub is aligned in such a way to prevent the hub fouling the constant gear of the countershaft gear cluster which is still lying in the gear casing.

12 Using a soft faced hammer, drive the mainshaft through the rear bearing making sure that reverse gear is held tight against 1st gear in the process.

13 Remove the mainshaft rear bearing from the gearbox casing.

14 Slacken reverse lever bolt so that the lever can be moved easily backwards and forwards.

15 Lift the mainshaft assembly upwards and out of the gearbox making sure that reverse gear does not slide off the end of the mainshaft. Fitting a small worm-drive clip to the shaft will prevent this happening.

16 The countershaft cluster gear assembly, needle rollers and retaining rings and thrust washers can now be extracted from the bottom of the gearbox.

17 Withdraw reverse idler shaft and lift out the gear noting the Woodruff key on the shaft.

5 Mainshaft - dismantling and reassembly

1 Before dismantling the mainshaft, note that the needle rollers must be kept in their individual gear sets as they are size graded for their individual locations and must not be mixed up.

2 Withdraw reverse gear from the mainshaft.

3 Withdraw 1st gear, retaining the 120 needle rollers, spacers and sleeve.

4 Withdraw 1st/2nd synchro. unit, retaining the two loose synchro.

Fig. 6.7. Driving mainshaft from rear bearing (Sec. 4)

Fig. 6.8. Removing mainshaft assembly (Sec. 4)

Fig. 6.9. Exploded view of geartrain (Sec. 5)

1 Mainshaft
2 Nut
3 Tab washer
4 Reverse gear
5 1st speed gear
6 Bearing sleeve
7 Needle rollers
8 Spacer
9 1st/2nd synchro. hub
10 Synchro. sleeve
11 Thrust washer
12 Plunger
13 Spring
14 Detent ball
15 Spring
16 Synchro. ring
17 2nd speed gear
18 3rd speed gear
19 Needle rollers
20 Spacer
21 Spacer
22 3rd/4th synchro. hub
23 Synchro. sleeve
24 Thrust washer
25 Plunger
26 Spring
27 Detent ball
28 Spring
29 Synchro ring
30 Nut
31 Tab washer
32 Plug
33 Constant pinion shaft
34 Roller bearing
35 Oil thrower
36 Nut
37 Tab washer
38 Reverse idler shaft
39 Key
40 Detent ball
41 Lever assembly
42 Setscrew
43 Fibre washer
44 Tab washer
45 Reverse slipper
46 Split pin
47 Countershaft
48 Key
49 Countergear cluster
50 Needle rollers
51 Retaining ring
52 Thrust washer
53 Thrust washer

rings. Withdraw 2nd speed gear, needles and spacer.

5   Grip the mainshaft securely in a vice fitted with jaw protectors, flatten the lock tab and unscrew the nut from the front end of the mainshaft. Draw off 3rd/4th synchro. unit and 3rd speed gear with 106 needles and spacer.

6   Examine all components for wear and gear endfloat detailed in 'Specifications' and renew as necessary.

7   Reassembly is a reversal of dismantling but make sure that needle rollers of one grading only are used for each gear. Finally retain the reverse gear on the shaft using a worm-drive clip or similar device pending installation in the gearbox of the complete mainshaft assembly. Tighten the mainshaft front nut to specified torque and use a lockwasher.

---

6   Synchromesh units - dismantling and reassembly

1   The synchromesh units are overhauled in the same way but their components parts, although similar in appearance are not interchangeable. The 3rd/top synchro. hub has a groove machined in it to identify it.

2   To dismantle a synchromesh unit, cover it with a stout piece of rag and push out the hub from the sleeve. Collect the balls, springs and other components.

3   Examine each part for wear particularly the contours of the teeth and grooves, renewing as necessary.

4   Commence reassembly by fitting the synchro. sleeve to the hub so that the deeper boss of the hub is on the same side as the narrow

chamfer of the sleeve.

5   Locate the three balls and springs in line with the teeth which have the three detent grooves on them.

6   Set the synchro. hub so that the holes for the balls and springs are exactly flush with the top of the sleeve (wider chamfer uppermost). Place a packing piece under the hub to set its height.

7   Install the three springs, plungers and their thrust members holding them in position with thick grease and depressing the thrust members as far as possible. Compress the springs using a worm-drive clip or piston ring clamp and then lift the synchro. assembly from the temporary packing piece. Depress the hub and at the same time push down the thrust members with a screwdriver until they engage in the groove in the sleeve (Figs. 6.14 and 6.15).

8   Using a soft-faced hammer, tap the synchro hub downwards until the balls can be heard and felt to engage in the neutral groove of the sleeve (Fig. 6.16).

---

7   Constant pinion shaft - dismantling and reassembly

1   Extract the roller bearing from inside the shaft.

2   Tap back the tab washer and remove the large nut, the tab washer and the oil thrower.

Fig. 6.12. Setting synchro. hub on sleeve ready for insertion of balls and springs (Sec. 6)

Fig. 6.10. Synchro. hub to sleeve relationship (Sec. 6)

Fig. 6.11. Synchro. sleeve tooth with three grooves (Sec. 6)

Fig. 6.13. Synchro. hub showing relative positions of ball, plunger and thrust member (Sec. 6)

Fig. 6.14. Using a clip to compress the synchro. spring (Sec. 6)

Fig. 6.15. Pushing down the synchro. thrust members (Sec. 6)

Fig. 6.16. Tapping the synchro hub fully into engagement (Sec. 6)

3   Tap the end of the shaft on the bench or strike it with a soft-faced hammer to dislodge the shaft bearing.
4   Reassembly is a reversal of dismantling but make sure that the shaft bearing is square and fully seated on the shaft.

---

8   Gearbox top cover - dismantling and reassembly

1   Unscrew the self-locking nut and remove the double coil spring, washers and fibre washer which secure the gearshift lever to the top cover.
2   Withdraw the gearlever.
3   Cut the locking wire and unscrew the selector rod retaining screws.
4   Withdraw 3rd/4th selector rod and extract the shift fork, spacer tube and interlock balls. Note the loose interlock pin at the front of the 1st/2nd selector rod.
5   Withdraw reverse selector rod and extract reverse fork, stop spring and detent plunger.
6   Withdraw 1st/2nd selector rod and extract the shift fork and the short spacer tube.
7   Reassembly is a reversal of dismantling but make sure that the interlock ball and pin are installed correctly when assembling the selector rods. Always renew the 'O' rings on the selector rods.
8   Install the reverse plunger and spring. Fit the ball and spring and start the screw and locknut on their threads. Press in the plunger as far as it will go and then tighten the screw to hold the plunger in its fully depressed state.
9   Release the screw until the plunger comes out far enough for the ball to engage in its circular groove. Hold the screw in this position and tighten the locknut.

---

9   Gearbox - reassembly

1   Fit one retaining ring to the front end of the counter gear. Using grease, locate 29 needle rollers in position and fit the inner thrust washer, making sure that the peg on the washer engages in the groove which is machined on the front face of the countergear.
2   Fit the second retaining ring and the 29 needle rollers to the rear end of the countershaft gear again using grease to retain the components.
3   Install the reverse idler gear, lever and idler shaft.
4   Using a dab of thick grease, stick the countergear rear thrust washer to the inside of the gearbox casing.
5   Stick the second thrust washer to the front of the countergear and then carefully lower the gear into position in the gear casing.
6   Using a rod which is slightly smaller in diameter than the countershaft, insert it through the gear casing so that it passes through the countergear without displacing the needle rollers or thrust washers.
7   Using feeler blades, check the clearance (endfloat) between the rear thrust washer and the end face of the countergear. This should be between 0.004 and 0.006 in (0.10 and 0.15 mm). Any adjustment which may be needed is carried out by changing the thrust washers. These are available in five thicknesses: 0.152 in (3.86 mm), 0.156 in (3.96 mm), 0.159 in (4.04 mm), 0.162 in (4.11 mm) and 0.164 in (4.17 mm).
8   Withdraw the rod from the countergear and lower the countergear to the bottom of the gear casing.
9   Install a new gasket to the front face of the gear casing.
10 Insert the reassembled mainshaft through the top of the gear casing and pass the rear of the mainshaft through the rear bearing aperture.
11 Insert the constant pinion shaft/bearing assembly through the bearing aperture at the front of the gear casing, making sure that the cut-away parts of the driving gear are at the top and bottom and that the internal roller bearing is in position.
12 Tap the constant pinion shaft into engagement with the front end of the mainshaft.
13 Hold the constant pinion shaft securely in position and then install the mainshaft rear bearing using a piece of tubing applied to its inner race to drive it home.
14 Carefully raise the countergear until its gears mesh with those of the mainshaft. Insert the countershaft from the rear of the gear casing, taking care not to displace the thrust washers or needle rollers. Fit the Woodruff key which locates the countershaft in the gear casing.
15 If the oil pump gears were removed, refit them to the oil pump in their original attitude as marked before removal. Coat the gears and interior of the pump body with oil. Insert the pump housing screws and stake them.

Gearbox without overdrive
16 Fit a new gasket to the rear face of the gear casing.
17 Install the distance piece and driving pin to the oil pump in the rear extension.
18 Locate the rear extension onto the gear casing and secure it with the setscrews.
19 Install the speedometer drive gear to the end of the mainshaft, fit the speedometer driven gear and bush so that the hole in the bush is in

line with the hole in the rear extension. Insert the speedometer pinion lock bolt.
20 Install the flange to the rear end of the mainshaft making sure that the coupling bolts are in position in the flange bolt holes before fitting the flange.
21 Fit a new tab washer and screw on the mainshaft nut. Lock two gears to prevent the mainshaft turning and then tighten to specified torque and bend over the locking tab.

Gearbox with overdrive
22 Refit the overdrive as described in Section 11.

All gearboxes
23 To install the top cover, first fit a new gasket. Check that the gears and top cover selectors are in the neutral position. Check that reverse idler gear is not in mesh by pushing reverse lever fully to the rear.
24 Lower the top cover onto the gear casing until the shift forks engage with the grooves in the synchromesh units.
25 Install and tighten the top cover bolts and nuts making sure that they are returned to their original positions.
26 Refit the clutch bellhousing complete with new constant pinion shaft oil seal (lip towards gearbox). Note that the two clutch bellhousing bolts adjacent to the clutch fork trunnions are locked with wire. The other bolts are locked with tab washers.
27 Refit the clutch release lever and bearing.

---

10 Overdrive unit - description, maintenance and adjustment

1   The overdrive unit consists of a hydraulically controlled epicyclic gear housed in a casing at the rear of the gearbox. When engaged, the overdrive unit reduces the engine speed in relation to the road speed so reducing engine wear and giving improved fuel economy.
2   The overdrive is operated by an electric solenoid which is acutated by a switch mounted on the gearshift knob and it can only be engaged when top gear has been selected due to the provision of an isolator switch.
3   Topping-up and changing the oil have been covered in conjunction with the gearbox in Section 2 of this Chapter.
4   Adjustment of the solenoid should not be regarded as routine but in the event of faulty operation of the overdrive unit, the adjustment should be checked.
5   The solenoid box is located on the left-hand side of the overdrive unit and is accessible from underneath the car.
6   Remove the solenoid cover plate (four screws) and expose the solenoid lever.
7   Move the lever to the right until a rod 3/16 in (4.76 mm) in diameter when pushed through the hole in the lever, will register with the hole in the overdrive casing. Now turn the plunger nut until the point is reached where the plunger is pushed right home in the solenoid and the nut just makes contact with the fork of the lever. Remove the rod.
8   Energise the solenoid by applying current to it from the car battery and recheck the alignment of the holes. If they are in correct alignment, refit the solenoid cover plate. Adjustment can be verified by connecting a 0 to 30 amp ammeter in series with the solenoid supply cable and when the solenoid is energised, the current consumption should be 1 amp.
9   The overdrive isolator switch should not normally require adjustment but if it becomes faulty then it must be renewed and adjustment of the new switch will almost certainly be required.
10 To renew the switch, disconnect the battery and remove the cover from the transmission tunnel.
11 Support the rear end of the engine using a hoist or a crossbar and threaded lifting eye supported on the top surfaces of the front wing valances.
12 Remove the four screws from the engine rear mounting bracket and then lower the rear of the engine by no more than 1 to 2 in (25.4 to 50.8 mm).
13 Disconnect the leads from the isolator switch which is located on the left-hand side of the gearbox. Unscrew the switch and retain the washers.
14 Install the new switch using the original washers and then connect a continuity meter between the switch terminals. Place the gearlever in neutral when the meter should indicate a very high resistance (open circuit). Now press the gearlever towards top gear when the meter

Fig. 6.17. Adjusting the overdrive unit solenoid (Sec. 10)

Fig. 6.18. Overdrive isolator switch (arrowed) (Sec. 10)

should indicate a short circuit immediately the gearlever moves. Add or remove washers from the switch as necessary to achieve this situation.
15 Reverse the removal operations to complete the fitting.

---

11 Overdrive unit - removal and refitting

1   Remove the engine and gearbox/overdrive unit together as described in Chapter 1.
2   Remove the gearbox from the engine also as described in Chapter 1.
3   Remove the nuts from the four short studs which retain the overdrive unit to the adaptor plate on the rear face of the gear casing. Also remove the two nuts from the long studs at the base of the overdrive unit.
4   Withdraw the overdrive unit from the mainshaft leaving the adaptor plate in positon.
5   The adaptor plate is held in position by seven nuts which can be removed if required.
6   To refit the overdrive unit to the gearbox, secure the unit upside-down in a vice.
7   With the internal splines correctly aligned (see Section 12), do not turn the output flange until the unit has been fitted to the gearbox.
8   Check that the cam is not worn and that the flat spring ring on the gearbox mainshaft is not distorted nor protrudes above the splines.
9   Turn the gearbox mainshaft so that the cam has its highest point uppermost. The lowest point will now align with the overdrive pump roller. Engage bottom gear and do not turn the mainshaft again until the overdrive unit has been fitted to the gearbox.
10 Locate a new gasket to the front face of the overdrive unit. Mate the gearbox carefully to the overdrive unit making sure that the pump roller rides up the chamfer of the cam and that the overdrive pushes fully up to the adaptor plate using hand pressure only. If the overdrive stands away from the adaptor plate by about 5/8 in (15.88 mm) then

86

Fig. 6.19.

Fig. 6.19. Exploded view of the overdrive unit (Sec. 12)

#	Part	#	Part	#	Part	#	Part
1	Adaptor plate	19	Plug	37	Cam	55	Retaining plate
2	Gasket	20	Washer	38	Operating piston	56	Spring
3	Stud	21	Oil pump plunger assembly	39	'O' ring	57	Clutch sliding member
4	Stud	22	Oil pump body	40	Bridge piece	58	Ball bearing
5	Front casing	23	Spring	41	Nut	59	Circlip
6	Shaft	24	Screw	42	Tab washer	60	Corrugated washer
7	Cam	25	Fibre washer	43	Accumulator piston	61	Circlip
8	Lever	26	'O' ring	44	Ring	62	Brake ring
9	Tension pin	27	Non-return valve	45	Spring	63	Sun wheel
10	'O' ring	28	Ball	46	Support rod	64	Planetary carrier assembly
11	Welch plug	29	Spring	47	Packing washer	65	Annulus assembly
12	Stop	30	Support rod	48	Plug	66	Oil thrower
13	Breather	31	Plug	49	Washer	67	Spring ring
14	Stud	32	Copper washer	50	Solenoid	68	Spring ring
15	Main operating valve	33	Oil filter	51	Gasket	69	Ball bearing
16	Ball	34	Magnetic ring	52	Nut	70	Circlip
17	Plunger	35	Plug	53	Gasket	71	Ball bearing
18	Spring	36	Washer	54	Thrust ring	72	Uni-directional clutch cage
						73	Roller
						74	Spring
						75	Clutch inner member
						76	Thrust washer
						77	Rear casing assembly
						78	Stud
						79	Thrust button
						80	Oil seal
						81	Speedometer driving gear
						82	Speedometer driven gear
						83	Bearing assembly
						84	'O' ring
						85	Screw
						86	Copper washer
						87	Connecting flange
						88	Bolt
						89	Nut
						90	Washer
						91	Split pin

this indicates that the internal splines have become misaligned. In this case, remove the overdrive unit and re-align the splines by turning the inner member of the uni-directional clutch in an anticlockwise direction. This can be done using a long screwdriver.

11 When the overdrive unit has been correctly fitted to the gearbox, tighten the four nuts (short studs) and the two nuts (long studs) at the base of the unit.

12 Connect the engine and gearbox and install in the car, as described in Chapter 1.

13 Top-up the gearbox (which will fill the overdrive unit) with the correct grade and quantity of oil.

12 Overdrive unit - overhaul

1 Absolute cleanliness must be observed in the following operations even to the extent of preventing particles from cleaning cloths remaining inside the unit. The operations described in paragraphs 9, 11, 12, 13, and 14 can all be carried out without removing the overdrive unit from the car provided the overdrive accumulator is first exhausted by switching on the ignition, engaging top gear and operating the overdrive switch between ten and twelve times.

2 With the unit removed from the car, clean away all external dirt.

3 Secure the unit in a vice fitted with jaw protectors so that the front casing is uppermost.

4 Flatten the tab washers which lock the four nuts which hold the operating piston bridge pieces. Remove the nuts, washers and bridge pieces.

5 Release the two solenoid retaining screws so that the front casing of the overdrive unit can be removed.

6 Remove the four nuts which secure the front and rear casings and then separate the casings. The brake ring is spigotted into the casings and will normally remain attached to the front casing but it may be extracted if necessary by applying a few taps with a soft-faced hammer.

7 Lift out the clutch sliding member complete with thrust-ring, bearing and sun wheel.

8 Lift out the planet carrier and gear train.

9 *To dismantle the operating valve*, remove the plug from the bottom of the unit (same side as the solenoid). Extract the spring, plunger and ball. Extract the operating valve by drawing it down with a piece of wire.

10 Remove the operating pistons by gripping their centre bosses with a pair of pliers and exerting a rotary pull.

11 *To remove the solenoid*, withdraw the cover plate (four screws), extract the two securing screws and ease the plunger out of the yoke of the valve operating lever.

12 *Access to the accumulator* is gained by removing the large plug from the bottom of the unit on the right-hand side. Once the plug is unscrewed to its full length, all spring compression is released and the spring, support pin and washer can all be withdrawn with the plug. The accumulator piston can be withdrawn by engaging a piece of wire in the groove in its bore.

Fig. 6.20. Extracting the accumulator piston from the overdrive unit (Sec. 12)

13 *To remove the pump non-return valve,* unscrew and remove the plug which is centrally located in the bottom of the unit. The valve body can only be extracted by using a special key (Tool no. L213). Extract the spring and ball.

14 *To remove the pump,* first withdraw the non-return valve as just described and then withdraw the pump body. A bolt can be screwed into the body and using a nut and distance piece, it can be extracted from its recess. The pump plunger and spring will come out at the same time.

15 *The oil filter* is accessible after removing the plug immediately below the solenoid cover plate. Extract the gauze filter. Four magnetic rings are located in the filter assembly - two in the plug recess and two in the casing recess.

16 *The clutch sliding member and sun wheel* are removable after withdrawing the circlip from the sun wheel and prising off the corrugated washer and sliding member.

17 *The planet carrier assembly* should be inspected for wear on the gear teeth and excessive clearance in the bearings. Any fault can only be rectified by renewing the carrier assembly complete as individual components are not supplied.

18 To dismantle *the rear casing and annulus,* refer to Fig. 6.19. Extract the spring ring (67) and oil thrower (66).

19 Remove the assembly ring from the uni-directional clutch and allow the rollers to come out. The hub will then be easily removable from the cage and leave the spring exposed. Extract the bronze thrust washer which is located between the hub of the clutch and the annulus.

20 To remove the annulus, remove the speedometer dowel screw (85), withdraw the speedometer drive bush (83) and the pinion (82).

21 Remove the coupling flange (87) and extract the oil seal. Press the annulus forward out of the rear casing. The front and rear bearings will remain in the rear casing with the speedometer drive gear sandwiched between them.

22 Extract the circlip (70) and drive out the speedometer gear and rear bearing. Finally drive out the front bearing.

23 With the overdrive dismantled, thoroughly clean each component and carry out a very detailed inspection for wear or damage paying particular attention to the following components:

24 Front casing and brake ring.
   Operating cylinder bores and accumulator (scoring or leaks).
   Sealing discs and plugged oil passages (leaks).
   Worn centre bush.
   Operating pistons (38) and sealing ring (39).
   Pump roller and bronze bush.
   Pump plunger (wear or scoring).
   Pump body, valve seat and ball (wear or scoring).
   Pump spring (distortion).
   Accumulator piston (scoring or broken rings).
   Accumulator spring (distortion or collapse).
   Operating valve (distortion).
   Restrictor jet (clear).
   Filter and magnetic rings (clean in petrol).
   Brake ring (62) (scoring or cracks).

25 Clutch sliding member.
   Friction lining (charring or wear). If worn, renew sliding member complete.
   Thrust ring bridge piece pins (tight or bent).
   Ball race (noisy or worn).
   Clutch springs (distortion or collapse).

26 Planet carrier and gear train
   Sun-wheel teeth (chipping or wear).
   Sun-wheel bush (wear). If worn renew sun-wheel complete.

27 Rear casing and annulus.
   Uni-directional clutch rollers (chipping or wear).
   Cage (ears distorted or bent).
   Bronze washers.
   Annulus gear teeth (damage or chipping).
   Speedometer pinion (wear or chipped teeth).
   Always renew the rear oil seal (80) at time of major overhaul.

28 Commence reassembly by inserting the pump plunger, spring and body in the central holes in the bottom of the front casing. Make sure that the flat on the plunger locates against the thrust button below the centre bush.

29 Tap the pump body home until its groove is in alignment with the screw hole in the front casing. Install the screw and its fibre washer.

30 Reseat the non-return valve ball using a copper drift and then screw in the non-return valve body. Fit the ball spring, pin, copper washer

and plug.

31 Insert the piston into the accumulator casing followed by the spring, pin, fibre washer and plug.

32 When installing the operating pistons, ease the rubber seals into the cylinder bores and make sure that the centre bosses of the pistons face towards the front of the unit.

33 Install the operating valve so that the rounded end engages with the flat of the small cam of the operating shaft. Insert the 5/16 in (7.93 mm) diameter ball, plunger and spring and screw in the plug with copper washer.

34 Refit the oil filter with two magnetic rings in the casing recess and two in the plug recess.

35 The front casing is now complete except for the solenoid and can be placed to one side ready for fitting to the unit later.

36 Press the front bearing into the rear casing and fit its circlip.

37 Support the inner track of the bearing and press in the annulus until the bearing abuts on the shoulder.

38 Fit the speedometer drive gear and then press the rear bearing onto the tailshaft and into the rear casing simultaneously. Install a new oil seal.

39 Fit the bolts to the coupling flange and press on the coupling flange. Fit the washer and castellated nut. Tighten the nut to specified torque and insert a new split pin.

40 Insert the speedometer pinion gear and bush making sure that the 'O' ring seal is in good condition.

41 Turn the annulus to engage the gear so aligning the holes in the casing and bush. Fit the locating screw and its copper washer.

42 Fit the spring into the roller cage of the uni-directional clutch and then insert the inner member into the cage and engage it with the other end of the spring. Engage the slots of the inner member with the roller cage tongues checking that the spring rotates the cage so that when the rollers are installed they will be pushed up the inclined faces of the inner member. The cage is spring-loaded in an anticlockwise direction when viewed from the front.

43 Position the assembly front face downwards and install the rollers at the same time turning the clutch clockwise. A narrow band or clip can be used to facilitate this operation.

44 Refit the uni-directional clutch, entering the rollers into the outer member of the annulus. Fit the oil thrower and retaining clip.

45 Assemble the planet carrier to the annulus and sun-wheel. To do this, turn each gear until the dot on one tooth of the large gear is located radially outwards.

46 Install the sun-wheel to mesh with the planet gears (without moving the position of the dots) and then insert the assembly to mesh with the internal gear in the annulus. Align the splines of the planet carrier

Fig. 6.21. Assembly position for planet carrier, annulus and sun-wheel. Note dots (arrowed) on one tooth of each gear (Sec. 12)

and the uni-directional clutch.

47 Press the thrust bearing into the thrust ring and then press this assembly onto the hub of the clutch sliding member. Secure the assembly with the circlip.

48 Slide the assembly onto the sun-wheel splines until the inner lining is in contact with the annulus and then fit the corrugated washer and circlip.

49 Fit the retaining plate over the bolts of the thrust ring bearing assembly. Apply jointing compound to both faces of the brake ring flange and tap the brake ring home into the front casing.

50 Install the clutch return springs into the front casing.

51 Offer the front casing/brake ring assembly to the rear casing making sure that the thrust ring bolts pass through the holes in the casing without jamming. The pressure of the clutch springs will tend to keep the two casings apart but the four securing nuts should be tightened progressively and in diagonally opposite sequence to overcome this.

52 Fit the two bridge pieces and new tab washers.

53 Engage the solenoid plunger in the fork of the operating lever and after fitting a gasket to the solenoid flange, fix the solenoid to the casing with its two screws.

54 Adjust the solenoid, as described in Section 10.

55 Install the solenoid cover plate and gasket (four screws).

56 The overdrive unit is now ready for installation to the gearbox, as described in Section 11.

13 Fault diagnosis - manual gearbox

Symptom	Reason/s
Ineffective synchromesh	Worn baulk rings or synchro hubs.
Jumps out of one or more gears (on drive or over-run)	Weak detent springs or worn selector forks or worn gears.
Noisy, rough, whining and vibration	Worn bearings and/or thrust washers (initially) resulting in extended wear generally due to play and backlash.
Noisy and difficult engagement of gears	Clutch fault (See Chapter 5).

Note: It is sometimes difficult to decide whether it is worthwhile removing and dismantling the gearbox for a fault which may be nothing more than a minor irritant. Gearboxes which howl, or where the synchromesh can be 'beaten' by a quick gearchange, may continue to perform for a long time in this state. A worn gearbox usually needs a complete rebuild to eliminate noise because the various gears, if re-aligned on new bearings will continue to howl when different wearing surfaces are presented to each other.

The decision to overhaul therefore, must be considered with regard to time and money available, relative to the degree of noise or malfunction that the driver has to suffer.

14 Fault diagnosis - overdrive unit

Symptom	Reason/s
Lack of engagement	Insufficient oil. Break in electrical circuit. Solenoid lever out of adjustment. Dirt on pump non-return valve seat. Worn accumulator. Choked filter.
Will not disengage *	Solenoid sticking. Blocked restrictor jet in operating valve. Solenoid lever out of adjustment. Clutch sticking (in overdrive unit).

* If these conditions occur on no account reverse the car as extensive damage will be caused.

Clutch slip when overdrive selected	Insufficient oil. Solenoid lever out of adjustment. Dirt on pump non-return valve seat. Worn accumulator. Operating valve incorrectly seated. Worn or glazed clutch linings (in overdrive unit).

Chapter 6 Part II: Automatic transmission

Contents

Specifications

Type ... ... Borg-Warner three element hydrokinetic torque converter with hydraulically operated planetary gear set to provide 3 forward and 1 reverse ratio

Application

Model 8	4.2 litre engined cars
Model 12	4.2 litre (Series 2) early models
Model 35F	2.8 litre engined cars
Model 65	4.2 litre (Series 2) engined cars, later models

Model 8

Ratios:

1st	2.40 : 1
2nd	1.46 : 1
3rd	1.00 : 1
Reverse	2.00 : 1
Maximum ratio of torque converter	2.00 : 1 (infinitely variable)

Shift speeds:

Selector	Throttle position	Upshift			Downshift	
		1–2	2–3	3–2	3–1	2–1
D1	Minimum	6-7 mph (10-11 kph)	10-12 mph (16-19 kph)	6-12 mph (10-19 kph)	— —	3-6 mph (5-10 kph
	Kickdown	42-46 mph (68-74 kph)	66-73 mph (106-117 kph)	59-67 mph (95-108 kph)	16-20 mph (26-32 kph)	16-20 mpl (26-32 kp
D2	Minimum	—	10-12 mph (16-19 kph)	6-12 mph (10-19 kph)	—	—
	Kickdown	—	66-73 mph (106-117 kph)	59-67 mph (95-108 kph)	—	—
L	Zero	—	Any speed	—	9-17 mph (14-27 kph)	—

Fluid capacity, including torque converter * ... ... 16.5 Imp. pints (9.4 litres/19.8 US pints)

* This cannot be completely drained at subsequent oil changes

Model 12

Ratios as model 8

Shift speeds (with 3.31 : 1 and 3.54 : 1 axle ratio):

Throttle position	Upshifts		Downshifts	
	1–2	2–3	3–2	2–1
Minimum	6-10 mph (9-16 kph)	14-18 mph (22-29 kph)	—	—
Full	39-45 mph (62-72 kph)	73-82 mph (117-132 kph)	—	—

Throttle position	Upshifts		Downshifts	
	1–2	2–3	3–2	2–1
Kick-down	–	–	63-73 mph (101-117 kph)	13-17 mph (21-27 kph)
Zero	–	–	–	7-17 mph (11-27 kph)
Part	–	–	20-26 mph (32-42 kph)	–

Shift speed (with 3.07 : 1 axle ratio)

Throttle position	Upshifts		Downshifts	
	1–2	2–3	3–2	2–1
Minimum	7-11 mph (11-18 kph)	16-20 mph (25-32 kph)	–	–
Full	45-51 mph (72–82 kph)	85-94 mph (136-151 kph)	–	–
Kick-down	–	–	73-83 mph (117-133 kph)	15-19 mph (24-30 kph)
Zero	–	–	–	9-19 mph (14-30 kph)
Part	–	–	23-29 mph (37-47 kph)	–

Fluid capacity as model 8

Model 35F
Ratios:
1st	...	2.40 : 1
2nd	...	1.46 : 1
3rd	...	1 : 1
Reverse	...	2.09 : 1
Torque converter ratio	...	2 : 1 to 1 : 1 (infinitely variable)

Shift speeds:

Selector	Throttle Position	Upshifts		Downshifts	
		1–2	2–3	3–2	2–1
D	Light	9-14 mph (14-22 kph)	14-20 mph (22-32 kph)	–	–
D	Full with kick-down	31-40 mph (49-64 kph)	60-65 mph (96-104 kph)	52-60 mph (83-96 kph)	19-26 mph (37-48 kph)
2	Zero	–	–	–	7-9 mph (11-14 kph)

Fluid capacity as model 8

Model 65
Ratios:
1st	...	2.39 : 1
2nd	...	1.45 : 1
3rd	...	1 : 1
Reverse	...	2.09 : 1
Torque converter ratio	...	1.91 : 1 to 1 : 1 (infinitely variable)
Fluid capacity	...	14.5 Imp. pints (8.2 litres/17.4 US pints)

Torque wrench settings

All transmissions except Type 65	lb f ft	Nm
Torque converter to driveplate bolts ...	30	41
Torque converter housing to engine bolts ...	35	48
Oil pan securing bolts ...	13	18
Output coupling flange nut ...	50	69
Oil cooler pipe unions ...	21	29
Filler tube union nut ...	25	35
Transmission case to torque converter housing ...	60	83
Selector lever to transmission casing nut ...	35	48

Type 65 transmission		
Transmission case to torque converter housing:		
Small bolts ...	25	35
Large bolts ...	40	55
Oil pan bolts ...	5	7
Oil pan drain plug ...	10	14
Output coupling flange bolt ...	80	111

15 General description

1   The automatic transmission unit used in all models is of Borg-Warner manufacture but different versions of this unit are fitted, according to the car engine capacity and date of production.
2   Application details are given in 'Specifications' Section but the main difference between the transmission units is that only cars equipped with the model 8 unit can be started by towing or running down an incline, due to the fact that they have an extra rear oil pump. This pump provided hydraulic fluid pressure at speeds over 20 mph (32 kph). The other model transmission units have a front pump only, and hydraulic fluid pressure is not generated unless the engine is running.
3   In the event of a breakdown, the propeller shaft on all cars except those equipped with model 8 transmissions must be disconnected before the car is towed otherwise serious damage to the transmission will occur.
4   There are certain minor differences between the different trans-mission units, mostly concerned with the speed selection arrangement but all units incorporate a fluid torque converter coupled to a hydraulically-operated planetary gearbox to provide three forward ratios and reverse.
5   All forward ratios are automatically engaged in accordance with accelerator position and car speed. Overriding control is still maintained by manual selection and a kick-down facility is provided for rapid change down.
6   Servicing and overhaul operations should be restricted to those described. Due to the complexity of the transmission unit and the need for special tools it is not recommended that major overhauls are undertaken.
7   In the event of a fault developing, always diagnose the problem **before** removing the unit from the car. This fault finding can be carried out either by referring to the 'Fault diagnosis' Sections in this Chapter or by consulting your Jaguar/Daimler dealer.
8   Factory reconditioned units are normally available through your dealer on an exchange basis, and in the case of a major fault developing in the original unit, this method of rectification can usually show a marked swing against overhaul charges.

16 Maintenance (all models)

1   The most important maintenance task is the regular checking of the fluid level.

2   At the intervals specified in 'Routine Maintenance', operate the car on the road for at least 5 miles (8 km) and then place it on a level surface and with the engine still running, move the speed selector lever through all positions finally placing the lever in 'P'.
3   Switch off the engine, withdraw the dipstick and wipe it clean on a piece of non-fluffy cloth. Re-insert it and then withdraw it for the second time and read off the fluid level. The operations described in this paragraph should be completed within one minute. Any instructions found in handbooks which suggest reading the oil level while the engine is running should be disregarded as this has been proved to be an impossible task, due to splash occurring within the transmission oil pan.
4   If necessary, add specified fluid to the combined dipstick/oil filler tube to bring the level up to the 'FULL' mark. The difference between the 'LOW' and 'FULL' marks is equivalent to 1½ Imp. pints (0.75 litres).
5   The only other maintenance items are to keep the exterior of the transmission casing clean to prevent the unit overheating and if an oil cooler is fitted, to periodically check the condition and security of the fluid flow and return pipes to the cooler which is located in the base of the cooling system radiator.

17 Model 8 transmission - adjustments

Speed selector linkage adjustment
1   In the event of faulty speed selection occurring or failure of the parking pawl to hold the car when 'P' is selected, first check the adjustment of the speed selector linkage.
2   Disconnect the selector rod from the actuating lever on the side of the transmission unit.
3   Pull the selector hand control into 'P', and then push the lever on the side of the transmission casing fully forward towards the front of the car.
4   Attempt to reconnect the selector rod to the actuating lever. When it is in perfect alignment, release the locknuts on the linkage tube and adjust the effective length of the linkage until the selector rod will connect with the actuating lever without having to deflect either component.
5   Refit the connecting nut, tighten the locknuts and then check the speed selection in all positions.

Kick-down cable adjustment
6   An oil pressure gauge will ideally be needed for this operation, although adjustment can be carried out on a trial-and-error basis as

Fig. 6.22. Sectional view of automatic transmission showing main components

1	Engine crankshaft	7	Rear clutch
2	Turbine	8	Front brake band
3	Impeller	9	Uni-directional
4	Stator		clutch
5	Input shaft	10	Rear brake band
6	Front clutch	11	Pinion carrier

12	Ring gear and output shaft
13	Sun-gear and shaft
16	Planet pinion
16	Planet pinion
17	Reverse sun gear

Fig. 6.23. Dipstick used on Type 65 transmission which permits checking fluid when cold (Sec. 16)

Fig. 6.24. Dipstick marking on all models except Type 65 (Sec. 16) follows:

7 Place the speed selector lever in 'D1' or 'D2' and using minimum accelerator pressure to cause the car to increase speed, check that the 2 to 3 upshift occurs at between 1100 and 1200 rev/min.

8 A momentary increase in engine speed between 200 and 400 rev/min during upshift indicates low fluid pressure.

9 A jerky upshift (or 2 to 1 downshift) indicates high fluid pressure.

10 To lower the pressure, release the locknut on the kick-down rod and turn it to reduce its length.

11 To increase the pressure, unscrew the rod to effectively lengthen it.

12 If a pressure gauge is available, connect it to the take-off point on the transmission casing. With the fluid at normal operating temperature, and 'D1' or 'D2' selected, apply the handbrake and increase the idling speed to 1250 rev/min. The pressure gauge should indicate between 70 and 75 lb/sq in (4.92 and 5.27 kg/sq cm). Adjust if necessary, as previously described.

Front band adjustment

13 This operation should be carried out after the first 1000 miles (1600 km) running of a new car or after a new transmission unit has been installed. It may also be necessary if indicated after reference to 'Fault diagnosis'.

14 Remove the drain plug from the oil pan and drain the oil into a clean container (Fig. 6.29). If the car has just come in off the road, be very careful as the oil can be extremely hot! If a drain plug is not fitted, remove the oil pan, keep it level and tip the fluid from it.

15 Unscrew the oil pan bolts and lift the oil pan from the transmission casing.

16 Release the locknut on the front servo adjusting screw, unscrew the screw and then slide a block (¼ in - 6.3 mm) thick between the servo piston pin and the end of the adjusting screw. Tighten the adjusting screw to a torque of 10 in/lb. If a torque wrench is not available, use a spring balance connected to a socket wrench (Fig. 6.30).

Fig. 6.25. Location of automatic transmission dipstick on 2.8 litre models (Sec. 16)

Fig. 6.26. Speed selector linkage (Model 8 transmission) A = locknuts (Sec. 17)

Fig. 6.27. Kickdown rod adjuster (Model 8 transmission) (Sec. 17)

Fig. 6.28. Pressure take off point (Model 8 transmission) (Sec. 17)

Fig. 6.29. Transmission drain plug (Model 8 transmission) (Sec. 17)

Fig. 6.30. Adjusting front brake band (Model 8 transmission) (Sec. 17)

Fig. 6.31. Speed selector lever (Model 12 transmission) (Sec. 18)

1 Cover	4 Selector lever
2 Cable clevis pin	5 Locknuts

17 Back off the adjusting screw 1½ turns exactly and tighten the adjusting screw locknut to between 20 and 25 lb/ft (28 and 35 Nm). Remove the spacer block.

Rear band adjustment
18 This will normally only be required if indicated after reference to 'Fault diagnosis' Section.
19 The rear brake band adjusting screw is located on the right-hand side of the transmission casing and access is provided through a hole in the transmission tunnel.
20 Release the adjuster screw locknut and unscrew it three or four turns.
21 Check that the adjuster screw turns freely and then screw it in using a torque wrench to a torque of 10 lb/ft (14 Nm).
22 Unscrew the adjusting screw exactly 1½ turns and tighten the locknut to a torque of between 35 and 40 lb/ft (48 and 55 Nm).

18 Model 12 transmission - adjustments and tests

Speed selector linkage adjustment
1 Working within the car, release the selector cover screws, raise the cover, turn it through 90° and lift it over the control lever.
2 Disconnect the selector cable from the control lever.
3 Move the lever on the side of the transmission casing fully to the rear (P) and then push it forward one notch to (R).
4 Move the hand control to position (R).
5 Release the locknuts on the selector cable and adjust its length until its connecting eye slips onto the pin on the hand control without any

Fig. 6.32. Starter inhibitor switch and reversing lamp switch (Model 12 transmission) (Sec. 18)

A Starter inhibitor switch	B Reversing lamp switch

need to move either component to ensure perfect engagement.
6 Tighten the locknuts, fit a new cable split pin and refit the selector cover.

Starter inhibitor switch adjustment (early models)
7 Check that the speed selector linkage adjustment is correct and then remove the cover from the speed selector lever.
8 Place the selector control in 'N' or 'P' and disconnect the lead from the inhibitor switch.
9 Connect a test-lamp and a small battery in series with the single terminal on the inhibitor switch.
10 Release the plunger switch locknut (A) (Fig. 6.32) and rotate the switch until the lamp just illuminates. Turn the plunger switch inwards (clockwise) for exactly ½ turn and retighten the locknut.
11 Disconnect the lamp and battery, remake the original connections, switch on the ignition and make sure that the starter motor will only operate in 'N' or 'P'.

Starter inhibitor switch adjustment (later models)
12 Later models have a different switch assembly. Connect a test-lamp and battery in series, as previously described in this Section.
13 Release the switch locknuts and with the selector lever in 'N' move the position of the switch until the test lamp lights up.
14 Tighten the switch locknuts and then recheck the switch operation with the test bulb and battery. The lamp should remain on in 'N' or 'P' and remain out in all other selector positions.
15 Remove the test rig and reconnect the electrical feed lead to the switch terminal.

Vacuum control unit adjustment
16 Speed selection is controlled partly by the car's roadspeed and partly by engine manifold depression acting on a vacuum control unit.
17 It can be suspected that the vacuum control unit diaphragm is ruptured if one of the following conditions is observed:

Fig. 6.33. Later type starter inhibitor switch arrangement (Model 12)
(Sec. 18)

2   Selector lever knob   8   Test circuit
3   Cover screws   9   Selector lever
7   Switch feed cable   10   Switch securing locknuts

Fig. 6.34. Pressure take off point (4) vacuum control unit (9) on
Model 12 automatic transmission (Sec. 18)

Fig. 6.35. Sectional view of vacuum control unit on Model 12
transmission showing adjuster screw (9) (Sec. 18)

Fig. 6.36. Kickdown solenoid terminal (1) on Model 12
transmission (Sec. 18)

(i)   Smoky exhaust due to oil being drawn from transmission
       through ruptured diaphragm into inlet manifold.
(ii)   Fluid level consistently falling at regular checks.
(iii) Rough or jerky upshifts or downshifts.

18 The vacuum control unit under these circumstances must be
renewed as a complete assembly.
19 To check and adjust the vacuum control unit, vacuum and pressure
gauges will be required.
20 Ensure that all engine adjustments are correct, also the ignition
settings. Have the engine and transmission at normal running temperature (operate on road for minimum 5 miles/8 km).
21 Connect the vacuum gauge to the heater control take off point at
the forward end of the inlet manifold.
22 Remove the hexagonal plug (4) from the front left-hand side of the
transmission casing and connect the pressure gauge (Fig. 6.34).
23 Start the engine, select '1' or 'R' and apply the hand and foot
brakes firmly. Increase the engine speed until vacuum gauge reads 9
to 10 in Hg (23 to 25 cm) at 1200 rev/min. The fluid pressure gauge
should read between 70 and 90 lb/sq in (4.92 and 6.32 kg/sq cm).
24 If the pressure reading is outside that specified, remove the vacuum
hose from the control unit and insert a screwdriver. Turn the internal
screw clockwise to increase pressure or anticlockwise to decrease it.
One full turn of the screw will vary the pressure by about 5 lb/sq in
(0.35 kg/sq cm) (Fig. 6.35).

Kick-down switch and solenoid adjustment
25 Disconnect the lead from the kick-down solenoid lead through
connector and insert a test bulb between the end of the lead and a
good earth (Fig. 6.36(,[

26 Switch on the ignition and depress the accelerator pedal to the
kick-down position.
27 If the circuit is satisfactory, the test-lamp will illuminate. If it does
not, release the locknut on the kick-down switch and turn the switch
until the lamp does light up. Tighten the lock nut (Fig. 6.37).
28 To test the kick-down solenoid, disconnect the lead from the
solenoid lead through connector terminal. Connect a jumper lead
momentarily between the battery positive terminal and the solenoid
lead through connector terminal. A distinct click should be heard if the
solenoid is operating satisfactorily. Renewal of the solenoid will
necessitate removal of the oil pan. Remove the solenoid by turning it
through 180° in an anticlockwise direction.

Rear brake band adjustment
29 This operation should be carried out after the first 1000 miles
(1600 km) running on a new car or when a new transmission has been
installed and at 24000 miles (38600 km) intervals thereafter.
30 The adjuster screw is located on the right-hand side of the transmission casing. Release the locknut and unscrew it two turns.
(Fig. 6.38).
31 Lubricate the adjuster screw and check that it turns freely. Tighten
the screw to a torque of 10 lb/ft (14 Nm) and then loosen it exactly
1¼ turns. Retighten the locknut to a torque of 35 lb/ft (48 Nm).
32 The front brake band on this type of transmission is self-adjusting.

---

19 Model 35F transmission - adjustments

Speed selector linkage adjustment
1   The adjustment procedure is very similar to that described in

Fig. 6.37. Kickdown switch (5) and locknut on Model 12 transmission (Sec. 18)

Fig. 6.38. Adjusting rear brake band (Model 12 transmission) (Sec. 18)

Fig. 6.40. Pressure take off point (Model 35F transmission) (Sec. 19)

Section 17, for the model 8 transmission, except that the connection of the selector rod to the lever should be carried out while both components are in the 'R' position.

Downshift (kick-down) cable adjustment
2   The downshift cable is preset in production by a stop which is crimped to it at the carburettor end. All that is necessary is to maintain a clearance of about 0.015 in (0.38 mm) between the crimped stop and the end face of the threaded cable adjuster. To do this, release the locknut and turn the cable adjuster in, or out, as necessary.
3   In the event of the crimped stop moving or a new cable being fitted (supplied with loose stop), then the cable must be adjusted by one of the following methods:
4   *Method 1:* Run the car on the road for a minimum of five miles (8 km) until the transmission attains normal operating temperature. Connect a pressure gauge to the take-off point on the rear of the transmission casing.
5   Select 'D' or '2' and increase the engine speed to 1000 rev/min. The pressure gauge should read between 95 and 100 lb/sq in (6.68 and 7.03 kg/sq cm). If the pressure indicated is lower than specified, increase the effective length of the downshift outer cable by turning the cable adjuster. If the pressure is higher, decrease the length of the cable by again turning the adjuster.
6   *Method 2:* Where a pressure gauge is not available, the oil pan can be removed (this must be done in any event if the cable is being renewed) and the cable adjusted to provide downshift valve cam settings as shown in the diagrams (Fig. 6.41).
7   Whichever method is used, when the cable adjustment is correct, crimp the cable stop so that it provides a clearance, as described in paragraph 2.

Starter inhibitor switch adjustment
8   This is carried out in a similar manner to that described in Section 18.

Fig. 6.39. Downshift cable adjustment (Model 35F transmission) (Sec. 19)

A Adjuster   B Crimped stop

Fig. 6.41. Downshift valve cam settings (Model 35F transmission) (Sec. 19)

Front brake band adjustment
9   Drain the transmission and carry out the adjustment, as described in Section 17, for the model 8 transmission.

Rear brake band adjustment
10   The operations are similar to those described for the model 12 transmission in Section 18, paragraphs 29 to 31 except that the adjuster screw should be released by only ¾ of a turn before locking it with the locknut.

---

20 Model 65 transmission - adjustments

Speed selector rod adjustment
1   Remove speed selector lever cover and release selector cable locknuts.
2   Disconnect cable from selector arm on the transmission and then set both components in '1'.
3   Adjust the effective length of the cable using the locknuts until the cable can be connected to the arm with the clevis pin eyes in both components in perfect alignment.

Downshift cable adjustment
4   Refer to Section 19, paragraphs 2 to 7.

Front brake band adjustment
5   Remove the transmission cover, carpet and remove the access plate.
6   Slacken the locknut on the adjustment screw then torque tighten the screw to 4 lb ft (7 Nm).
7   Back the screw off ¾ of a turn then hold it stationary in this position whilst tightening the locknut.
8   Fit the access plate and replace the carpet.

Rear brake band adjustment
9   Drive the car onto a ramp or raise it on jacks. Apply the handbrake.
10   Select 'P', raise the ramp and slacken the adjuster locknut.
11   Torque tighten the screw to 5 lb ft (7 Nm) then back it off ¾ of a turn.
12   Hold the screw stationary in this position and tighten the locknut.
13   Lower the car to the ground.

---

21 Stall speed test

---

1   Should the performance of the automatic transmission not appear to be up to standard, the following stall test can be carried out and the necessary conclusions drawn from the test results.
2   The stall speed is the maximum speed at which the engine can drive the torque converter impeller while the turbine is being held stationary.
3   Run the car on the road for at least 5 miles (8 km) until both the engine and the transmission are at normal operating temperature.
4   Apply the handbrake fully and chock the roadwheels.
5   Select '1' or 'R' and depress the accelerator fully. Note and record the maximum reading on the tachometer.
6   Do not extend the stall test beyond 10 seconds or repeat it at less than half hourly intervals as overheating of the transmission may occur.
7   Use the following table to compare the tachometer readings obtained.

Model 8, 12 or 35F

Rev/min obtained	Condition indicated
Under 1000	Stator free wheel slipping
1350 to 1550	Engine not developing full power
1600 to 1700	Conditions normal
Over 2100	Clutch slip or brake band fault

Model 65

Rev/min obtained	Condition indicated
Under 1400	Stator free wheel slipping
1600 (approx)	Engine not developing full power
2200	Conditions normal
Over 2400	Clutch slip or brake band fault

Fig. 6.42. Speed selector cable and adjuster nuts on Model 65 transmission (Sec. 20)

Fig. 6.43. Adjusting front brake band (Model 65 transmission) (Sec. 20)

1   *Cover plate*   3   *Locknut*
2   *Adjuster screw*

Fig. 6.44. Rear brake band adjuster (Model 65 transmission) (Sec. 20)

1   *Adjuster screw*   2   *Locknut*

22 Rear oil seal - renewal

1   Leakage of fluid from the rear end of the transmission extension housing will almost certainly be from a worn output shaft oil seal.
2   Disconnect the front end of the propeller shaft (see Chapter 7) and place the shaft to one side.
3   Unscrew and remove the output shaft coupling flange nut. The nut may be secured by a split pin or a tab washer. The coupling flange will have to be held quite still while the nut is unscrewed. Make up a lever for this which can be bolted to the coupling flange using the original bolts which will still be in position in the flange.
4   Withdraw the coupling flange and washer.
5   Prise out the oil seal and then tap in a new one using a piece of tubing as a drift.
6   Apply grease to the coupling flange surfaces which will be in contact with the lips of the oil seal, install the coupling, tighten the nut to specified torque and fit a new split pin or bend over the tab washer.
7   Reconnect the propeller shaft and then check and top-up the fluid level in the automatic transmission unit.

23 Automatic transmission - removal and installation

1   The recommended method of removing the automatic transmission is to remove the engine and transmission as a combined unit and then separate them.
2   The necessary operations are described in Chapter 1, Sections 6 and 8.
3   Reconnection of the transmission to the engine and installation are described in Chapter 1, Sections 52 and 53.

24 Fault diagnosis - automatic transmission

Symptom	Reason/s
Engine will not start in 'N or 'P'	Faulty starter or ignition circuit. Incorrect speed selector linkage adjustment. Incorrectly adjusted inhibitor switch.
Engine starts in selector positions other than 'N' or 'P'	Incorrect speed selector linkage adjustment. Incorrectly adjusted inhibitor switch.
Severe bump when selecting	Idling speed too high.
'D' or 'R' or excessive creep when handbrake released	Downshift cable incorrectly adjusted. Vacuum circuit fault (Type 12). Solenoid fault (Type 12).
Poor acceleration and low maximum speed	Incorrect fluid level. Incorrect linkage adjustment. Incorrect downshift cable adjustment.
No movement when 'R' selected	Incorrect rear band adjustment.
Poor upshift quality	Front band requires adjustment.
No movement in 'D'	Front brake band requires adjustment. Fault in one-way clutch.

Chapter 7 Propeller shaft

Contents

Specifications

Type ... ... Two section open with needle roller universal joints and flexible mounted centre bearing. Sliding joint incorporated in front section

Shaft diameter
Early cars:
Automatic or manual gearbox ... ... 2 in (50.8 mm)
Later cars:
Automatic transmission ... ... 2 in (50.8 mm)
Manual gearbox ... ... Front 3 in (76.2 mm), Rear 2 in (50.8 mm)

Torque wrench settings	lb f ft	Nm
Propeller shaft flange nuts	34	47
Centre bearing baseplate bolts	18	25

1 General description

1 An open propeller shaft is fitted which is divided in the centre. The forward end of the rear section is supported on a rubber-mounted ball race and a universal joint is fitted at its rear end.

2 The front section has a universal joint at each end and incorporates a sliding spline within a flexible gaiter.

3 No lubrication or maintenance is required as all joints and bearings are prepacked with grease during production.

2 Propeller shaft (front section) - removal and refitting

Early cars
1 Unscrew and remove the four self-locking nuts from the front and rear flanges of the propeller shaft.

2 Compress the shaft at the sliding splines section and withdraw the propeller shaft towards the rear of the car.

3 Refitting is a reversal of removal but make sure that the mating faces of the flanges are clean and free from particles of grit.

Fig. 7.1. Front section of propeller shaft - exploded view (Sec. 2)

Series 2 models

4   Removal of the propeller shaft from these models will necessitate
supporting the weight of the rear of the engine on a suitable hoist or
a cross bar and threaded lifting eye.

5   With the engine weight supported, remove the exhaust intermediate
pipe.

6   Remove the rear and intermediate heat shields.

7   Disconnect the engine rear mounting plate by withdrawing the
setscrews, spacers and washers.

8   Place a jack under the gearbox (suitably insulated from damage with
a block of wood) and release the self-locking nut which secures
the engine rear mounting. If the car is equipped with automatic
transmission, do not position the jack under the oil pan but place it
with a block of wood under the cast section of the transmission casing.

9   Remove the bracket and engine mounting plate from the gear
casing.

10 Disconnect the gearbox/propeller shaft coupling flange and the
flanges just forward of the centre bearing and lift the front section of
the propeller shaft from the car.

11 Refitting is a reversal of removal.

Fig. 7.2. Method of supporting weight of engine while engine
mountings are dismantled (Sec. 2)

3   Propeller shaft (rear section) - removal and refitting

1   On Series 2 models, remove the exhaust intermediate pipe and the
rear heat shield.

2   Unscrew and remove the four self-locking nuts from the front and
rear flanges of the rear section of the propeller shaft. Mark the
relative position of the centre bearing support bracket to the underside
of the body.

3   Remove the four setscrews which secure the support bracket.
Retain any shims which are located between the bracket and body,
noting carefully their position.

4   Withdraw the propeller shaft towards the rear of the car.

5   Refitting is a reversal of removal but make sure that the connecting
flange faces are clean and return any centre bearing support bracket
shims to their original positions.

6   Check the alignment of the propeller shaft, as described in Section 5.

4   Centre bearing - removal, overhaul and refitting

1   Remove the rear section of the propeller shaft complete with
centre bearing as described in the preceding Section.

Fig. 7.3. Propeller shaft centre bearing support plate (Sec. 3)

3   *Coupling flanges of front and*   5   *Support plate*
    rear sections of propeller shaft   *bolts*
4   *Propeller shaft to final drive*
    pinion drive flange

Fig. 7.4. Exploded view of the propeller shaft centre bearing (Sec. 4)

2   The flange coupling is secured to the rear propeller shaft by two Woodruff keys and a castellated nut (early cars) or by splines (later cars). Withdraw the nut and pull off the coupling.

3   Extract the Woodruff keys (early cars) and outer dust cover.

4   Using a soft-faced mallet, drive the shaft through the bearing and its housing and then press the bearing from the housing.

5   Remove the two self-locking nuts and bolts which secure the body mounting bracket to the centre bearing plate.

6   Remove the four bolts and lockwashers which secure the mounting rubbers to the body mounting bracket.

7   Renew any worn components and reassemble and refit by reversing the removal and dismantling process.

8   Check the alignment of the propeller shaft as described in Section 5.

---

5   Propeller shaft - alignment

1   Whenever the propeller shaft has been removed or the centre bearing disturbed, its alignment must be checked in the following way. It is advisable to check the alignment also if the engine/transmission has been removed and refitted. Incorrect alignment of the propeller shaft can cause judder when taking off from a standing start.

2   Make up an alignment jig in accordance with the dimensions given in the diagram (Fig. 7.5).

3   First check the *horizontal alignment* by holding up the jig to the shaft. The sides of all three legs should contact the propeller shaft simultaneously, two legs on the rear section of the shaft and one leg

on the front section.

4   Any adjustment needed to make sure that all three legs contact simultaneously, should be carried out by releasing the setscrews which secure the centre bearing bracket to the propeller shaft tunnel and moving the bracket sideways.

5   To check the vertical alignment, again use the jig and hold it against the bottom face of the shafts. The ends of all three legs should make contact with the shaft simultaneously. If they do not, add or extract shims between the centre bearing bracket and the propeller shaft tunnel.

6   On later cars equipped with a manual gearbox which have a 3 in (76.2 mm) diameter front propeller shaft section the vertical alignment (with shims) should be checked and adjusted as just described, but the horizontal alignment differs from earlier cars. The jig previously described should be modified so that its centre leg is increased in width by 1/8 in (3.175 mm). Also modify the front leg of the jig to accommodate the greater diameter of the front section of the shaft.

7   Use the jig as previously described so that the wider centre leg will give an offset of the centre bearing to the left-hand side of the car. Movement of the centre bearing can be carried out by releasing the setscrews and pushing the bearing within the travel permitted by the elongated bolt holes of its support bracket.

8   On completion, tighten the centre bearing setscrews.

9   This offset alignment of the propeller shaft in the horizontal plane also applies to cars with automatic transmission built from 1973 onwards even though with this type of transmission, the diameter of both sections of the propeller shaft is still 2 in (50.8 mm).

Fig. 7.5. Propeller shaft alignment jig (manual gearbox cars with 2.0 in (50.8 mm) dia. rear section shaft and automatic transmission up to 1973) (Sec. 5)

Fig. 7.6. Checking propeller shaft horizontal alignment (Sec. 5)

Fig. 7.7. Checking propeller shaft vertical alignment (Sec. 5)

Fig. 7.8. Ejecting a universal joint bearing cup (Sec. 6)

Fig. 7.9. Alternative method of removing a universal joint bearing cup (Sec. 6)

Fig. 7.10. Separating universal joint yoke from spider (Sec. 6)

Fig. 7.11. Propeller shaft sliding joint alignment marks (Sec. 6)

6 Universal joints - overhaul

1 Wear in the needle roller bearings is characterised by judder and vibration in the transmission on over-run, 'clonks' on taking up the drive, and in extreme cases of lack of lubrication, metallic squeaking and ultimately grating and shrieking sounds as the bearings break up.

2 It is easy to check if the needle roller bearings are worn; with the propeller shaft in position, try to turn the shaft with one hand and with the other hand hold the rear axle flange and repeat this procedure for the other joints. Any movement between the shaft and the front, centre or rear couplings is indicative of bearing failure and/or wear in the spider. The old bearings will have to be discarded and replaced by a new universal joint assembly.

3 Remove the propeller shaft, in the manner described in Sections 2 and 3.

4 Thoroughly clean all dirt from the snap rings and the top of the bearing surfaces.

5 Remove all the snap rings by pinching with a pair of pliers and at the same time prising out with a screwdriver. If a ring proves difficult to remove it may be because it is jammed by the end of the bearing race so lightly tap the end of the race to relieve the pressure.

6 Hold the joint in the hand and with a hide faced or other type of soft hammer, tap the yoke lug as shown in Fig. 7.8. This will cause the top bearing to work outwards until it can finally be removed with the fingers. If the top bearing proves obstinate it can be tapped out from inside with a small diameter punch or piece of bar but be careful not to damage the bearing if this is not being renewed.

7 Repeat the above procedure for the opposite bearing.

8 The splined sleeve yoke to flange can now be separated from the shaft yoke as depicted.

9 Rest the two trunnions which are now exposed, on wood blocks and tap the yoke with a soft nosed hammer to remove the two remaining races.

10 It is now advisable to look carefully at the yoke cross holes. It is a very rare event but these holes have been known to wear to a certain degree of ovality. If this has occurred the defective item will have to be renewed.

11 On early model cars it is advisable to fit new cork gaskets and gasket retainers on the spider using a tubular drift.

12 Smear the wall of the race with grease to keep the rollers in position in the housing for assembly.

13 Insert the spider in the yoke holes, place the bearings in position and then lightly tap it home using a soft flat faced drift slightly smaller than the yoke hole in diameter.

14 Repeat the above for the opposite bearing in the yoke.

15 Fit new snap rings to the bearings and ensure they correctly located in the grooves.

16 Now place the mating yoke in position on the spider and fit the bearings and snap rings in the same manner as described above. It is essential that the sliding joint is refitted with its fixed yoke in line with the fixed yoke at the end of the propeller shaft; arrows are stamped on the two items to facilitate alignment. Apply grease to the mating surfaces of the sliding section of the shaft.

17 Make sure that the joint moves freely in all directions, if it appears to bind tap lighly with a wooden mallet to relieve any pressure of the bearings on the end of the spider.

18 Refit the propeller shaft to the car as described in Sections 2 and 3.

7 Fault diagnosis - propeller shaft

Symptom	Reason/s
Judder on take-off	Shaft out of alignment.
Vibration when vehicle running on road	Out of balance or distorted propeller shaft. Backlash in splined shaft. Loose flange securing bolts. Worn universal joint bearings.

Chapter 8 Final drive

Contents

Specifications

Type	Independently mounted with open universally-jointed halfshafts

Axle ratios (early models)

	2.8 litre	4.2 litre
Standard	4.27 : 1	3.54 : 1
Overdrive	4.55 : 1	3.77 : 1
Automatic transmission	4.27 : 1	3.54 : 1

Axle ratios (later models)

	2.8 litres	3.4 litres	4.2 litres
Standard	4.09 : 1	3.54 : 1	3.31 : 1
Automatic transmission	4.09 : 1	3.54 : 1	3.31 : 1
N. America (standard)	—	—	3.54 : 1
N. America (auto. transmission) ...	—	—	3.07 : 1

Differential tolerances

Output shaft endfloat	0.001 to 0.003 in (0.02 to 0.07 mm)
Backlash (as etched on pinion gear):	
Pinion bearing preload (early)	8 to 12 lb in (0.09 to 0.14 kg m)
Pinion bearing preload (later)	25 to 30 lb in (0.3 to 0.35 kg m)
Oil capacity	2¾ Imp. pints (1.5 litres/3¼ US pints)

Torque wrench settings

	lb f ft	Nm
Output shaft nut	100	138
Caliper mounting bracket bolts (later cars)	70	97
Pinion nut (early cars)	120 to 130	166 to 179
Pinion nut (later cars) initial setting	100	138
Crownwheel bolts	80	111
Differential bearing cap bolts	60	83
Differential carrier bolts	75	104

1 General description

1 The final drive unit is mounted independently from the hubs. Short driveshafts having a universal joint at each end transmit power from the final drive output shafts to the roadwheels.
2 The output shafts of the final drive unit are carried on double row, angular contact ball bearings. The inner, or splined, ends of the shafts engage in mating splines in the side gears of the differential assembly.
3 Later cars have final drive units which may differ from earlier models in the following respects:

(i) Pinion shaft bearings preloaded by a collapsible spacer instead of shims.
(ii) Driveshaft oil seals integral with caliper mounting bracket.
(iii) Modified crownwheel and pinion design.
(iv) Optional limited slip differential unit available as an option.

4 In view of the special tools required it is not recommended that servicing operations extend beyond those described in this Chapter. In the event of complete overhaul to the final drive unit being required, it is better to renew the unit on a factory exchange basis rather than 'mix' new and old components even assuming that final drive components can be obtained without undue delay. Where this recommendation is followed, it should be noted that reconditioned units are supplied without driveshafts, hubs or brake components and these items should therefore be retained from the original unit. When carrying out operations to the drive train on cars equipped with a limited slip differential unit (Powr-Lok), never jack-up one rear wheel and turn the wheel while the opposite one is still on the ground. Always jack-up both rear wheels otherwise damage to the unit may be caused.

2 Rear hub - removal, overhaul and refitting

1 Jack-up the rear end of the car and support it securely under the bodyframe on axle stands. Remove the roadwheel.
2 Remove the suspension outer pivot grease nipple, withdraw the split

pin and unscrew and remove the castellated nut and washer from the end of the axle halfshaft.

3   Using a suitable extractor withdraw the hub and hub carrier assembly from the splined end of the halfshaft. Note the location of the inner oil seal track and the endfloat spacer.

4   Unscrew and remove the nuts from the ends of the lower wishbone outer pivot shaft (arrowed Fig. 8.1) and drive out the pivot shaft. Remove the hub and hub carrier.

5   Turn the hub carrier upside-down so that the hub inner bearing is at the top and then press out the hub. Discard the outer oil seal.

6   Remove the three setscrews and withdraw the water deflector. Prise out the inner oil seal and remove the inner track from the inner bearing.

7   Drive out the inner and outer bearings if these are to be renewed. Use a suitable extractor to withdraw the inner track of the outer bearing.

8   If new hub bearings are being fitted, press the new outer tracks of the inner and outer bearings into the hub carrier. Apply wheel bearing grease to the bearing components.

9   Hold the hub carrier so that the outer bearing is at the top. Locate the inner race of the outer bearing and then press a new outer oil seal into its recess.

10 Fit the water deflector and press the hub complete with outer seal track into the inner track of the outer bearing until the hub is fully home.

11 Hold the hub and hub carrier vertically so that the inner end of the hub is uppermost.

12 Locate the inner track of the inner bearing on the hub followed by the special collar of the official tool no. J.15. Press the track onto the hub until its inner face is flush with the special collar.

13 Mount a dial gauge as shown Tap the hub carrier downwards, zero the dial gauge and then use two levers inserted between the hub and hub carrier to move the carrier upwards. Record the maximum reading on the dial gauge.

14 Remove the Special Collar and then fit a spacer (if necessary) to give endfloat of between 0.002 in and 0.006 in (0.051 to 0.152 mm). Spacers are supplied in thicknesses of 0.109 to 0.0151 in steps of 0.003 in (0.076 mm) and are lettered 'A' (smallest) to 'R' (largest) omitting letters 'I' and 'N' as given in the following table:

Letter	Thickness in.	mm
A	0.109	2.77
B	0.112	2.85
C	0.115	2.92
D	0.118	3.00
E	0.121	3.07
F	0.124	3.15
G	0.127	3.23
H	0.130	3.30
J	0.133	3.38
K	0.136	3.45
L	0.139	3.53
M	0.142	3.61
P	0.145	3.68
Q	0.148	3.75
R	0.151	3.87

Fig. 8.1. Rear hub showing hub extractor and lower wishbone outer pivot shaft (arrowed) (Sec. 2)

Fig. 8.2. Pressing rear hub from carrier (Sec. 2)

Fig. 8.3. Pressing in rear hub inner track of inner bearing using special collar of official tool (Sec. 2)

Fig. 8.4. Checking rear hub bearing endfloat (Sec. 2)

15 For example, assume that the endfloat measured with the collar in position is 0.25 in (0.64mm). Take the mean permissible endfloat as 0.004 in (0.10 mm) and subtract this from the measured endfloat. giving 0.021 in (0.53 mm). The Special Collar is 0.150 in (3.81 mm) thick so the thickness of the spacer to be fitted will be 0.150 - 0.021 in ie; 0.129 in (3.28 mm). The nearest spacer in thickness to this is 0.130 in (3.30 mm) so fit a letter 'H' spacer in place of the Special Collar.

16 Fit the inner oil seal and its seating ring.

17 Locate the hub assembly between the jaws of the suspension wishbone, install the pivot shaft and nuts.

18 Clean the splines of the hub and halfshaft with a suitable solvent and then apply a thin coating of thread locking compound to the splines.

19 Engage the hub with the halfshaft splines, fit the washer and castellated nut and tighten to specified torque.

20 Install a new split pin to the castellated nut and refit the outer pivot grease nipple.

21 It is worth rechecking the hub bearing endfloat again at this stage by attaching the dial gauge as shown and levering the hub outwards. (Fig. 8.5).

22 Where possible, do not drive the car for a period of between 4 and 12 hours in order to allow the thread locking compound to harden.

23 Remove the hub bearing grease cap and inject wheel bearing grease until no more will go in. Do not pressurise the grease, or it will be forced past the oil seals. Refit the cap.

24 Refit the roadwheel and lower the car to the ground.

3 Axle halfshaft - removal and refitting

1 Remove the rear suspension assembly, as described in Chapter 11, Section 19 and then remove the hub assembly as described in the preceding Section.

2 Remove the rear shock absorber which is nearest the front of the car. To do this, remove the upper and lower mounting pivot nuts and drive out the pivot pin until the shock absorber mounting is released.

3 Unscrew and remove the four self-locking nuts which secure the halfshaft inner universal joint to the output flange of the final drive unit.

4 Withdraw the halfshaft but extract and note the exact location of any shims which are used for camber purposes.

5 Refitting is a reversal of removal but make sure that the camber shims are returned to their original locations.

4 Halfshaft universal joints - overhaul

1 The procedure is very similar to that described in Chapter 7 for the overhaul of propeller shaft universal joints to which reference should be made.

5 Output shaft oil seal and bearing (earlier cars) - renewal

1 Remove the halfshaft as described in Section 3.

Fig. 8.5. Re-checking bearing endfloat with hub installed to car (Sec. 2)

Fig. 8.6. Rear hub grease cap (Sec. 2)

Fig. 8.7. Rear shock absorber mountings. Outer pivot grease nipple (1) (Sec. 3)

Fig. 8.8. Withdrawing a halfshaft (Sec. 3)

2   Cut the locking wire and remove the two bolts which secure the brake caliper to the final drive unit.

3   Remove the brake discs, noting carefully the number of shims located between the disc and the driveshaft flange.

4   *On earlier cars,* a locking ring is used to retain the output shaft. With this design, extract the two bolts and the locking plate which retain the locking ring to the caliper mounting bracket. **On no account remove the other three adjacent bolts** which secure the caliper mounting bracket which must not be disturbed.

5   Release the locking ring by tapping it with a hammer and brass or copper drift engaged in the slots in the ring.

6   When the ring is completely free, withdraw the shaft assembly through the caliper mounting bracket and do not disturb the setting of the mounting as the operation is carried out.

7   Bend down the lock tab and unscrew the bearing nut, extract the bearing from the shaft.

8   The oil seal on this type of earlier assembly is fitted inside the locking ring and renewal should be carried out by renewing the seal and ring as an assembly.

9   Refitting is a reversal of the removal and dismantling operations.

6   Output shaft oil seal and bearing (later cars) - renewal

1   Repeat the operations described in paragraphs 1, 2 and 3, of the preceding Section.

2   Cut the locking wire and remove the five bolts which secure the caliper mounting bracket. Support the caliper.

3   Withdraw the output shaft together with the caliper mounting bracket shims, ball bearing and the square section oil seal from the ball bearing housing.

4   Flatten the tab on the locking plate and unscrew the nut from the output shaft.

5   Withdraw the ball bearing and caliper mounting bracket from the output shaft. The oil seal is integral with the caliper mounting bracket and the assembly must be renewed complete.

6   Smear the new oil seal with oil and press it squarely into its seat in the bearing housing.

7   Apply hypoid gear oil to the square section seal, fit the four special flange bolts and position the caliper mounting bracket and oil seal assembly over the output shaft. Slide the ball bearing onto the shaft, a new tab washer and the nut. Tighten nut to torque and bend up the tab of the lockwasher.

8   Oil the splines of the output shaft and fit it into the differential housing.

9   Insert and tighten (finger-tight) the five bolts which retain the caliper mounting bracket.

10   It should be noted that the oil seal is slightly oversize so that it will be compressed when all bolts are fully tightened.

11   Using feeler blades, measure between the inner face of the caliper mounting bracket and the differential housing (A).

12   Shims are available in the following thicknesses:

0.003 in (0.076 mm), 0.005 in (0.127 mm), 0.010 in (0.254 mm), 0.030 in (0.762 mm)

Select those which are of a thickness which when subtracted from the measurement (A) will leave a gap of 0.003 in (0.076 mm). When the bolts are tightened, this is the required 'nip' for bearing and oil seal.

13   Remove the output shaft, apply a thin coat of jointing compound to the shims (which have just been selected) and to the mating faces of the flanges. Insert the output shaft with coated shims, insert bolts and tighten to specified torque in diagonally opposite sequence.

14   Wire the five bolts to lock them.

15   Install the brake discs to the output shaft flanges, refitting any shims to their original locations.

16   Install the caliper to the mounting bracket. Check that the brake disc is central in the jaws of the caliper. This can be done using feeler blades. Any adjustment which may be required should be carried out by altering the shim pack which is located between the drive flange and the disc.

17   Lock the caliper bolts with wire.

18   Refit the halfshaft, as described in Section 3.

7   Pinion oil seal (early models with bearings preloaded with shims) - renewal

1   Disconnect the propeller shaft rear flange from the final drive unit pinion companion flange.

2   Make up a suitable lever, 3 or 4 ft (0.9 or 1.2 m) in length and drilled so that by bolting it to the companion flange, the flange can be held still while the flange nut is unscrewed.

3   Remove the nut, washer and flange and then prise out the defective oil seal.

4   Fit the new oil seal gasket into the seal recess, fit the oil seal so that its lip is towards the final drive unit and its dust-excluding face is visible when installed.

5   Fit the companion flange, washer and nut and holding the flange quite still, tighten the nut to a torque of between 120 and 130 lb ft (166 and 179 Nm).

6   Reconnect the propeller shaft.

7   Top-up the final drive unit.

Fig. 8.11. Sectional view of output shaft flange and bearing (Sec. 6)

3 Brake disc	*5 Bearing and oil seal*
4 Caliper mounting bracket	*6 Output shaft nut*
bolt	*7 Special flange bolt*

Fig. 8.9. Output shaft locking ring (earlier cars) (Sec. 5)

Fig. 8.10. Output shaft (caliper mounting) bracket on later cars (Sec. 6)

8 Pinion oil seal (later models with bearing collapsible spacer) - renewal

1   Disconnect the propeller shaft from the final drive pinion companion flange. Disconnect the halfshafts from the output flanges of the final drive unit.
2   Wind a cord round the companion flange of the pinion and attach it to a spring balance. Check and record the force required to start the flange moving. Take the average of several recordings.
3   Hold the companion flange still by fitting a tool similar to the one described in the preceding Section.
4   Unscrew and remove the pinion nut and washer and withdraw the companion flange.
5   Prise out the faulty oil seal and install the new one.
6   Refit the companion flange (complete with propeller shaft flange bolts) the washer and screw on the pinion nut.
7   Tighten the nut to 100 lb/ft (138 Nm) holding the flange still with the tool to prevent it turning.
8   Check the rotating force required to turn the flange using the cord and spring balance. Tighten the pinion nut, *only a fraction of a turn at a time,* until the force recorded on the spring balance matches that recorded before dismantling.
9   If the nut is overtightened, the collapsible tyre spacer which is located between the pinion bearings will be overcompressed and a new spacer will have to be fitted. It is not good attempting to reduce the preload by backing off the nut. A new spacer can only be fitted after almost complete dismantling of the final drive unit.

Fig. 8.12. Final drive unit mounting bolts (Sec. 9)

9 Final drive unit - removal and installation

1   Remove the rear suspension as described in Chapter 11, Section 19. Drain the oil from the final drive unit.
2   Invert the suspension assembly on the bench and remove the 14 bolts which secure the tie plate.
3   Disconnect the four shock absorber/roadspring assemblies but do not dismantle them.
4   Remove the four self-locking nuts which secure the halfshaft inner universal joint flange to the brake disc and final drive output flanges.
5   Withdraw the halfshafts noting the number and location of the camber shims.
6   Remove a nut from one end of the suspension inner wishbone pivot shafts and drive out the shafts.
7   Withdraw the hubs, halfshafts and radius arm assemblies.
8   Disconnect handbrake levers from the compensator.
9   Disconnect the brake lines from the caliper units.
10 Turn the final drive assembly over and cut the locking wire from the differential carrier bolts. Unscrew the bolts and remove the crossbeam from the carrier by tilting the crossbeam forward over the nose of the pinion.
11 Installation is a reversal of removal but observe the following points:

Fig. 8.13. Separating crossbeam from final drive unit (Sec. 9)

Tighten the differential carrier bolts to the specified torque and lock the bolts with new wire.

Never substitute nylon type self-locking nuts for the all metal type used on the output shaft flange studs.

10 Fault diagnosis - final drive

Symptom	Reason/s
Noise on drive or overrun	Low oil level. Loose crownwheel bolts. Loose bearing cap bolts. General wear in bearings or gearteeth.
Noise on turn	Seized, broken or damaged pinion or side gear or thrust washers.
Knock during gearshift or when taking up drive	Excessive crownwheel to pinion backlash. Worn gears. Worn halfshaft splines. Drive pinion nut loose. Loose crownwheel bolts or bearing cap bolts. Worn side gear splines. Wear in halfshaft universal joints.

Chapter 9 Braking system

Contents

Specifications

Type	4 wheel disc, hydraulic. Dual circuit with vacuum servo assistance. Handbrake mechanical to rear wheels
Caliper type	Girling
Disc diameter	
Front	11.18 in (28.4 cm)
Rear	l0.395 in (26.3 cm)
Disc thickness	
Front (all models except Series 2)	0.5 in (12.7 mm)
Front (Series 2)	0.95 in (24.13 mm)
Rear (all models)	0.5 in (12.7 mm)
Master cylinder bore diameter	0.875 in (22.23 mm)
Servo unit	Girling Type 100
Total area rubbed by friction material	448 sq in (2890 sq cm)

Torque wrench settings	lb ft	Nm
Disc retaining bolts	35	48
Caliper retaining bolts:		
Front	55	76
Rear	50	69
Brake pedal pivot bolt	18	25
Master cylinder banjo bolt	23	32
Master cylinder tipping valve nut	40	55

1 General description

1 The braking system is of four wheel disc type. The hydraulic system is of dual circuit type with a tandem master cylinder. Servo assistance is provided.

2 The rear calipers and discs are mounted inboard on the differential housing and output flanges.

3 The handbrake operates through mechanical linkage to the rear calipers which incorporate automatically adjustable handbrake mechanism.

2 Disc pads - inspection and renewal

1 At the intervals specified in 'Routine maintenance', examine the thickness of the friction material on the disc pads.

2 In the case of the front brakes, remove the roadwheels.

3 The pads are clearly visible through the aperture in the caliper units and if the friction material has worn down to 1/8 in (3.2 mm) or less then they must be renewed (photos).

4 Always renew the pads in axle sets.

5 Withdraw the spring clips and pull out the pad retaining pins. On

later models, anti-chatter springs are fitted to the pads.

6   Withdraw the pads from the caliper, gripping their edges with a pair of pliers if they are hard to remove (photo).

7   Brush out any dust from the interior of the caliper and then depress the caliper pistons squarely into their bores in order to accommodate the new, thicker pads. Depressing the pistons will cause the fluid level to rise in the master cylinder reservoir and eventually overflow, so it is advisable to draw off some of the hydraulic fluid from the reservoir before commencing operations. A poultry baster or an old hydrometer is useful for drawing off some fluid. Do not spill any hydraulic fluid on the paintwork as it acts as a paint stripper!

8   Install the new pads making sure that the friction lining is against the disc, insert the retaining pins and spring clips.

9   Apply the footbrake several times to bring the pads into contact with the discs and then top-up the fluid reservoir to the indicated level.

10 For renewal of handbrake friction pads, see Section 12.

---

3   Front caliper - removal, overhaul and refitting

1   Jack-up the front of the car and remove the roadwheel.

2   Disconnect the hydraulic hose at the junction with the rigid brake pipe (see Section 6). Plug the pipes.

3   Cut the locking wire, remove the caliper mounting bolts and withdraw the caliper. Withdraw the disc pads.

4   Clean away all external dirt. **On no account unscrew the bolts which secure the two halves of the caliper body together.**

5   Detach the rubber dust excluders from the locating grooves.

6   Place a pad of rag between the piston end faces and apply air from a tyre pump to the fluid union on the caliper body. This will eject the pistons far enough so that they can be extracted with the fingers. There are two outer and one inner piston, on calipers fitted to early cars, later cars are fitted with four piston calipers.

7   Examine the surfaces of the pistons and the cylinders for scoring or 'bright' wear areas. If these are evident, renew the caliper complete.

8   Where the components are in good condition, extract and discard the seals which are located in the cylinder grooves.

9   Obtain a repair kit which will contain the new seals and other renewable items. Manipulate the new seals into their cylinder grooves using the fingers only.

10 Dip each piston in clean hydraulic fluid and enter it squarely into its cylinder.

11 Refit the dust excluders and engage their lips in the cylinder grooves. Depress the pistons fully into their cylinders.

12 Refit the caliper to the stub axle carrier and tighten the bolts to the specified torque wrench setting. Lock the bolts with new wire.

13 Refit the disc pads.

14 Reconnect the hydraulic hose and bleed the front circuit, as described in Section 10.

15 Refit the roadwheel and lower the car to the ground.

2.3A Front disc caliper

2.3B Rear disc caliper

Fig. 9.1. Removing disc pads (Sec. 2)

2.6 Removing a disc pad

Fig. 9.2. Exploded view of a front disc caliper (earlier three piston type) (Sec. 3)

1	Caliper body	6	Piston seal	11	Bleed nipple
2	Outer pistons	7	Dust excluder	12	Dust cap
3	Inner piston	8	Friction pad	13	Mounting shim
4	Piston seals	9	Pad retaining pin	14	Anti-chatter spring
5	Dust excluder	10	Clip		(later models)

Fig. 9.3. Exploded view of a rear disc caliper (Sec. 4)

1	Caliper body	11	Handbrake mechanism	22	Hinge pin
2	Piston	12	Pad carrier assembly	23	Split pin
3	Piston seal	13	Pad carrier assembly	24	Protection cover
4	Dust excluder	14	Anchor pin	25	Protection cover
5	Friction pad	15	Operating lever	26	Bolt
6	Pad retaining pin	16	Return spring	27	Washer
7	Clip	17	Pawl assembly	28	Bolt
8	Bridge pipe	18	Tension spring	29	Split pin
9	Bleed nipple	19	Anchor pin	30	Bolt
10	Dust cap	20	Adjuster	31	Retraction plate
		21	Friction spring	32	Tab washer

4 Rear caliper - removal, overhaul and refitting

Early cars

1   Remove the rear suspension assembly as described in Chapter 11, Section 19. Support the suspension on blocks placed centrally under it.

2   Extract the split pin and clevis pin and disconnect the handbrake cable from the compensator linkage. Disconnect the pull-off springs.

3   Lift the lock tabs and withdraw the pivot bolts together with the retraction plate.

4   Remove the handbrake friction pad carriers from the caliper bridges by moving them to the rear round the discs and then withdrawing them from the rear of the suspension assembly (refer to Section 12, of this Chapter).

5   Disconnect the hydraulic hose from the caliper body and plug the hole.

6   Remove the disc pads, as described in Section 2.

7   Cut the locking wire and remove the two bolts which secure the caliper to the final drive unit.

8   Withdraw the caliper through the aperture in the front of the crossmember.

Series 2 cars

9   Remove the handbrake caliper in the following way. Remove the nuts and bolts which secure the tie plate to the rear suspension unit and withdraw the tie-plate.

10 Fully release the handbrake and remove the split pin and clevis pin which secure the handbrake cable to the caliper operating lever on one side of the car and then disconnect the cable from the opposite caliper.

11 Disconnect the return spring from the handbrake operating lever.

12 Flatten the caliper mounting bolt lock tabs, unscrew and remove the bolts, the tab washer and the retraction lever. **On no account unscrew the bolts which secure the two halves of the caliper body together.**

13 Slide the caliper around the brake disc and withdraw it through

the gap exposed by the removal of the tie-plate.

14 Disconnect the hydraulic line from the caliper and plug the open ends to prevent loss of fluid and entry of dirt.

15 Withdraw the disc pads from the caliper and then cut the locking wire from the caliper mounting bolts and unscrew and remove the bolts.

16 Slide the caliper around the brake disc and withdraw it through the gap exposed by removal of the tie-plate.

17 Overhaul of the caliper is similar to that described for the front caliper in Section 3, except that only two pistons are employed in the rear unit. Refer also to Sections 12 and 13, of this Chapter.

18 To refit the caliper, locate it in position and secure it with two mounting bolts. Lock the bolts with new wire. Check that the brake disc is central within the caliper opening. If necessary, adjustment can be carried out by adding or removing brake disc shims.

19 Reverse the rest of the removal operations and when installation is complete, bleed the rear brake circuit as described in Section 10.

5 Master cylinder (early cars) - removal, overhaul and refitting

1   Remove the cap from the master cylinder reservoir and draw off as much fluid as possible by syphoning or using a poultry baster or old hydrometer.

2   Disconnect the brake lines from the master cylinder body.

3   Unscrew and remove the two flange nuts and withdraw the master cylinder from the front face of the vacuum servo unit.

4   Clean away all external dirt.

5   Extract the two screws and their washers and withdraw the tipping valve cover and seal.

6   Remove the tipping valve securing nut, depress the primary plunger and withdraw the tipping valve.

7   Eject the remainder of the internal components, either by carefully shaking them out or by applying air pressure from a tyre pump at one fluid inlet union while holding a finger over the second inlet.

8   Examine the surfaces of the plungers and the cylinder bore for scoring or 'bright' wear areas. If these are evident, renew the master

Fig. 9.4. Exploded view of the master cylinder (earlier cars) (Sec. 5)

1   Body
2   Tipping valve
3   Tipping valve securing nut
4   Tipping valve cover seal
5   Cover
6   Screw
7   Spring washer
8   Gland seal
9   Primary plunger
10 Intermediate spring
11 Ring seal
12 Secondary plunger
13 Thimble
14 Spring
15 Valve spacer
16 Spring washer
17 Valve stem
18 Valve seal

H.5685

cylinder complete.

9   If these components are in good condition then separate the plungers and intermediate spring. Lift the leaf of the spring retainer and withdraw the spring and valve sub-assembly from the secondary plunger.

10 Extract the spring, valve spacer and spring washer from the valve stem, also the seal from the valve head.

11 Discard all rubber seals and obtain a repair kit which will contain all the renewable items.

12 Install the new seals using the fingers only to manipulate them into position on the primary and secondary plungers.

13 Fit the valve seal (smallest diameter first) onto the valve head. Position the spring washer on the valve stem so that it flows away from the valve stem shoulder.

14 Fit the valve spacer, legs first, then attach the spring retainer to the valve stem so that the key hole end is first.

15 Slide the secondary spring over the retainer and then position the sub-assembly on the secondary plunger. The spring must be compressed whilst the leaf of the retainer is depressed behind the head of the plunger. This operation will be made easier if the sub-assembly is carefully secured in a vice and the vice jaws closed to compress the spring until it is nearly coil bound. Use a small screwdriver to press the spring retainer back against the secondary plunger. Depress the leaf of the retainer behind the head of the plunger.

16 Fit the intermediate spring between the primary and secondary plungers. Dip the plungers in clean hydraulic fluid and insert them into the cylinder bore (valve end leading).

17 Depress the primary plunger from the bore and install the tipping valve assembly. Fit the seas and screw in the tipping valve securing nut to a torque of 40 lb/ft (55 Nm). Install the tipping valve cover and a new seal.

18 Fit the master cylinder to the vacuum servo unit.

19 Reconnect the brake lines and bleed the complete hydraulic system (both circuits), as described in Section 10.

---

6   Master cylinder (later cars) - removal, overhaul and refitting

---

1   Slacken the clips which secure the reservoir hoses to the master cylinder adaptors, disconnect the hoses and plug them.

2   Disconnect the rigid brake lines from the master cylinder body and plug the lines.

3   Unbolt the master cylinder from the servo unit (photo).

4   Clean away all external dirt.

5   Prise the reservoir hose adaptors from their sealing grommets on the master cylinder body. Prise out the grommets.

6   Depress the primary piston into the bore of the master cylinder and extract the secondary piston stop pin from the grommet housing nearest the front of the master cylinder.

7   Extract the circlip from the end of the master cylinder and tap the flange end on a block of wood to eject the primary piston and spring and the secondary piston and spring. If these components are difficult to remove, apply air from a tyre pump at the fluid outlet port.

8   Keep the piston assemblies separate noting that the secondary piston spring is thicker and longer than the primary spring.

9   Examine the surfaces of the pistons and cylinder bore for scoring or 'bright' wear areas. If these are evident, renew the master cylinder complete.

10 If these components are in good condition, remove the spring, spring seat, recuperating seal and washer from the secondary piston. Also prise the seals from the rear of the secondary piston.

11 Dismantle the primary piston in a similar way.

12 Discard all the seals and obtain a repair kit.

13 Use only the fingers to manipulate the seals into position and commence reassembly by fitting the secondary piston inner seal into its groove so that its lip faces the front of the master cylinder.

14 Install the second seal to the secondary piston with its lip in the reverse direction to the first one fitted.

15 Fit the washer, recuperating seal, spring seat and the spring over the front end of the secondary piston.

16 Install primary piston rear seal (lip away from circlip) and then fit the washer, recuperating seal, spring seat and spring over the front end of the piston.

17 Apply hydraulic fluid to the piston assemblies and insert the secondary piston and spring into the master cylinder followed by the primary piston. Depress the piston and fit the circlip.

6.3 Brake booster and master cylinder

Fig. 9.5. Later type master cylinder (Sec. 6)

2   Fluid pipe adaptor
3   Grommets
4   Lock pin
20 Secondary piston
21 Primary piston

18 Depress the primary piston and fit the secondary piston stop pin.

19 Refit the grommet and adaptors and install the master cylinder to the servo by reversing the removal operations. Bleed the system.

7 Flexible hydraulic hoses, inspection, removal and refitting

1 Periodically, inspect the condition of the flexible brake hoses. If they appear swollen, chafed or when bent double with the fingers tiny cracks are visible, then they must be renewed.
2 Always uncouple the rigid pipe from the flexible hose first, then release the end of the flexible hose from the support bracket. Now unscrew the flexible hose from the caliper or connector. If this method is followed, no kinking of the hoses will occur.
3 When installing the hose, always use a new copper sealing washer.
4 When installation is complete, check that the flexible hose does not rub against the tyre or other adjacent components. Its attitude may be altered to overcome this by releasing its bracket support locknut and twisting the hose in the required direction by not more than one quarter turn.
5 Bleed the hydraulic system (Section 10).

8 Rigid brake lines - inspection, removal and refitting

1 At regular intervals wipe the steel brake pipes clean and examine them for signs of rust or denting caused by flying stones.
2 Examine the fit of the pipes in their insulated securing clips and bend the tongues of the clips if necessary to ensure a positive fit.
3 Check that the pipes are not touching any adjacent components or rubbing against any part of the vehicle. Where this is observed, bend the pipe gently away to clear.
4 Any section of pipe which is rusty or cafed should be renewed. Brake pipes are available to the correct length and fitted with end unions from most Jaguar/Daimler dealers and can be made to pattern by many accessory suppliers. When installing the new pipes use the old pipes as a guide to bending and do not make any bends sharper than is necessary.
5 The system will of course have to be bled when the circuit has been reconnected.

9 Front brake disc - inspection, removal and refitting

1 Jack-up the front of the car and remove the roadwheels.
2 Withdraw the disc pads.
3 Examine the discs for deep grooves or scoring or cracks. If these are evident, renew the disc. Light scoring is normal.
4 Check the disc for 'run-out'. A dial gauge should be used for this although feeler blades placed between the face of the disc and a fixed point are a satisfactory substitute.
5 Turn the disc and check that the 'run-out' or out of true does not exceed 0.004 in (0.10 mm). If it does the disc must be renewed.
6 It is most important that for optimum brake efficiency the hub endfloat is as specified in Chapter 11.
7 To remove a disc, disconnect the flexible hydraulic hose at the support bracket. Plug the pipes.
8 Remove the caliper, as described in Section 3.
9 Remove the hub by prising off the end cap and extracting the split pin from the castellated nut. Unscrew the nut and thrust washer.
10 Separate the disc from the hub by unscrewing the five setscrews.
11 Refitting the disc is a reversal of removal but adjust the hub endfloat as described in Chapter 11, and bleed the hydraulic circuit, as described in Section 10, of this Chapter.

10 Rear brake disc (except Series 2) - inspection, removal and refitting

1 Repeat the operations described in the preceding Section, paragraphs 2 and 5.
2 Remove the rear suspension assembly, as described in Chapter 11, Section 19, if the brake disc must be renewed.
3 Remove the brake caliper, as described in Section 4, of this Chapter.
4 Turn the suspension assembly upside-down and remove the hydraulic shock absorber/spring units, also as described in Chapter 11.
5 Release the clip and slide back the halfshaft inner universal joint shield.
6 Remove the four self-locking nuts which secure the inner universal joint and brake disc to the output shaft flange.

Fig. 9.6. Flexible to rigid hydraulic hose connection (Sec. 7)

A Flexible hose and fitting   B Locknut

7 Withdraw the halfshaft noting the camber shims between the universal joint and brake disc.
8 Tap the bolts which secure the halfshaft universal joints and brake disc back as far as possible.
9 Lift the suspension lower wishbone, hub carrier and halfshaft assembly upwards until there is enough clearance to withdraw the brake disc from its mounting bolts.
10 For optimum brake performance it is most important that the endfloat of the rear hubs is as specified in Section 2, of Chapter 8.
11 Refitting is a reversal of removal but make sure that the rear brake hydraulic circuit is bled as described in Section 11.

11 Rear brake disc (Series 2) - inspection, removal and refitting

1 Refer to paragraphs 3, 4 and 5 of Section 9. If the brake disc must be renewed, jack-up the car and remove the roadwheel from the side of the car concerned.
2 Support the bodyframe securely on stands.
3 Remove the brake caliper, as previously described.
4 Drive out the shock absorber lower mounting pin and then cut the locking wire from the radius arm locking bolt and remove the bolt.
5 Unscrew and remove the grease nipple from the hub pivot shaft and then support the hub on wooden blocks.
6 Lever the radius arm from the spigot anchor point.
7 Release the clip which secures the halfshaft inner universal joint cover and slide the cover clear of the joint.
8 Disconnect the inner universal joint from the brake disc, by unscrewing the securing nuts, tapping the bolts towards the final drive unit and carefully retaining the camber shims.
9 Lift out the brake disc. It may be necessary to jack up the car a little higher to facilitate removal of the disc.
10 Refitting is a reversal of removal but the disc must run central in the caliper aperture. If this is not the case, add or remove shims located between the disc and the final drive output flange. Compensate for this by adding or subtracting a shim of similar thickness from the camber angle shim pack.

12 Pressure differential warning actuator

1 The purpose of this device which is fitted to certain models is to monitor the pressures in the front and rear brake hydraulic circuits and to give a visual warning when a drop in pressure occurs in either circuit. Such a drop in pressure may be due to a leak in the hydraulic pipes or hoses, a failed seal in the caliper or master cylinder and the cause should be sought and rectified immediately.
2 The device is essentially a piston which is kept in balance by the

equal pressures of the two circuits of the hydraulic system. When pressure in one circuit falls, the piston is displaced and completes an electrical circuit to illuminate a warning lamp.

3   Early types of pressure differential warning actuator need resetting after being displaced but later models have an integral automatic reset.

Early type

4   To reset the early type actuator, check that the master cylinder reservoir is full.

5   Switch on the ignition and run the engine at idling speed.

6   Attach a bleed tube to the front right-hand caliper bleed nipple, placing the open end of the tube in a suitable container.

7   Apply gentle pressure to the brake pedal and have an assistant slowly open the bleed nipple as pressure on the pedal is increased. When the actuator warning lamp goes off, the device is reset and depressing the brake pedal must cease. Hold the pedal in its partly depressed state and tighten the bleed nipple.

8   If you were slow in stopping the pressure increase on the brake pedal and the actuator piston was displaced in the opposite direction and the warning lamp comes on again, repeat the operations previously described on the left-hand rear caliper.

9   Remove the bleed tube, switch off the engine and top-up the reservoir.

10 Any fault in a pressure differential warning actuator should only be rectified by renewing the unit, no overhaul is possible.

13 Hydraulic circuit - bleeding

1   Removal of air from the hydraulic system is essential to the correct operation of the brakes. Whenever either of the hydraulic circuits has been 'broken' or a component removed and replaced, the system must be bled.

2   If only one circuit of the dual line hydraulic system has been disconnected then only that circuit need to be bled. If the master cylinder has been removed and refitted then both circuits will of course require bleeding.

3   An indication of air in the system is a 'spongy' pedal or when the pedal travel is reduced by repeated applications of the brakes. In the latter case, the trouble may be due to a worn or faulty master cylinder and this should be rectified immediately.

4   If there is any possibility of incorrect fluid having been put into the system, drain all the fluid out and flush through with methylated spirit. Renew all piston seals and cups since these will be affected and could possibly fail under pressure.

5   Gether together a clean glass jar, a length of tubing which fits tightly over the bleed nipples and a tin of the correct brake fluid.

6   To bleed the system on cars not equipped with a pressure differential warning actuator, clean the areas around the bleed nipples and then attach a bleed tube to the nipple on the left-hand rear caliper.

7   Place the end of the tube in a clean glass jar containing sufficient fluid to keep the end of the tube submerged during the operation.

8   Open the bleed valve with a spanner and quickly press down the brake pedal. After slowly releasing the pedal, pause for a moment to allow the fluid to recoup in the master cylinder and then depress again. This will force air from the system. Continue until no more air bubbles can be seen coming from the tube. At intervals make certain that the reservoir is kept topped up, otherwise air will enter at this point again. Tighten the bleed valve when the pedal is fully depressed.

9   Repeat the operations on the right-hand rear caliper and then follow with the front caliper.

10 On cars which are fitted with an early type pressure differential warning actuator (not with automatic reset), bleeding must be carried out so that the following conditions apply:

   a) *Use only light pressure on the footbrake.*
   b) *Do not depress the brake pedal fully to the floor.*
   c) *Never check the 'feel' of the brake pedal until the hydraulic system has been completely bled.*

11 On cars which are fitted with the later automatic reset type actuator, the foregoing precautions need not be observed.

Always discard fluid which has been bled from the system and top-up the system with fluid which has been stored in an airtight container and has remained unshaken for the preceding 24 hours.

Fig. 9.7. Pressure differential warning actuator (Sec. 12)

3 *Electrical connector*	5 *Actuator mounting*
4 *Fluid pipe unions*	*bolt*

14 Handbrake cable - adjustment

1   Under normal circumstances, the self-adjusting characteristic of the disc brake caliper units is applied to the handbrake mechanism and no further adjustment is required. However, due to cable stretch, some supplementary adjustment may be needed after high mileages when the handbrake control has excessive travel when applying the brake fully.

2   Working under the car, slacken the locknut at the forked end of the cable threaded adjuster.

3   Extract the split pin, clevis pin and washer and disconnect the fork from the handbrake lever.

4   Check that the handbrake actuating arms at the rear calipers are fully released by pressing them in towards the calipers.

5   Unscrew the clevis fork on the end of the handbrake cable until it can be reconnected to the handbrake lever and the clevis pin inserted without any tendency for the cable to pull on the caliper actuating levers.

6   Refit the washer and split pin to the clevis pin.

15 Handbrake friction pads - renewal

1   The friction pads for the handbrake are quite separate from the disc pads which are actuated by the hydraulic system. Under normal conditions, the handbrake pads will last indefinitely. Where they are in need of renewal proceed as follows:

2   Disconnect the handbrake cables by removing the split pin and clevis pin and detaching the fork end on one lever so that the outer cable can be withdrawn from the trunnion on the other lever.

3   Raise the locktabs and withdraw the pivot bolts and retraction plate.

4   Remove the friction pad carriers by withdrawing them to the rear around the brake disc and out at the rear of the suspension assembly. On Series 2 cars, it is easier to remove the tie-plate from the rear suspension and remove the carriers through the gap provided.

5   Repeat for the second caliper.

6   With the friction pad carriers removed, extract the worn pads by slackening the nuts on the outer face of each carrier and inserting a suitably hooked tool in the hole in each pad securing plate.

7   Install the new pads so that the exposed part of the pad backplate is uppermost.

8   Fit new retraction fingers and assemble the carrier to the main caliper body. Leave the pivot bolts slack (refer to paragraphs 4 to 9, of Section 13).

9   Pull and release the handbrake control several times until the ratchet ceases to operate which will indicate that the mechanism is now fully adjusted.

10 Apply the handbrake fairly hard and then tighten the pivot bolts and

Fig. 9.8. Handbrake cable adjustment (Sec. 14)

A   Locknut   *B   Cable end fitting*

Fig. 9.9. Cutaway view of the handbrake mechanism attached to the rear caliper (Sec. 15) (Refer also to Fig. 9.3)

1   Operating lever   *4   Adjuster nut*
2   Pad carrier assembly   *5   Adjuster bolt*
3   Pawl assembly   *6   Friction pad*

lock the tab washers.

11 Reconnect the handbrake linkage to the operating levers and check the handbrake adjustment, as described in Section 11.

16 Handbrake friction pad carrier - dismantling and reassembly

1   With the carrier removed as described in the preceding Section, remove the cover securing screw, discard the split pin and withdraw the pivot clevis pin and detach the dust cover.
2   Remove the split pin from the screwdriver slot and unscrew the adjuster bolt from the ratchet nut. Withdraw the nut and bolt.
3   Detach the pawl return spring and remove the pawl over the locating dowel. Detach the operating lever return spring and remove the operating lever and lower cover plate.
4   Reassembly is a reversal of dismantling but if new components have been fitted, refit the friction pad carrier in the following way.
5   Ensure that the handbrake pivot bolts are slack.
6   Set the adjuster bolt until there is ¼ in (6.35 mm) free-movement between the head of the bolt and the outer pad carrier.

Fig. 9.10. Handbrake cable attachment to rear caliper operating lever (Sec. 15)

7   Pull the inner and outer pad carriers away from the disc and then bend the brass retraction fingers until there is 1/16 in (1.6 mm) clearance between each pad and the disc.
8   Take up the free-movement of the adjuster bolt until the head of the bolt is just in contact with the seating of the outer pad carrier.
9   Fit a new split pin to lock the adjuster bolt.
10 Repeat the operations described in paragraphs 9, 10 and 11 of Section 12.

17 Handbrake cable and control - removal and refitting

1   To renew the handbrake cable assembly, work underneath the car and disconnect the cable from the operating levers of the rear calipers.
2   Disconnect the clevis fork at the forward end of the cable from the intermediate lever.
3   Remove the cable clips from the body and withdraw the cable.
4   If the handcontrol must be removed, disconnect the primary cable from the intermediate lever.
5   Slip the primary cable nipple out of the clevis fork.
6   Working within the car, pull back the carpet to gain access to the handbrake control support bracket. Remove the two bracket setscrews.
7   Working within the engine compartment, remove the plastic grommet from the lower end of the handbrake control.
8   Disconnect the two leads from the handbrake warning lamp switch and then withdraw the control into the car interior.
9   Refitting is a reversal of removal but adjust the handbrake on completion, as described in Section 11.

18 Combined brake warning lamp - description

1   A warning lamp is located on the instrument panel which is connected to three switches, the handbrake 'OFF' switch and the two fluid level switches one of which is fitted in each of the master cylinder reservoirs.
2   When the ignition is switched on, the lamp will light up if the handbrake is applied. Once the handbrake is released, if the lamp fails to go out, then either the brake hydraulic fluid is at a low level and must be immediately replenished or the handbrake 'ON' switch is in need of adjustment.

19 Handbrake 'ON' switch - adjustment

1   The switch is screwed into the lower end of the handbrake control

H.5693

Fig. 9.11. Handbrake control (1) showing warning switch (2) primary cable (3) intermediate lever (4) and secondary cable (5). Earlier versions had a pulley into which primary cable was engaged (Sec. 17)

outer tube, see Fig. 9.11.

2   When the handbrake is fully released, the switch plunger is depressed to break the warning lamp circuit.

3   If the lamp remains on, remove the handbrake control and primary cable as described in Section 14. Disconnect the switch terminals.

4   Release the locknut and unscrew the switch.

5   Check that the handbrake control is in the fully released position and then screw the switch right in. Unscrew the switch exactly ½ a turn, temporarily connect the switch leads and check the operation of the switch with the ignition on.

6   If the operation is satisfactory, tighten the switch locknut and refit the handbrake control and the primary cable.

20 Vacuum servo unit - description

1   A vacuum servo unit is fitted into the brake hydraulic circuit in series with the master cylinder, to provide assistance to the driver when the brake pedal is depressed. This reduces the effort required by the driver to operate the brakes under all braking conditions.

2   The unit operates by vacuum obtained from the induction manifold and comprises basically a booster diaphragm and non-return valve. The

servo unit and hydraulic master cylinder are connected together so that the servo unit piston rod acts as the master cylinder pushrod. The driver's braking effort is transmitted through another pushrod to the servo unit piston and its built in control system. The servo unit piston does not fit tightly into the cylinder, but has a strong diaphragm to keep its edges in constant contact with the cylinder wall, so assuring an air tight seal between the two parts. The forward chamber is held under vacuum conditions created in the inlet manifold of the engine and, during periods when the brake pedal is not in use, the controls open a passage to the rear chamber so placing it under vacuum conditions as well. When the brake pedal is depressed, the vacuum passage to the rear chamber is cut off and the chamber opened to atmospheric pressure. The consequent rush of air pushes the servo piston forward in the vacuum chamber and operates the main pushrod to the master cylinder.

3   The controls are designed so that assistance is given under all conditions and, when the brakes are not required, vacuum in the rear chamber is established when the brake pedal is released. All air from the atmosphere entering the rear chamber is passed through a small air filter.

4   Under normal operation conditions the vacuum servo unit is very reliable but should a fault develop then the complete assembly must be

renewed as repair kits or internal components are no longer supplied. Operations must therefore be restricted to the maintenance tasks described in the next Section.

5 It must be emphasised that failure of a servo unit will not affect the safety of the braking system, merely cause higher pedal pressures than are normally required.

21 Vacuum servo unit - maintenance

1 Occasionally check the security and condition of the vacuum hose to the inlet manifold.

2 At specified intervals (see 'Routine Maintenance') or when the foot brake pedal seems to be sluggish in operation, renew the air filter.

3 Remove the brake vacuum servo unit, as described in Section 19 of this Chapter.

4 Remove the dust cover, detach the end cap and withdraw the filter and filter felt rings. Cut the filter rings to permit them to press over the clevis fork.

5 Fit the new filter felts by cutting them cleanly again so that they will pass over the clevis fork. Ensure that the cuts in the various filter rings are not in line but stagger their position.

6 Refit the end cap and dust cover.

7 Refit the brake vacuum servo unit, as described in Section 19.

8 Deterioration of the non-return valve grommet on the front face of the vacuum servo unit may cause a vacuum leak and consequent loss of servo assistance. Should this happen, prise out the non-return valve by inserting a screwdriver between the valve and the grommet.

9 Pull out the grommet gripping it with pliers.

10 Apply rubber grease to the internal bore of the new grommet and push the non-return valve into it. Push the grommet complete with non-return valve into the front face of the servo unit.

Following this method there is reduced risk of the grommet being pushed into the interior of the servo unit which would probably require complete dismantling of the unit to retrieve it.

22 Vacuum servo unit - removal and refitting

1 The vacuum servo unit is removed in conjunction with the pedal box and hydraulic master cylinder.

2 Disconnect the brake lines from the master cylinder and plug the lines.

3 Disconnect the vacuum pipe from the servo unit.

4 Working inside the car above the brake pedal arm, remove the four setscrews and lockwashers from the bottom mounting of the pedal box.

5 Remove the four self-locking nuts and washers which secure the pedal box to the vertical face of the engine compartment rear bulkhead.

6 Withdraw the pedal box as an assembly complete with vacuum servo unit, master cylinder and reservoir.

Fig. 9.12. Brake vacuum servo air filter components (Sec. 21)

27 Rear shell
28 Filter felts
29 Air filter

30 Filter retainer
31 Dust cover
32 Clevis fork

Fig. 9.13. Sectional view of brake vacuum servo unit showing various modes of operation (Sec. 20)

1 *Brake pedal released*   2 *Brake pedal applied*   3 *Brake held applied*   4 *Brake being released*

7   Refitting is a reversal of removal but bleed the hydraulic system on completion, as described in Section 10.

23 Brake pedal - dismantling and reassembly

1   Remove the pedal box, vacuum servo and master cylinder assembly as described in the preceding Section.
2   Remove the two rubber sealing plugs from the sides of the pedal box.
3   Disconnect the vacuum servo pushrod from the pedal lever by removing the split pin and the clevis pin.

4   Remove the vacuum servo unit from the pedal box (four self-locking nuts).
5   Remove the self-locking nut and washer from the pedal pivot bolt and drive out the bolt. Retain the fibre washers which are located on the pedal pivot bolt.
6   Withdraw the pedal lever shaft locking pin and spring washer and extract the lever shaft.
7   Withdraw the pedal and lever assembly from the pedal box.
8   Extract the two split pins, clevis pins and links and disconnect the pedal from the pedal lever.
9   Reassembly is a reversal of dismantling.

H.5689

Fig. 9.14. Pedal box assembly (Sec. 23)

1   Brake pedal with manual gearbox
2   Brake pedal with automatic transmission

24 Fault diagnosis - braking system

Symptom	Reason/s
Pedal travels almost to floor before brakes operate	Brake fluid level too low. Caliper leaking. Master cylinder leaking (bubbles in master cylinder fluid). Brake flexible hose leaking. Brake line fractured. Brake system unions loose. Pad linings over 75% worn.
Brake pedal feels springy	New pads not yet bedded-in. Brake discs badly worn or cracked. Master cylinder securing nuts loose.
Brake pedal feels 'spongy' and 'soggy'	Caliper leaking. Master cylinder leaking (bubbles in master cylinder reservoir). Brake pipe line or flexible hose leaking. Unions in brake system loose.
Excessive effort required to brake car	Pad linings badly worn. New pads recently fitted — not yet bedded-in. Harder pads fitted than standard causing increase in pedal pressure. Pads or discs contaminated with oil, grease or hydraulic fluid. Servo unit inoperative or faulty.
Brakes uneven and pulling to one side	Pads or discs contaminated with oil, grease or hydraulic fluid. Tyre pressures unequal. Radial ply tyres fitted at one end of the car only. Brake caliper loose. Brake pads fitted incorrectly. Different type of pads fitted at each wheel. Anchorages for front suspension or rear suspension loose. Brake discs badly worn, cracked or distorted.
Brakes tend to bind, drag or lock-on	Air in hydraulic system. Caliper pistons seized. Handbrake cables too tight.

Chapter 10 Electrical system

Contents

Specifications

System	12 volt, negative earth with battery and alternator

Battery

Early models	12 volt, 60 a/hr (20 hr rate)
Series 2	12 volt, 66 a/hr (20 hr rate)

Alternator (without air-conditioning)

Type:	
Early models	Lucas 11AC
Series 2	Lucas 18ACR
Voltage	12
Output:	
11AC	43 amps
18ACR	45 amps
Stator phases	3
Phase connection	Star
Resistance/phase at 68°F (20°C) ± 5%	0.107 ohms
Resistance of rotor winding in ohms at 68°F (20°C)	3.8 ± 5%
Control unit (11AC only)	Lucas 4TR
Warning lamp control unit (11AC only)	Lucas 3AW

Alternator (early air-conditioning systems)

Type	Butec
Nominal voltage	12
Maximum output	60 amps
Maximum operating speed	4500 rev/min (engine speed)
Resistance of rotor coil	3.6 to 4 ohms
Regulator	Butec R2

Alternator (later air-conditioning systems)

Type	Lucas 20ACR
Voltage	12
Output	66 amps
Rotor winding resistance	3.6 ohms
Integral control unit	Lucas 11TR

Starter motor (2.8 litre early models)

Type	Lucas M45G inertia drive

Starter motor (3.4 and 4.2 litre, early models)

Type	Lucas M45G pre-engaged

Starter motor (later 2.8 litre and Series 2 models)

Type	Lucas 3M100 pre-engaged or inward or outward inertia type

Fuses (all models except Series 2)

No.	Circuit protected	Capacity (amps)
1	Screen washer, instruments, horn relay, tachometer	35
2	Map reading lamp, interior lamp, air-conditioning relay	35
3	Windscreen wiper, flasher, heater motor, stop lamps	35
4	Horns	50
5	Left-hand side and tail lamps	10
6	Outer headlamp	35
7	Inner headlamps (main beam)	35
8	Outer headlamp (LH dip)	35
9	Outer headlamp (RH dip)	35
10	Right-hand side and tail lamps	10
11 Separate	Hazard warning circuit	35
12 in-line	Heated rear window	15
13 fuses	Overdrive solenoid/reversing lamp	8

Fuses (Series 2)

No.	Circuit protected	Capacity (amps)
1	Fog lamps	25
2	Hazard warning	35
3	Map, interior lamps, cigar lighter, electrically operated aerial	35
4	Instruments, choke warning lamp	10
5	Stop lamps, flashers, battery cooling, horn relay, kick-down switch (automatic transmission)	35
6	Reversing lamps	10
7	Panel lamps	10
8	Left-hand side/tail	10
9	Right-hand side/tail	10
10	Air-conditioning/heater motors	35
11	Air-conditioning relay, windscreen wipers, windscreen washer	35
12	Heated rear window	25
In-line	Headlamp main beam	25
type	Headlamp dipped beam	10
fuses	Horn relay	17

Bulbs

Description of lamp	Wattage
Outer headlamp UK	60/45
(sealed beam unit) N. America	37.5/50
Inner headlamps UK ...	50
(main beam sealed beam units) N. America	37.5
Front parking/flasher	6/21
Front parking (N. America)	6
Front rear indicators (N. America)	21
Sidemarker	6
Stop/tail	6/21
Rear number plate	6
Reversing	21
Interior and door pillar	10
Map reading	6
Luggage compartment	6
Instrument illumination	2.2
Warning lamps	1.5
Switch indicator strips	2
Automatic transmission indicator	2
Opticell light unit (Series 2)	6
Centre console (Series 2)	2.2
Cigar lighter	2.2
Choke warning lamp { Emission control	2.2
Choke handle lamp { cars only	2.0

1 General description

All models have a 12 volt negative earth electrical system.

The major components comprise a battery which is located under the bonnet against the rear bulkhead, an alternator and output control unit which may be integral or externally mounted according to alternator type, and an inertia or pre-engaged type starter motor.

On cars equipped with an air-conditioning system, a heavy duty alternator is fitted.

The battery supplies a steady current for the ignition, lighting and other electrical circuits and provides a reserve of electricity when the current consumed by the electrical equipment exceeds that being produced by the charging system.

Although full instructions for the periodic overhaul and minor servicing of the various electrical components are given in this Chapter it must be appreciated that rectification of major faults will require specialised knowledge and equipment and therefore, where such faults arise, the defective item should be removed and replaced with a serviceable item which can usually be obtained on an exchange basis.

Wiring diagrams covering the various models will be found at the end of the Chapter.

2 Battery - maintenance and inspection

1 Keep the top of the battery clean by wiping away dirt and moisture.
2 Remove the plugs or lid from the cells and check that the electrolyte level is just above the separator plates. If the level has fallen, add only distilled water until the electrolyte level is just above the separator plates.
3 As well as keeping the terminals clean and covered with petroleum jelly, the top of the battery, and especially the top of the cells, should be kept clean and dry. This helps prevent corrosion and ensures that the battery does not become partially discharged by leakage through dampness and dirt.
4 Once every three months, remove the battery and inspect the battery securing bolts, the battery clamp plate, tray and battery leads for corrosion (white fluffy deposits on the metal which are brittle to touch). If any corrosion is found, clean off the deposits with ammonia and paint over the clean metal with an anti-rust/anti-acid paint.
5 At the same time inspect the battery case for cracks. If a crack is found, clean and plug it with one of the proprietary compounds marketed for this purpose. If leakage through the crack has been excessive then it will be necessary to refill the appropriate cell with fresh electrolyte as detailed later. Cracks are frequently caused to the top of battery cases by pouring in distilled water in the middle of

winter *after* instead of *before* a run. This gives the water no chance to mix with the electrolyte and so the former freezes and splits the battery case.
6 If topping up the battery becomes excessive and the case has been inspected for cracks that could cause leakage, but none are found, the battery is being over-charged and the voltage regulator will have to be checked.
7 With the battery on the bench at the three monthly interval check, measure its specific gravity with a hydrometer to determine the state of charge and condition of the electrolyte. There should be very little variation between the different cells and if a variation in excess of 0.25 is present it will be due to either:

a) *Loss of electrolyte from the battery at some time caused by spillage or a leak, resulting in a drop in the specific gravity of electrolyte when the deficiency was replaced with distilled water instead of fresh electrolyte.*
b) *An internal short circuit caused by buckling of the plates or a similar malady pointing to the likelihood of total battery failure in the near future.*

8 The specific gravity of the electrolyte for fully charged conditions at the electrolyte temperature indicated, is listed in Table A. The specific gravity of a fully discharged battery at different temperatures of the electrolyte is given in Table B.

Table A

Specific Gravity - Battery Fully Charged

1.268 at 100°F or 38°C electrolyte temperature
1.272 at 90°F or 32°C electrolyte temperature
1.276 at 80°F or 27°C electrolyte temperature
1.280 at 70°F or 21°C electrolyte temperature
1.284 at 60°F or 16°C electrolyte temperature
1.288 at 50°F or 10°C electrolyte temperature
1.292 at 40°F or 4°C electrolyte temperature
1.296 at 30°F or-1.5°C electrolyte temperature

Table B

Specific Gravity - Battery Fully Discharged

1.098 at 100°F or 38°C electrolyte temperature
1.102 at 90°F or 32°C electrolyte temperature
1.106 at 80°F or 27°C electrolyte temperature
1.110 at 70°F or 21°C electrolyte temperature
1.114 at 60°F or 16°C electrolyte temperature
1.118 at 50°F or 10°C electrolyte temperature
1.122 at 40°F or 4°C electrolyte temperature
1.126 at 30°F or-1.5°C electrolyte temperature

3 Battery - removal and refitting

Cars excluding Series 2
1 The battery is located within the engine compartment. It may be on the left or right-hand side according to which side the steering is positioned.
2 Disconnect the negative terminal first whenever servicing the battery.
3 Then remove the positive terminal, and remove the battery frame holding-down screws and lift the frame away.
4 Lift out the battery carefully to avoid spilling electrolyte on the paintwork.
5 Replacement is a reversal of removal procedure but when reconnecting the terminals, clean off any white deposits present and smear with petroleum jelly.

Series 2 cars
6 The battery incorporates a cooling fan on these cars; remove the battery in the following way:
7 Peel back the flexible covers from the battery terminals, release the pinch bolts and disconnect the leads from the battery terminals.
8 Disconnect the leads to the battery cooling fan by detaching them

Fig. 10.1. Battery with cooling fan (Sec. 3)

3 Fan securing screw	*5 Keeper plate and screws*
4 Impeller	*6 Electric motor*

at the snap connectors.

9 Slacken the battery holding down bolts.

10 Prise the flexible outlet pipe from the cooling jacket grommet.

11 Detach the battery positive lead from the clip on the cooling jacket.

12 Ease the battery and its cooling jacket forward until the jacket can be withdrawn from the battery.

13 Lift the battery from the car.

14 The cooling fan can be removed from the cooling jacket after withdrawing the seven securing screws. The nylon impeller can be levered from the motor shaft.

15 Reassembly and refitting are reversals of removal and dismantling.

4   Electrolyte replenishment

1 If the battery is in a fully charged state and one of the cells maintains a specific gravity reading which is 0.25 or more lower than the others, and a check of each cell has been made with a voltage meter to check for short circuits (a four to seven second test should give a steady reading of between 1.2 to 1.8 volts), then it is likely that electrolyte has been lost from the cell with the low reading at some time.

2 Top up the cell with a solution of 1 part sulphuric acid to 2.5 parts of water. If the cell is already fully topped up draw some electrolyte out of it with a hydrometer.

3 When mixing the sulphuric acid and water **never add water to sulphuric acid** - always pour the acid slowly onto the water in a glass container. **If water is added to sulphuric acid it will explode.**

4 Continue to top up the cell with the freshly made electrolyte and then recharge the battery and check the hydrometer readings.

5   Battery charging

1 In winter time when heavy demand is placed upon the battery, such as when starting from cold, and much electrical equipment is continually in use, it is a good idea to occasionally have the battery fully charged from an external source at the rate of 3.5 or 4 amps (see Section 7).

2 Continue to charge the battery at this rate until no further rise in specific gravity is noted over a four hour period.

3 Alternatively, a trickle charger at the rate of 1.5 amps can be safely used overnight.

4 Specially rapid 'boost' charges which are claimed to restore the power of the battery in 1 to 2 hours are most dangerous as they can cause serious damage to the battery plates.

6   Alternator - general description and maintenance

1 Briefly the alternator comprises a rotor and stator. Current is generated in the coils of the stator as soon as the rotor revolves. This current is three-phase alternating which is then rectified by positive and negative silicon diodes and the level of voltage required to maintain the battery charge is controlled by a regulator unit.

2 Maintenance consists of occasionally wiping away any oil or dirt

which may have accumulated on the outside of the unit.

3 No lubrication is required as the bearings are grease sealed for life.

4 Check the drivebelt tension periodically to ensure that its specified deflection is correctly maintained. The correct tension of the belt is indicated when the mid point of the top run of the belt can be depressed ½ in (12.7 mm). Adjustment is carried out by releasing the alternator pivot mounting bolts and the adjustment link bolts and moving the alternator away from or towards the engine. Retighten the bolts on completion.

5 On cars which are equipped with power steering or/and air-conditioning the drivebelt arrangement is complex and although all the belts should be tensioned as just described, renewal of an inner belt will necessitate removal of the outer belts first.

7   Alternator - special precautions

Take extreme care when making circuit connections to a vehicle fitted with an alternator and observe the following. When making connections to the alternator from a battery always match correct polarity. Before using electric-arc welding equipment to repair any part of the vehicle, disconnect the connector from the alternator and disconnect the positive battery terminal. Never start the car with a battery charger connected. Always disconnect both battery leads before using a main charger. If boosting from another battery, always connect in parallel using heavy cable.

8   Alternator (Lucas 11AC type) - testing in-situ

1 Disconnect the lead from the negative terminal of the battery.

2 Disconnect the lead from the main output terminal of the alternator and connect a moving coil DC ammeter (range up to 75 amps) between the main output terminal and the end of the lead which was originally connected to it.

3 Detach the terminal connector block from the base of the control unit and then connect the black and the brown/green cables together by a short jump lead.

4 Reconnect the lead to the battery negative terminal, switch on the ignition and start the engine. Slowly increase the engine speed until the engine speed is about 2000 rev/min indicated on the tachometer. Check the ammeter which should record approximately 40 amps.

5 A low current reading will mean a faulty alternator or poor circuit connections. If the circuit connections are checked and found to be in order, measure the resistance of the rotor coil by means of an ohmmeter connected between the field terminal blades, having first disconnected the external wiring. The indicated resistance must be approximately 3.77 ohms. Where an ohmmeter is not available, connect a 12 volt supply with an ammeter in series between the field terminals, when the indicated reading should be 3.2 amps (Fig. 10.5). If a zero reading is shown on the ammeter or infinity on the ohmmeter, an open circuit is indicated in the field system which includes the brush gear, slip-rings or windings. If the meters record readings much above or below the valves specified, there may be a short circuit in the rotor winding which will necessitate a new rotor/slip ring assembly.

Fig. 10.2. Alternator mounting and adjustment link bolts (Sec. 6)

Fig. 10.3. Drivebelt arrangement on cars equipped with optional systems (Sec. 6)

1   Water pump/power steering   2   Air compressor drivebelt
    pump drivebelt   (air conditioning system)
                                   8   Alternator drivebelt

Fig. 10.4. Lucas 4TR alternator control unit (Sec. 8)

Fig. 10.5. Circuit for testing 11AC type alternator with ammeter (Sec. 8)

Fig. 10.6. Brushgear (early type 11AC alternator) (Sec. 10)

Fig. 10.7. Brushgear (later type 11AC alternator) (Sec. 10)

9 Alternator - removal and installation

1   Disconnect the leads from the slip ring end cover, making sure to mark the cables for exact refitting.
2   Slacken the alternator mounting bolts and adjuster link bolts, push the unit in towards the engine, slip the drivebelt off the pulleys and then remove the mounting bolts and lift the alternator away.
3   *On cars equipped with an air-conditioning system,* the air compressor and its mounting bracket will have to be disconnected in order to gain access to the alternator. *On no account disconnect any of the air-conditioning system hoses* but release the compressor mountings and bracket and support the compressor without moving it any more than is absolutely necessary.
4   Installation is the reversal of removal but adjust the alternator drivebelt as described in Section 6 of this Chapter, also the air compressor belt as described in Chapter 12, Section 29.

10 Alternator (Lucas 11AC type) - overhaul

1   Remove the alternator from the car as described in Section 9.
2   An exploded view of the slip ring end cover is given in Fig. 10.10 but where figures are quoted in the following paragraphs the reference is to Fig. 10.8.
3   Take off the shaft nut (1) and its spring washer (21).
4   Withdraw the fan (20).
5   Break the staking of the nuts to the bolts (3) and then unscrew the bolts. Examine the threads of the bolts and if they are damaged discard the bolts.
6   Mark the drive end bracket (4).
7   Withdraw the drive end bracket (4) and the rotor (16) from the stator (8).
8   It is advisable not to separate the rotor from the drive end bracket unless the bearing is suspect or the rotor is to be replaced. In this event, first remove the shaft key (5) and the collar (2). Now use a hand press to remove the rotor from the drive end bracket.
9   Remove the terminal nuts and their washers and insulating pieces, the brush box screws and the hexagon headed setscrew from the slip ring end cover and the stator and diode heat sink assemblies can now be withdrawn.
10 Close up the retaining tongue at the root of each field terminal blade and withdraw the brush spring together with the terminal assemblies from the brushbox.
11 There are detail differences between the brush gear on earlier and later type alternators which should be noted.
12 *On earlier type brush gear,* check the length of the brushes which should not be below 5/32 in (3.97 mm). Discard them if they are at, or are approaching that dimension. New brushes are supplied complete with spring and terminal blade and have merely to be pushed in until the tongue registers; but, to be sure that the terminal is properly retained, carefully lever up the retaining tongue so that it makes an angle of 30° with the terminal blade.
   See that the brushes are in good condition, that they are not chipped or showing any obvious defect.
   Check that the brushes move freely in the holders. If they appear sluggish, clean the bearing sides with a cloth moistened with petrol and if this does not effect a cure, polish the sides with a smooth file but make sure that all trace of dust is removed before refitting to the holders.
   If you have suitable equipment available, it is a good idea to check the brush spring pressures. With the brush spring compressed to 25/32 in (19.84 mm) the brush spring pressure when fitted to the holder should be 4 - 5 ozs (113 - 114 grms), and 7½ - 8½ ozs (212 - 242 grms) with the spring compressed to 13/32 in (10.31 mm).
13 *On later type brush gear,* check that the brushes protrude beyond the brush box moulding (when in the free position) by not less than 0.2 in (5.0 mm). If they do not, renew them. New brushes are supplied complete with brush spring and terminal blade and each brush is secured in position by a plate and screw.
14 Examine the slip rings. The surfaces should be smooth and free from oil or other foreign matter. They can be cleaned with a cloth moistened in petrol but if there is any evidence of burning it is permissible to use fine glass paper. **Do not** use emery cloth or similar abrasive.
15 It is unlikely that the slip rings will be scored or pitted but discard

Fig. 10.8. Exploded view of Lucas 11AC alternator (Sec. 10)

1	Pulley nut	6	Field winding (rotor)	11	Needle roller bearing
2	Collar	7	Slip rings	12	Brush box
3	Tie bolts	8	Stator	13	Brushes
4	Drive end bracket	9	Silicon diodes	14	Diode heat sink
5	Key	10	Slip ring end bracket	15	Stator windings

16	Rotor
17	Bearing retaining plate
18	Ball bearing
19	Rivets
20	Fan
21	Spring washer

them if they are in this condition. Do not try to rectify them by machining as any resultant eccentricity could adversely affect the high speed performance of the alternator.

16 Check the rotor windings by connecting an ohmmeter or 12 volt DC supply between the slip rings in the manner described in Section 8 paragraph 5, where this test was then made with the brush gear in circuit. Reading should be the same as given in those paragraphs.

17 Test for defective insulation between each of the slip rings and one of the rotor poles using a mains low wattage test lamp for the purpose. If the lamp lights it indicates that the coil is earthing and the rotor/slip ring assembly must be replaced.

18 Unsolder the three stator cables from the heat sink assembly but take care not to overheat the diodes.

19 Identify the three cables as 'A', 'B', and 'C' and this gives three pairs of cables 'AB', 'AC' and 'BC' for testing the stator windings.

20 Measure the voltage drop across each of these pairs of cables in turn whilst passing a 20 amp current between the cable ends. The voltage drop should be about 4.3 volts in each of the three measurements. If any reading is outside of that value, the stator must be renewed.

21 Using a mains test lamp, check for defects in the insulation between the stator coils and lamination pack, by connecting the lamp between any of the three cable ends and the lamination pack. If the lamp lights, the stator coils are earthing and a replacement stator must be fitted.

22 Check the diodes before you re-solder the cables to the heat sink assembly.

23 Check each diode by connecting it in series with a 1.5 watt test bulb across a 12 volt DC supply and then reverse the connections. The lamp should light and current should flow in one direction only. If the lamp lights when current is flowing in either direction or it does not light at all, the diode is defective.

24 Diodes are not individually replaceable but are supplied already pressed into the appropriate heat sink portion which, as already described, consists of two mutually insulated assemblies, one of positive and the other of negative polarity. The positive assembly carries three cathode base diodes marked in black.

25 When soldering the interconnections, use 'M' grade 45/55 tin/lead solder. Be careful not to overheat the diodes or bend their pins. It is advisable to lightly grip the diode pins with a pair of long nosed pliers when soldering so that the pliers will absorb excess heat.

26 After soldering, the connections must be neatly arranged around the heat sinks as shown and tacked down with 'MMM' EC 1022 adhesive where shown in the figure in order to ensure adequate clearance for the rotor (Fig. 10.10).

27 The stator connections must pass through the appropriate notches at the edge of the heat sink.

28 When reassembling the alternator, take care that a clearance of

Fig. 10.9. Soldering alternator diodes using pliers as a heat sink (Sec. 10)

·045"GAP

Fig. 10.10. Slip ring end cover layout (11AC alternator) (Sec. 10)

0.045 in (1.143 mm) is maintained between the positive and negative heat sinks as shown in Fig. 10.10.

29 Renew any bearings which are so worn that they permit excessive side movement of the rotor shaft.

30 The needle roller bearing in the slip ring end cover is supplied complete with end cover.

31 If the drive end bearing requires renewal, file flat the heads of the three retainer plate rivets and punch out the rivets. Press the bearing from the bracket.

32 Pack the new bearing with high melting point grease, press it into position and fit the retaining plate using the new rivets supplied.

33 When reassembling, remember not to overtighten the brushbox screws, make sure that the drive end bracket, slip ring end bracket and lamination pack alignment marks are correctly located and re-stake the tie bolts after having tightened the nuts.

11 Alternator (Butec type) - testing in-situ

1 The following tests will indicate a faulty alternator but before carrying them out, remove the sensing diode block.

2 Check the stator phase for earthing to the alternator frame. Connect 110 or 230 volt supply and test lamp as shown in Fig. 10.12. The circuit should not be completed, if it is and the bulb lights up, then the stator is of delta connected type, all phases will indicate earthing.

3 Now carry out a stator winding continuity test. Using an ohmmeter or test lamp, check the continuity of each phase as shown in Fig. 10.13. Each phase should indicate a similar reaction.

4 To carry out an alternator phase test, run the engine at an idling speed of 460 rev/min. Connect an AC voltmeter or a 12 volt test lamp between two of the three AC terminals in turn. Voltage or lamp brilliance should be nearly the same across phases 1—2, 2—3 and 1—3. Any pronounced difference indicates earthed or shorted stator terminals.

Fig. 10.11. Terminal identification (Butec alternator) (Sec. 11)

1 AC output tappings   4 Negative DC terminal
2 Sensing diode terminal   5 Positive DC terminal
3 Field terminal

Fig. 10.13. Checking stator winding for continuity (Butec alternator) (Sec. 11)

Fig. 10.12. Checking stator phase for earthing (Butec alternator) (Sec. 11)

Fig. 10.14. Carrying out alternator phase test (Butec type) (Sec. 11)

12 Alternator (Butec type) - overhaul

1 Unscrew and remove the nut and washer and then with a suitable extractor, withdraw the fan/pulley assembly and extract the Woodruff key.
2 Remove the brushes, washer, insulating cover, gasket and jumper leads having first removed the two field terminal nuts.
3 Unscrew the four brush holder screws and remove the brush holder from the slip ring end housing.
4 Unscrew and remove the three self-locking nuts and the tie bolts which hold the alternator together.
5 Using a hammer and a brass drift held against the end of the rotor shaft, remove the slip ring end housing and the stator.
6 To disconnect the stator from the slip ring end housing, remove the three AC terminal nuts and stator connections and separate the stator from the housing with a soft-faced mallet.
7 With a suitable extractor, remove the rotor from the drive end housing.
8 With the alternator dismantled, the following tests can be carried out if suitable meters or test bulb circuits are available.
9 To test the rotor coil resistance, place the probes from an ohmmeter, one on each of the slip rings. The coil resistance should be between 3.6 and 4 ohms. No resistance indicates an open circuit in the rotor coil. Shorted turns in the coil can be suspected if on inspection the brush springs are found to have collapsed.
10 It is not recommended that any of the diodes are tested as special equipment is needed and there is also a great risk of damaging servicable components. If a diode fault is suspected, have them checked out by your dealer.
11 Clean the stator with a fuel soaked cloth and then check each AC terminal to each of the other two terminals using a test lamp rig to see that a complete circuit is made in each case. Also test for insulation breakdown between each terminal and the stator case (Figs. 10.17 and 10.18).
12 The drive end housing bearing can be renewed by removing the four screws from the bearing retainer plate and tapping out the bearing.

Press in the new bearing but apply pressure to the outer track only.
13 Rotor slip rings and bearing can be renewed by extracting them with a two or three-legged puller. When fitting the new slip ring assembly warm it slightly before pressing it onto the rotor shaft. Make sure that the slots in the slip rings align with the slot in the shaft which carries the cables from the rotor coil. The slip ring coil leads will require unsoldering and resoldering for this operation.
14 Commence reassembly by assembling the rotor and drive end housing.
15 Install the stator over the rotor and line up the tie bolt holes.
16 Secure the three stator connections to the insulator block in the slip ring end housing.
17 Place the housing assembly into position using the tie bolts to align the housing with the stator.
18 Tighten the tie bolts to the specified torque wrench setting.
19 Refit the brush holder assembly and renew the 'O' ring seal.
20 Insert the brushes. If they are less than 0.19 in (4.76 mm) in length, renew them. Let the brushes rest on the slip rings, place the tab jumpers over the terminal screws and brush springs (compressed). Fit a new gasket, insulating cover, washers and nuts.
21 Refit the Woodruff key, fan and pulley, washer and nut.

Fig. 10.15. Separating rotor and drive end housing (Butec alternator) (Sec. 12)

Fig. 10.16. Exploded view of Butec type alternator (Sec. 12)

1 *Drive end bracket*	3 *Rotor*	5 *Tie bolts*
2 *Slip ring end bracket*	4 *Stator*	6 *Brush assembly*

Fig. 10.17. Checking stator windings for continuity (Butec alternator) (Sec. 12)

Fig. 10.18. Checking stator windings for insulation breakdown (Butec alternator) (Sec. 13)

13 Alternator (Lucas type 11AC) relay and output control unit 4TR description, checking and adjusting

1   In the interest of safety and as a protection to the alternator, a relay is incorporated in the ignition switch/steering column lock circuit to isolate the field windings.

2   The relay is located just below the 4TR control unit within the engine compartment.

3   The 4TR output control unit is an electronic type unit in which switching is achieved by transistors, not mechanical contacts.

4   Check and adjustment of the control unit can only be carried out satisfactorily if the alternator and associated circuits are correct and a well charged battery is in use.

5   Leave the existing connections to the alternator and the control unit undisturbed but move the tags sufficiently on the control unit to allow connection of a high quality voltmeter between the positive and negative terminals. It is advisable to use a voltmeter of the suppressed zero type capable of reading to 12 - 15 volts.

6   Run the alternator, whether testing in-situ or on the bench, at charging speed for eight minutes.

7   Switch on an electrical load of approximately 2 amps (side and tail lights will give this loading).

8   Now run the engine at 1500 rpm when the voltmeter should show a reading of 13.9 to 14.3 volts with an ambient temperature of 20 to 26° C (68 to 78° F).

9   If the reading is outside the above limits, but has risen to some degree above battery terminal voltage before finally reaching a steady value, the unit can be adjusted to bring it within limits.

10 If the voltmeter reading remains steady at battery terminal voltage or if, on the other hand, it increases in an uncontrolled manner, the control unit is faulty and as it cannot be serviced it must be replaced.

11 To adjust the control unit, first stop the engine and then take out the control unit mounting screws, leave the voltmeter connected.

12 Lift the control unit away from the bulkhead and if you look at the rear you will find a blob of sealing compound which conceals a potentiometer adjuster. Carefully chip away the sealing compound.

13 Check that the voltmeter is still firmly connected between positive and negative terminals of the control unit.

14 Start the engine and again run it at 1500 rpm. Turn the potentiometer by means of the slot, in a clockwise direction to increase, and in an anticlockwise direction, to decrease the setting. The potentiometer should be turned only a small amount at a time as you will find that a small movement will make a considerable difference to the voltage reading.

15 When the voltage reading is within limits (see paragraph 8), stop the engine. Now check the setting by restarting the engine and again checking at 1500 rpm with a load of 2 amps.

16 If the readings are correct, remove the voltmeter and then refit the control unit after sealing the potentiometer.

Fig. 10.19. Location of relay fitted in conjunction with Lucas 11AC alternator) (Sec. 13)

Fig. 10.20. 4TR control unit fitted in conjunction with Lucas 11AC alternator) (Sec. 13)

A   =   Adjuster

14 Alternator (Lucas 11AC) warning lamp control unit 3AW - description and testing

1 This device is connected to one of the pairs of diodes in the alternator and operates in conjunction with the ignition warning lamp to verify that the alternator is charging.
2 The device is mounted adjacent to the output control unit within the engine compartment.
3 A lamp control unit can often be damaged by excessive voltages resulting from a faulty diode or open circuit in the alternator or an open circuit in the alternator to battery circuit.
4 Before renewing a lamp control unit, use a moving coil voltmeter to check the voltage between the alternator 'AL' terminal and earth. This should be between 6 and 7.5 volts with the engine running at 1500 rev/min.
5 If a higher voltage is recorded, check that all circuit connections are clean and tight.
6 The warning lamp control unit is a sealed unit rather similar in appearance to a flasher unit and it can only be renewed as a sealed component.

15 Alternator (Butec) regulator R2 - description and testing

1 This type of regulator is fully transistorised without any moving parts.
2 Output voltage adjustment can be carried out by turning a screw which is accessible after extracting a socket screw from the front of the unit.
3 **Never disconnect the battery leads while the engine is running or the alternator and the regulator will be damaged.**
4 If low voltage output is suspected because of a discharged battery, remove the plug from the base of the regulator and bridge the 'Negative' and 'Field' contacts on the plug itself. This action will permit the alternator to run full field and if the low voltage condition persists, it must indicate a faulty alternator, not the regulator.
5 If the low voltage condition continues, check the regulator adjustment. To do this, check that (engine running at 1500 rev/min) at least 12 volts exists between the positive (+) and negative (—) terminals on the regulator. If necessary remove the socket screw and adjust the screw located behind it to give 14 volts on normal engine load. Note the setting of the adjuster screw then rotate it fully clockwise and measure the voltage between the field and the negative terminals which should be less than 1.5 volts. If it is as specified, return the adjuster screw to its original position. If the voltage is not as specified, remove the regulator and have your dealer bench test the internal diodes and transistors and printed circuit.
6 Individual faulty components can be removed and renewed but it is recommended that this work is left to your dealer.

16 Alternator (Lucas 18ACR and 20ACR) - testing in-situ

1 This heavier duty type alternator is substituted for the Butec model previously used on cars with an air-conditioning system. It differs from earlier Lucas types by having an integral regulator unit.
2 A moving coil ammeter and a moving coil voltmeter will be required to carry out these tests.
3 Start the cold engine and run it at 3000 rev/min for 3 or 4 minutes.
4 Disconnect the lead from the battery negative terminal.
5 Connect the ammeter in series with the alternator main output cable and starter solenoid.
6 Remove connectors from the alternator, detach the moulded end cover and then re-make the connections.
7 Connect a jump lead to short out the 'F' and '—' terminals of the control unit.
8 Reconnect the lead to the battery negative terminal.
9 Switch on all the car lights with the headlamps on main beam. Switch on the ignition and check that the warning lamp is on.
10 Start the engine, slowly increase its speed to 3000 rev/min. The reading on the ammeter should be equivalent to the alternator maximum rated output which is 45 amps (18ACR type) or 66 amps (20ACR type). If it is not, the alternator requires overhaul and reconditioning.
11 Having completed the output test, now check for voltage drop.

Fig. 10.21. Lucas 3AW warning lamp control unit fitted in conjunction with Lucas 11AC alternator (Sec. 14)

Fig. 10.22. Butec type voltage regulator (Sec. 15)

Fig. 10.23. Alternator output test (Lucas type 20 ACR) (Sec. 16)

2 Ammeter   4 Jump lead

12 Connect a voltmeter between the battery positive terminal and the alternator main output terminal.
13 Switch on all the car lights including the headlamps on main beam. Start the engine and run at 3000 rev/min. Record the voltmeter reading and then switch off the engine.
14 Transfer the voltmeter connections to the battery negative terminal and the alternator negative terminal.
15 Repeat the operations described in paragraph 13, and again note the reading on the voltmeter. The readings recorded should not exceed 0.5 volts for the positive side. Higher readings indicate high resistance in the circuit.

Fig. 10.24. Voltage drop test (Lucas type 20 ACR) between positive terminals (Sec. 16)

Fig. 10.25. Voltage drop test (Lucas type 20 ACR) between negative terminals (Sec. 16)

Fig. 10.26. Control unit test (Lucas type 20 ACR alternator) (Sec. 16)

1 Ammeter   2 Voltmeter

16 To test the control unit, first make sure that all connections are clean and secure and the battery in a fully charged condition (charge from an outside source if necessary).
17 Connect an ammeter in series with the starter solenoid and the alternator main output cable.
18 Connect the voltmeter between the battery terminals.
19 Start the engine and run it at 3000 rev/min until the ammeter reads less than 10 amps. The voltmeter reading should be between 13.6 and 14.4 volts. If the reading fluctuates or is outside the range specified, then the control unit is faulty.

17 Alternator (Lucas 18ACR and 20ACR) - overhaul

1 The main difference between the two alternators lies in the control unit. The following description relates to the model 20ACR but applies equally to the 18ACR provided reference is made to the appropriate illustration.
2 With the alternator removed from the car, remove the pulley retaining nut and washer and draw off the pulley. Remove the fan, spacer and Woodruff key.
3 Remove the moulded cover plate.
4 Unscrew the brush holder screws noting they also secure the radio interference suppression capacitor and black earth cable.
5 Disconnect the red leads from the 'IND' and '+' terminals of the alternator.
6 Withdraw the brush moulding complete with control box.
7 Disconnect the three stator windings from their respective heatsinks.
8 Remove the four screws which secure the heatsink/terminal block assembly and the small screw which connects the earth strap to the alternator frame.
9 Unscrew and remove the three tie bolts from the alternator frame.
10 Separate the slip ring end bracket and stator from the rotor and drive end bracket. To do this, insert a lever and prise them apart.
11 With the alternator dismantled, check the brushes for wear. The brushes must protrude beyond the holder by at least 0.32 in (8 mm) otherwise renew them noting the location of the leaf spring at the side of the inner brush.
12 The slip rings should normally only require cleaning with a fuel soaked cloth but if essential, they can be burnished with finest grade glasspaper (not emery).
13 To test the servicability of the rotor, connect an ohmmeter between the slip rings. Resistance should be 3.6 ohms at 20°C (68°F).
Alternatively, where an ohmmeter is not available, connect an ammeter and 12 volt supply between the slip rings, the ammeter should indicate about 3 amps.
14 To test for defective insulation between the slip rings and the rotor

Fig. 10.27. Control unit on Lucas 18 ACR alternator (Sec. 17)

3 End cover screws   6 Regulator securing screws
5 Rectifier plate cables   7 Brushgear/regulator assembly

Fig. 10.28. Exploded view of Lucas 20 ACR alternator (Sec. 17)

1 Pulley nut and washer	5 Brush fixing screws	7 Brush moulding and control box
3 Spacer	6 Leads to 'Ind' and '+'	8 Stator winding terminals
4 Cover	terminals	9 Heatsink/terminal block and earth strap screws
		10 Tie bolts
		11 Rotor/drive end bracket
		12 Slip ring end bracket

Fig. 10.29. Checking slip ring resistance (Lucas 20 ACR) (Sec. 17)

1 Battery   2 Ammeter

Fig. 10.30. Checking insulation of slip rings and rotor (Lucas 20 ACR) (Sec. 17)

Fig. 10.31. Checking stator continuity (Lucas 20 ACR) (Sec. 17)

Fig. 10.32. Checking insulation of stator (Lucas 20 ACR) (Sec. 17)

poles, a 110 volt supply should be connected with a 15 watt test lamp between the slip rings and rotor poles in turn. If the lamp lights then the coil is earthed to the rotor core. In this event a new rotor/slip ring assembly will be required.

15 The stator can be tested for continuity by connecting any two of the three stator cables in series with a 12 volt battery supply and a 36 watt test lamp. The lamp should light up.

16 Repeat the test by moving the test lamp circuit to the third stator cable. Failure of the lamp to light on either of these tests indicates an open circuit and the stator must be renewed.

17 The insulation of the stator can be checked with a 110 volt test lamp rig. Connect the leads to the laminated yoke and to any one of the three stator cables. If the lamp lights up, the stator coils are earthed and the stator must be renewed.

18 To test the diodes, connect one battery terminal to the heatsink under test. Connect the other battery terminal in series with the test lamp (1.5W) and each diode pin in turn. Reverse the connections between the heatsinks and the diode pins in turn. The lamp should light in one direction only. If he lamp lights in both directions or does not light up at all, a new rectifier heatsink is needed.

19 When soldering the diode assemblies, carry out the operations, as described in Section 10, of this Chapter, paragraphs 25 and 26.

20 Reassembly is a reversal of dismantling but the following points must be observed.

21 If the rotor and drive end bracket have been separated, support the inner track of the drive end bearing using the distance collar. Do not use the drive end bracket as a support while fitting the rotor to it or it may crack.

22 Tighten the tie bolts evenly and make sure that the brushes are correctly located before refitting the brush moulding.

23 It is very important that the aluminium casing of the control unit does not touch the alternator body when it is installed in its final position. This would cause the field circuit to be fully switched on and the alternator would then supply maximum output irrespective of battery charge conditions.

18 Starter motors - general description

1 The starter motor used may be of inertia drive or pre-engaged type depending upon the car model, engine capacity, type of transmission used and the date of production of the vehicle.

2 The pre-engaged type of starter motor incorporates a solenoid mounted on top of the starter motor body. When the ignition switch is operated, the solenoid moves the starter drive pinion, through the medium of the shift lever, into engagement with the flywheel or driveplate starter ring gear. As the solenoid reaches the end of its stroke and with the pinion by now fully engaged with the flywheel ring gear, the main fixed and moving contacts close and engage the starter motor to rotate the engine.

   This fractional pre-engagement of the starter drive does much to reduce the wear on the flywheel ring gear associated with inertia type starter motors.

19 Starter motor - testing in position in the car

   The following tests cover both types of starter motor:

1 Switch on the lights and the ignition. Ensure that the selector lever of automatic models is in the 'P' or 'N' position.

2 Operate the starter control, if the lights go dim but the motor is not heard to operate, it shows that current is flowing through the motor windings but that, for some reason, the armature is not rotating. It may be that the pinion has not disengaged from the starter ring on the flywheel in which case the motor will have to be removed from the car for examination.

3 If, when the starter is operated, the lamps retain their full brilliance and the motor does not operate, check the circuit for continuity starting with the battery connections (especially the earth connection), then look carefully at the engine earth connection followed by the connections to the motor and the starter switch. If it is established that voltage is getting to the motor when the switch is operated, an internal fault in the motor is indicated.

4 Sluggish or a slow action of the motor is usually caused by a loose connection resulting in high resistance in the circuit, check as described in paragraph 3.

5 If the motor is heard to operate but it does not turn the engine, a fault in the drive is indicated which will involve removal of the motor for rectification.

20 Starter motor (inertia type) - removal and refitting

1 Disconnect the lead from the battery negative terminal.

2 Withdraw the three union connections from the lower face of the inlet manifold, release the hose clips at the centre junction and remove the inlet manifold rear starting pipe.

3 Remove the overflow pipe from the rear carburettor.

4 Remove the two nuts which secure the starter motor to the crankcase and withdraw the linked bolts.

Fig. 10.33. Testing diodes (Lucas 20 ACR) (Sec. 17)

5 On cars equipped with automatic transmission, the dipstick must be withdrawn from the transmission unit, also the dipstick/filler tube.

6 Withdraw the starter motor forward and then remove it rearwards through the chassis frame.

7 Refitting is a reversal of removal.

21 Starter motor (pre-engaged type) - removal and refitting

1 Disconnect the lead from the battery negative terminal.

2 Disconnect the lead from the oil pressure switch and then remove the switch from the oil filter body.

3 Disconnect the solenoid electrical leads, also those from the starter motor terminals. Remove the air cleaner.

4 Remove the two setscrews which secure the starter motor to the crankcase.

5 Withdraw the starter motor forwards to clear the starter drive and then remove it to the rear and upwards between the manifold and the wing valance. Retrieve the spigot plate.

6 Refitting is a reversal of removal but ensure that the spigot plate is correctly located on its positioning pins.

22 Starter motor (inertia type) - overhaul

1 Before completely dismantling the motor to check for a fault, first make sure that the brushes are not the cause of the trouble. This can be done by slackening the nut and bolt securing the 'window' cover band, slide the band clear of the 'windows' and the brushes can now be lifted out for examination. It is also possible to check the weight of the brush spring (correct tension 30-40 ozs) using a spring balance through the window.

2 Leave the brushes out of their holders if they are satisfactory and further dismantling is necessary.

3 Remove the nuts from the terminal post at the commutator end bracket.

Fig. 10.34. Checking brush gear (inertia type starter) (Sec. 22)

Fig. 10.35. Checking brush spring tension (inertia type starter) (Sec. 22)

Fig. 10.36. Inertia drive type starter motor (Sec. 18)

1	Terminal nuts and washers	3	Cover band	5	Bush	7	Brush spring
2	Tie bolts	4	Terminal post	6	Bush	8	Brushes

Fig. 10.37. Pre-engaged type starter motor (Sec. 18)

1	Solenoid	7	Bronze bush	13	Pole shoes	19	Thrust washer
2	Return spring	8	Thrust collar	14	Armature	20	Bronze bush
3	Clevis pin	9	Jump ring	15	Yoke	21	Brake shoes and cross peg
4	Pivot pin	10	Thrust ring	16	Commutator	22	Brake ring
5	Engagement lever	11	Armature shaft extension	17	Cover band	23	Brushes
6	Roller clutch	12	Field ring	18	Commutator end bracket		

4   Unscrew the two through bolts, and making sure that the brushes do not foul the yoke, remove the commutator end bracket from the yoke.

5   Relate the brushes, if they are serviceable, to their respective holders and then undo the lead securing screws and remove the brushes. (Fig. 10.38).

6   Withdraw the driving end bracket, complete with the armature and drive, from the yoke.

7   Now refer to Fig. 10.39 for dismantling of the drive.

8   Take out the split pin from the shaft nut (B), hold the squared end of the shaft with a spanner and then unscrew the nut. Some models have a jump ring instead of a split pin. Use a compressor to compress the spring.

9   Take off the main spring (C) followed by the remainder of the

Fig. 10.38. Brush connections (inertia type starter) (Sec. 22)

Fig. 10.39. Inertia type starter motor drive (Sec. 22)

components.

10 Renew any worn components, noting particularly the following:

*The minimum permissible length of the brushes is 5/16 in (7.9 mm).
The insulators between the commutator segments must not be
undercut.
No attempt should be made to machine the armature core or to
true a distorted armature shaft.
If either the screwed sleeve or the pinion of the drive are worn or
damaged, they must be replaced as a pair, not separately.*

11 Reassembly is a reversal of dismantling.

23 Starter motor (pre-engaged type) - overhaul

Type M45G

1 Before completely dismantling the motor to check for a fault, first
make sure that the brushes are not the cause of the trouble. This can be
done by slackening the nut and bolt securing the window cover band and
then sliding the band clear of the windows. The brushes can now be
lifted out for examination. They should be free in their holders,
undamaged, a minimum length of 5/16 in (7.94 mm) and the spring
tension, on a new brush, should be 52 ozs (1.47 kg).

2 Disconnect the copper link between the lower solenoid terminal
and the yoke of the motor.

3 Take off the two solenoid unit securing nuts, detach the extension
cables and withdraw the solenoid from the drive end bracket. Be careful
when disengaging the solenoid plunger from the starter drive engagement
lever.

4 If you have not already done so, slacken the nut and bolt securing
the cover band, slide the band clear of the windows, lift off the brush
springs and then remove the brushes from the holders.

5 Unscrew and remove the two through bolts from the commutator
end bracket.

6 The commutator end bracket and yoke can now be removed from the
intermediate and drive end bracket.

7 Remove the rubber seal from the drive end bracket.

8 Slacken the nut on the starter drive engagement lever eccentric pivot
pin and then unscrew and remove the pin.

9 Separate the drive end bracket from the armature and intermediate
bracket assembly.

10 Using a mild steel tube of suitable bore, remove the thrust washer
from the end of the armature shaft extension.

11 Prise the jump ring out of its groove and then slide the drive
assembly and the intermediate bracket from the shaft.

12 Prise out the jump ring and separate the operating bush and
engagement spring.

13 The commutator should appear in a burnished condition, free from
pitting or burning. It may be cleaned with a fuel soaked cloth or
polished with fine glass paper if absolutely necessary. Do not undercut
the insulators between the segments.

14 The porous bronze bearings in the commutator and drive end
brackets should be renewed if they are worn. They are best removed
by tapping a thread into them and then screwing in a bolt to extract
them.

15 Soak the new bearings in clean engine oil for 24 hours before

.005" – .015" (.127 – .381 mm)

Fig. 10.40. Setting starter motor pinion (pre-engaged starter) (Sec. 23)

installing them. No reaming is required.

16 Reassembly is the reverse of the above sequence but when refitting
the commutator end bracket, ensure that the moulded brake shoes seat
squarely and then turn them so that the ends of the cross peg in the
armature shaft engage correctly with the slots in the shoes.

17 After final assembly it will be necessary to check for correct
movement of the pinion, and for opening and closing of the starter
switch contacts.

18 To check pinion movement, refer to Fig. 10.40 and connect the
solenoid Lucas terminal to a **6 volt** battery as shown (do not use a 12
volt supply otherwise the armature will turn).

19 Measure the distance between the pinion and the thrust washer on
the extension of the armature shaft when the pinion is lightly pressed
towards the armature. This dimension should be 0.005 in to 0.015 in
(0.13 to 0.38 mm).

20 If the setting is outside of those limits, disconnect the battery.

21 Now adjust the setting by first slackening the nut on the eccentric
pivot pin (inset at Fig. 10.40) and then turn the pin clockwise to
decrease and anticlockwise to increase the gap. The head of the arrow
stamped on the end of the pin should be set only between the limits
of the arrows cast in the drive end bracket.

22 Tighten the pin securing nut and then reconnect the battery and
recheck the setting.

23 Having correctly set the pinion travel, the next task is to check the
opening and closing of the starter switch contacts.

24 Refer to Fig. 10.41, remove the copper link connecting the solenoid
'STA' with the starter motor terminal.

25 Connect a switched 10 volts DC supply between the solenoid Lucar
terminal and the large terminal 'STA'. **Do not** close the switch at this
stage.

26 Connect a separately energised test lamp across the solenoid main

Fig. 10.41. Pre-engaged type starter solenoid switch (Sec. 23)

A Core	G Starter terminal
B Shunt winding	H Solenoid terminal
C Series winding	I Battery terminal
D Plunger	J Accessories terminal
E Clevis pin	K Spindle and moving
F 'Lost motion' device	contact assembly

Fig. 10.43. Components of the Lucas 3M100 starter motor (Sec. 23)

3 Electrical link	9 Tie bolts
5 Solenoid	10 Brushes
6 Piston/engagement lever	11 Yoke/field coil
connection	12 Pivot pin and spire
7 End cap seal	ring
8 Spire ring and bush	13 Armature shaft

position.

31 Switch off and observe the test lamp. The solenoid contacts should open as indicated by the test lamp extinguishing.

32 Examine the roller clutch drive assembly. If it is in good condition it should take up the drive instantaneously in one direction and should rotate easily and smoothly in the other. There should be no roughness or tendency to bind in movement around or along the shaft splines. Similarly, the operating bush must be free to slide smoothly along the driving sleeve when the engagement spring is compressed. Make sure that the trunnion blocks pivot freely on the pegs of the engaging lever.

33 Finally, lubricate all moving parts of the roller clutch drive with general purpose grease.

Type 3M100

34 The operations described in the foregoing paragraphs generally apply to the later type of starter motor but the following differences must be noted.

35 There is no brush cover band on this type of starter.

36 The spire retaining rings must be renewed on reassembly.

37 The commutator end cover is removed after withdrawing it enough to be able to disengage the two field coil brushes from the brush box.

38 The minimum length of the brushes before renewal is 0.375 in (9.5 mm). When renewing the brushes, note which field coil conductor is fitted with the long or short brush flexible connector. Unsolder the old brushes and use resin cored solder to attach the new ones.

39 Drive the spire ring onto the armature shaft so that there is a clearance between the retaining ring and the bearing bush shoulder of no more than 0.010 in (0.25 mm).

Fig. 10.42. Roller clutch drive components (pre-engaged starter) (Sec. 23)

A Alternative construction (pinion	E Driving member
pressed and clear-ringed into	F Bush
driven member)	G Engagement spring
B Spring loaded rollers	H Operating bush
C Cam tracks	I Driving sleeve
D Driven member (with pinion)	

24 Fuses

1   The fuse units are located behind the instrument panel.

2   Access to the fuses is obtained by removing the screws from the top left and top right-hand corners of the instrument panel. The panel then hinges downward.

3   The fuses and the circuits which they protect are listed in 'Specifications' at the beginning of this Chapter.

4   Always renew a blown fuse with one of similar rating and if it blows for a second time, trace the cause before renewing it again.

5   Where a heated rear window and an air-conditioning system are installed, separate fuses in independent fuse holders are located also behind the instrument panel.

6   On cars equipped with an overdrive, a separate in-line fuse is located just above the steering column.

terminals.

27 Use a tool, an open ended spanner is ideal with its jaws passing over the armature shaft extension, to act as a stop and so restrict the pinion travel to its out of mesh clearance which is normally 1/8 in (3.17 mm).

28 Now energise the shunt winding using a 10 volt DC supply and then close the switch in the series winding circuit. The solenoid contacts should close fully and remain closed, a steady beam from the test lamp will indicate that this is so.

29 Switch off and remove the stop.

30 Switch on again and hold the pinion assembly in the fully engaged

Fig. 10.44. Fuse arrangement (for 'Key' see Specifications Section) (Sec. 24)

25 Flasher (direction indicator) unit - checking and renewal

1   The flasher unit which controls the direction indicators is located behind and to the right of the steering column.
2   Any fault in the system should first be checked out by testing the bulbs in the indicator lamps and the security of the wiring.
3   If these are in order, remove the old unit and then connect together the leads which have been removed from terminals 'B' and 'L' of the flasher unit. Turn on the ignition switch and turn the direction indicator switch first to the left and then to the right. Check that the appropriate bulbs light up. If they do then the bulbs and wiring are in good order.
4   Any difference in the speed of flashing between one side of the car and the other may be due to a gradual internal collapse of the unit. Exceptionally fast flashing of an indicator bulb usually means that a bulb is failing.

26 Hazard warning flasher unit

1   The system operates in conjunction with the four direction indicator lamps.
2   The hazard warning system actuates all four flasher lamps simultaneously.
3   The flasher unit is located close to the direction indicator flasher unit.
4   The system indicator lamp is accessible for renewal after removing the warning lamp cluster which is located between the speedometer and the revolution counter.
5   If one bulb in the system fails, the remaining three bulbs in the system will still function.

27 Bulbs - renewal

The design of the lamps illustrated in this Section may vary

Fig. 10.45. Location of overdrive unit fuse (Sec. 24)

Fig. 10.46. Location of hazard warning (A) and direction indicator flasher unit (B) (Sec. 25)

according to the model and date of production but the bulb renewal operations apply to all versions.

Headlamps

1   The headlamps are of sealed beam type. To renew an outer lamp unit, remove the upper retainer screw and withdraw the headlamp embellisher noting the two retaining lugs at the lower edge. On Series 2 cars, the embellisher incorporates a mesh filter covering a fresh air intake (photo).
2   Unscrew the three retaining screws and the headlamp retaining rim (photo).
3   Withdraw the headlamp sealed beam unit and detach the socket from the rear of the headlamp (photo).
4   Refitting is a reversal of removal but on no account alter the setting of the headlamp adjusting screws.

27.1 Removing headlamp embellisher

27.2 Removing headlamp sealed beam unit

27.3 Disconnecting headlamp unit

Fig. 10.47. Headlamp components (Sec. 27)

27.5 Removing front parking lamp lens

27.7 Removing rear lamp lens

27.8 Removing reversing lamp lens

27.9 Removing rear number plate lens

Front parking, direction indicator, side marker, flasher repeater lamps
5   Access to all these bulbs is obtained by removing the lamp lens securing screws and withdrawing the lens. Not all these lamps are fitted to all cars. The specification depends upon operating territory (photo).

Rear lamp and direction indicator lamp
6   Remove the three lens securing screws and withdraw the lens.
7   When refitting the tail/stop lamp bulb which is of twin filament type, note the offset pins (photo).

Reversing lamp
8   Remove the two lens securing screws and withdraw the lens and the festoon type bulb (photo).

Rear number plate lamp
9   Remove the two screws which are located in the centre section of the rear bumper and withdraw the lens (photo).

Interior lamp
10 Remove the lens cover by inserting a screwdriver under the bright plated part.
11 The bulb is of festoon type.
12 Replace the lens by inserting the top edge into the base and then snapping the bottom edge into place.

Map reading lamp
13 Press in the side clips of the bulb holder which is located under the centre of the screen rail above the instrument panel. Withdraw the holder downwards (Fig. 10.49).
14 The bulb is accessible through a hole in the base of the lamp.

Fig. 10.48. Interior lamp bulb (Sec. 27)

Warning lamps
15 The bulbs for these lamps are housed in a cluster which is located between the speedometer and the revolution counter. Prise the cover plate off and remove the capless type bulbs.

Indicator strip lamps
16 These bulbs are removable simply by pulling them out of their sockets along the bottom rear edge of the instrument panel.

Fig. 10.49. Map reading lamp bulb (Sec. 27)

Fig. 10.50. Warning lamps (Sec. 27)

A Direction indicators   D Brake warning
B Hazard warning   E Oil pressure warning
C Ignition warning

Fig. 10.51. Luggage compartment lamp bulb (Sec. 27)

Fig. 10.52. Automatic transmission speed selector bulb (Sec. 27)

Fig. 10.53. Opticell assembly (Sec. 27)

3 Bulb holder   4 Bulb

Fig. 10.54. Rear view of Series 2 clock (Sec. 27)

Luggage compartment lamp
17 Open the luggage compartment lid and remove the bulb by reaching through the aperture in the luggage compartment lid inner panel.

Automatic transmission indicator bulb
18 Remove the securing screws which retain the cover on the speed selector control. On Series 2 cars, prise out the window lift switch panel.
19 Remove the control lever knob by unscrewing the two halves in opposing directions.
20 Withdraw the two screws and remove the speed position indicator cover.
21 Remove the bulb cover and the bulb.

Door pillar lamp
22 These lamps are fitted to the top of the door pillars on Series 2 cars.
23 The lens is squeezed slightly and pulled from the lamp base to gain access to the festoon type bulb.

Fibre optic (Opticell) illumination system (Series 2 cars)
24 This system provides illumination to the ignition, lighting and heater/air-conditioning control switches from a central light source through fibre elements and diffuser lenses.
25 To renew the bulb, disconnect the battery, remove the centre console escutcheon and the window control switch panel. Pull the bulb holder from the opticell reflector and extract the bayonet type bulb.

Speedometer and tachometer bulbs
26 The bulbs can be withdrawn from the rear of these instruments after the instruments have been partially withdrawn as described in Section 38 or 39.

Clock illumination bulb (Series 2 cars)
27 A separate clock illuminating bulb is used on Series 2 cars and this is accessible only after first disconnecting the battery and dropping the centre oddments tray. Pull the bulb holder from the back of the clock case.

Fig. 10.55. Headlamp adjusting screws (Sec. 28)

A Outer vertical   C Inner vertical
B Outer horizontal   D Inner horizontal

28 Headlamp beam alignment

1 It is recommended that the headlamps are aligned on modern optical beam setting equipment at a service station.
2 However, where these facilities are not available or in an emergency, proceed in the following way.
3 Place the car on a level surface (during the hours of darkness) 25 ft (7.6 m) from and square to a wall or screen.
4 Switch the headlamps to full beam and observe the light patterns from the four headlamps on the wall. These patterns should have their centres at the same height on the wall as their lens centre points are from the ground and at the same horizontal distances from each other as the headlamp lens centres are from each other on the car.
5 If adjustment is required, remove the headlamp surround by removing the retaining screw and springing the surround from the bottom clips. Turn the appropriate adjuster screws as required.

29 Steering column ignition/starter switch and lock

1 The ignition/starter switch has five positions:

   1 Lock; 2 Park; 3 Accessories; 4 Ignition; 5 Start

2 In the 'Lock' position, the key can be removed but the steering wheel cannot be turned.
3 In the 'Park' position the key can be removed and the car can be pushed and steered for repair purposes.
4 In the 'Accessories' position, the radio and electrically-operated windows (where fitted) can be operated.
5 In the 'On' position, the ignition is switched on.
6 In the 'Start' position, the starter motor is actuated. On releasing the key it returns to the 'On' position. This arrangement gives enough time for the engine and starter motor drive to stop should a second attempt have to be made to start the engine, otherwise damage could be caused to the starter drive and flywheel ring gear.
7 The ignition section of the lock assembly can be removed by disconnecting the connector plug and removing the contact plate (two screws). It should be noted that two relays are incorporated in the circuits which are controlled by the ignition switch to prevent over-loading of the switch contacts. The relays are located under the fascia panel. Always check these components if a fault develops in the ignition/starter circuit.
8 The steering lock is secured to the upper end of the steering column by two shear-headed bolts. If the lock must be removed for any reason, the original bolts must be drilled out.
9 When refitting the new lock, check the operation of the lock tongue in the column cut-out before finally tightening and shearing the new securing bolts.

Fig. 10.56. Ignition key positions (Sec. 29)

1 Lock   3 Accessories
2 Park   4 Start

30 Direction indicator switch - removal and refitting

1 Disconnect the lead from the battery negative terminal.
2 Remove the steering wheel as described in Chapter 11.
3 Remove the three screws which secure the direction indicator switch and cowl to the steering outer column.
4 Disconnect the cables which run to the switch by separating the plug connectors.
5 Refitting is a reversal of removal.

Fig. 10.57. Steering column lock and ignition switch (Sec. 29)

31 Overdrive switch - removal and refitting

1 Disconnect the lead from the battery negative terminal.
2 Insert a thin knife blade or similar tool between the switch cover and the gear lever knob. Gently prise away the cover (with switch attached) from the snap ring retainer.
3 Disconnect the two cables from the switch connectors and separate the switch from the cover by removing the two securing screws.
4 Refitting is a reversal of removal.

32 Horns and relay

1 The twin horns are mounted just below and to each side of the radiator.
2 The horn circuit incorporates a relay and actuation is by means of the steering wheel horn ring or centre button.
3 The horns only sound when the ignition is switched on.
4 If the horns fail to work, first check the fuse and then the wiring and connections. If these are in order and the battery is fully charged, then the relay is probably the cause and it should be renewed. The relay is located within the engine compartment on the right-hand side towards the front.

33 Windscreen wiper blades and arms - removal and refitting

1 To remove a wiper blade, release the small tag which secures it to the wiper arm and pull the blade from the arm (photo).
2 The wiper arms can be removed from the splined driving spindles after first pulling the arms away from the windscreen until they lock.

3 When refitting the wiper arms, make sure that the wiper motor is in the parked position, having been switched off by the wiper control switch (not the ignition key) and set the arms complete with blades, parallel with the lower edge of the windscreen before pressing the arm fully onto its spindle.

34 Windscreen wiper motor and linkage - removal and refitting

1 Remove the wiper arms from their driving spindles.
2 Disconnect and remove the battery.
3 Unscrew the large nut which connects the driving cable conduit to the wiper motor (photo).
4 Withdraw the electrical plug connector from the socket in the motor.
5 Remove the two setscrews, washers and clamp strap and then withdraw the motor and driving cable by drawing the cable through its conduit (photo).
6 If the driving spindle assemblies are worn they can only be removed after first withdrawing the screen rail fascia. To do this, inseet a thin blade under the edge of the loudspeaker grille and lever up the fascia. The grille is retained by plastic pegs. Remove the two screws now exposed also the two other screws from the underside of the screen fascia roll (just above the fresh air outlets).
7 Unscrew and remove the two nuts which secure the wheelbox backplate and withdraw the cable drive conduit.
8 Unscrew the nuts which secure the wheelbox to the scuttle and withdraw the wheelbox, spacer and seals.
9 Refitting the wheelboxes is a reversal of removal except that the flared ends of the conduit tube must register with the narrow slots in the cover plate.
10 After refitting the wiper motor, the wiper arms must be installed in

Fig. 10.58. Removing the overdrive switch (Sec. 31)

Fig. 10.59. Location of horn relay (Sec. 32)

33.1 Disconnecting wiper blade from arm

34.3 Windscreen wiper driving cable conduit unit

34.5 Withdrawing wiper driving cable

the following way:
11 Switch on the ignition and then switch on the wiper switch to slow speed. Switch off the wiper switch so that the driving spindles will stop in the 'Parked' position. Install the wiper arms so that they lie parallel with the lower edge of the windscreen.

Fig. 10.60. Wiper motor mounting bolts (Sec. 34)

35 Windscreen wiper motor - overhaul

1 With the motor removed from the car as described in Section 34, withdraw the gearbox cover screws and remove the cover.
2 Prise the circlip from the groove in the gearwheel crankpin and extract the flat washer, conical spring, friction plate, connecting rod assembly and its flat washer.
3 Remove the circlip and washer which secure the shaft to the gearbox.
4 Draw the gear from the shaft, collecting the dished washer from the underside of the gearwheel.
5 Note the gearbox to yoke alignment marks and then withdraw the two fixing bolts and detach the yoke assembly and the armature from the gearbox. Take care that once removed, the yoke does not come near any swarf or iron filings which might be attracted to its pole pieces.
6 Mark the location of the moulded slider block in relation to the terminal assembly as this controls the wiper parking position.

Fig. 10.61. Windscreen wiper wheelbox (Sec. 34)

Fig. 10.62. Exploded view of the windscreen wiper motor (Sec. 35)

1	Gearbox cover	11	Slider block
2	Screw	12	Gearbox
3	Circlip	13	Limit switch
4	Washer	14	Screws
5	Spring	15	Bush
6	Friction plate	16	Brush gear
7	Crankarm	17	Armature
8	Gear	18	Yoke
9	Dished washer	19	Tie bolts
10	Cable rack		

7   Remove the screws which secure the brushgear and the terminal and limit switch assembly and withdraw the assemblies.
8   Inspect the brushes for wear. The main (diametrically opposite) brushes should be renewed if they are worn to 3/16 in (4.8 mm) or less. If the narrow section of the third brush is worn to the full width of the brush, it must be renewed. Check that the brushes move freely in their holders.
9   Clean the commutator of the armature with a fuel soaked rag or polish it with very fine glasspaper.
10 Renew any gearbox components which are worn.
11 Reassembly is a reversal of dismantling but check the following points.
12 Before refitting the armature to the yoke, check that the thrust disc and felt lubricating disc are in position in the yoke bearing. The thrust disc should be located flat against the endface of the bearing, followed by the felt washer which has a hole in its centre to allow the ball in the end of the armature shaft to contact the thrust disc. Prior to fitting the components, apply oil to the felt washer.
13 Apply grease liberally to all gearbox components.
14 If new parts have been fitted, check the armature endfloat which must be between 0.002 and 0.008 in (0.05 and 0.2 mm). With the wiper motor completely assembled and the thrust screw released and in the uppermost position, tighten the screw until it just makes contact and then unscrew it one quarter of a turn and tighten the locknut.

36 Windscreen washer - description and jet adjustment

1   The washer assembly comprises a plastic fluid container, an independently mounted motor, twin jets and an operating switch.
2   It is recommended that a reliable brand of washer solvent is mixed with water in the container instead of using plain water.
3   The motor/pump unit is mounted on the engine compartment rear bulkhead.
4   The jets can be removed for cleaning, if required, by unscrewing them from the jet holder.
5   Adjustment is carried out by moving the jets with a thin screwdriver blade (photo).

Fig. 10.63. Wiper motor armature endfloat adjuster screw and locknut (Sec. 35)

36.5 Adjusting windscreen washer jet

37 Speedometer cable - renewal

1   Reach up behind the instrument panel and unscrew the knurled ring from the back of the speedometer. Withdraw the cable and ring.
2   Disconnect the opposite end of the speedometer cable from the gearbox or automatic transmission and then detach the cable from its securing clips.
3   Withdraw the inner cable from the outer conduit.
4   Before installing the new inner cable, smear the lower two thirds of its length with a thin coating of multi-purpose grease.
5   Connect the cable assembly to the transmission and then position the cable in its original contour without moving the position of the securing clips.
6   Rotate the inner cable with the fingers to ensure that it is correctly engaged at the transmission end and then check that the inner cable projects by 3/8 in (9.5 mm) from the end of the outer conduit at the speedometer head end.
7   Engage the cable assembly with the back of the speedometer and tighten the knurled ring with the fingers.

38 Speedometer - removal and refitting

1   Disconnect the lead from the battery negative terminal.
2   Disconnect the speedometer cable from the rear of the speedometer, as described in the preceding Section.
3   Disconnect the trip control cable by unscrewing the knurled ring.
4   Apply hand pressure against the speedometer bezel, turn it in an anticlockwise direction until it stops and then withdraw it.
5   Disconnect the headlamp main beam warning lamp and the two instrument illumination lamps.
6   Refitting is a reversal of removal.

39 Tachometer - removal and refitting

1   The tachometer is of impulse type and is wired in circuit with the S/W terminal on the ignition coil and the ignition switch.
2   The instrument can be removed by applying hand pressure against the bezel and turning it in an anticlockwise direction.
3   Withdraw the instrument far enough to be able to punch the prongs of the socket retainer clip together and to withdraw the plug and

Fig. 10.64. Windscreen washer pump location (Sec. 36)

Fig. 10.65. Speedometer inner cable projection at speedometer head end (Sec. 37)

socket assembly.
4   Refitting is the reverse of removal.

40 Instrument sub-panel - removal and refitting

1   Disconnect the lead from the battery negative terminal.
2   Remove the two screws from the top of the main instrument panel and hinge it downwards (photos).
3   Withdraw the electrical harness plug.
4   Remove the four setscrews and withdraw the sub-panel complete with instruments.
5   If the individual instruments are to be removed, first withdraw the instrument voltage regulator.
6   Unscrew and remove the six cross-headed screws, disconnect the two electrical leads from the clock and then remove the base panel complete with the instruments mounted on it.
7   Individual instruments can be removed after extracting their securing screws but take great care not to damage the printed circuit.
8   Refitting is a reversal of removal.

Fig. 10.66. Removing tachometer (Sec. 39)

40.2A Removing instrument panel screw

40.2B Instrument panel hinged downward to expose fuses

Fig. 10.67. Exploded view of instrument sub-panel (Sec. 40)

1   Front casing
2   Battery condition indicator
3   Oil pressure gauge
4   Clock
5   Water temperature gauge
6   Fuel gauge
7   Screw
8   Printed circuit and backplate
9   Nut
10   Washer
11   Screw
12   Nut
13   Washer
14   Bulb
15   Bulb holder
16   Dust cover
17   Voltage stabiliser
18   Voltage stabiliser cover
19   Washer
20   Blade connector

41 Switch sub-panel - removal and refitting

1   Disconnect the lead from the battery negative terminal.
2   Remove the two screws from the top of the main instrument panel and hinge it downwards.
3   Disconnect the leads from the switches marking any that need it to ensure exact reconnection later.
4   Unscrew the four screws and detach the sub-panel.
5   The switches are secured in the sub-panel by plastic locking tabs which should be depressed to release the switches.

42 Electric clock - removal and refitting

1   The clock can be removed after carrying out the operations described in Section 40, paragraphs 1 to 6.
2   Refitting is a reversal of these operations.

43 Heated rear window

1   The heating element on all but the earliest cars is applied to the inside surface of the glass. Great care must be taken not to damage the element with sharp objects or, when cleaning the glass, with rings on the fingers.
2   Use only water to clean the glass and never stick labels onto the inside of the rear window if they are likely to cover any of the fine wires of the element.

44 Seatbelt warning system

1   This system is installed in cars destined for operation in North America.
2   Audible and visual alarm signals are given if the front seats are occupied but the belts not fastened and with the engine started, a gear is engaged or speed position (automatic transmission) selected.
3   Any fault in the system should be checked out by testing the circuit fuse and the wiring and connections.
4   On Series 2 cars, the system is modified so that the engine will not start unless the following operations have been carried out (front seat/s occupied).

> *Handbrake fully applied.*
> *Selector lever in 'N' or 'P' (automatic transmission) or neutral (manual gearbox).*
> *Seatbelt fastened.*

5   If the front seat passenger leaves the car while the engine is running, the warning devices will operate for seven seconds and then cease.
6   If the driver leaves his seat while the engine is running no warning signals will be given when he returns and selects a gear without refastening his seatbelt.
7   The engine can be started for purposes of maintenance or tuning by reaching inside the car and turning the starter switch so that no weight is applied to either front seat. Under these conditions, no warning or starter cut-out will be operative.
8   The seatbelt warning system buzzer/control unit is located under the fascia panel on the passenger side. The unit is mounted on the heater blower casing and on Series 2 cars, the fascia side panel and the glove compartment liner must both be removed first.

45 Electrically operated windows

1   These devices are supplied as optional equipment but are factory installed at time of production.

Driver's control switches
2   To remove the driver's control switches, first disconnect the lead from the battery negative terminal.
3   Lift the centre armrest lid and remove the screws which secure it to the console. Withdraw the nylon catch and withdraw the pocket from the console.
4   Remove the switch escutcheon panel by pressing it out from the

Fig. 10.68. Instrument panel rocker switches showing locking tabs (Sec. 41)

Fig. 10.69. Driver's electrically-operated window control panel (Sec. 45)

A   Right-hand rear
B   Left-hand rear
C   Front right-hand (and master switch)
D   Front left-hand

rear. On Series 2 cars, the switch panel can simply be levered from its location in the centre console.
5   If one switch is to be renewed, remove the control button from it and then extract the three screws which secure the console panel to the console.
6   Remove the four screws which secure the switch carrier plate to the console panel and move the panel to one side.
7   Extract the two screws and washers which secure the switch to the carrier plate, disconnect the leads and remove the switch.
8   Refitting a new switch is a reversal of the removal operations but make sure that the leads are correctly connected to the switch terminals.

Rear passenger's control switches
9   Remove the armrest from the door interior panel.
10 Disconnect the leads from the switch, identifying them so that they can be correctly refitted.
11 Remove the switch escutcheon plate and detach the switch from the armrest. On Series 2 cars, the switch panel is located below the heater air outlet. Prise the switch from its location.
12 Refitting is a reversal of removal.

Front window motors
13 To remove a front window motor, first disconnect the lead from the battery negative terminal.
14 Remove the door interior panel and the armrest as described in Chapter 12.
15 Disconnect the leads from the motor by separating the plug and socket connection.
16 Extract the two setscrews and remove the gearbox which controls the swivelling quarterlight ventilator.
17 Remove the upper bolt which secures the glass channel to the door

inner panel.

18 Remove the four setscrews and remove the window regulator mechanism from the door panel. Slide the mechanism towards the hinged edge of the door in order to clear the regulator arm roller from the channel. Now lift the regulator arm so that it passes on the outer side of the glass channel.

19 Withdraw the assembly through the aperture in the door interior panel.

20 The motor can be separated from the regulator after removing the three securing screws but on Series 2 cars do not let the spring

disengage suddenly as this could cause damage or injury.

21 Refitting is a reversal of removal.

Rear window motors

22 Remove the door interior panel and the armrest, as described in Chapter 12.

23 Disconnect the lead from the battery negative terminal.

24 Disconnect the leads from the window motor by separating the plug and socket.

25 Remove the four setscrews and detach the regulator mechanism from the door panel.

26 Adjust the position of the window glass until the regulator arm can be removed from the channel. Withdraw the regulator through the aperture in the door. It may be necessary to remove the door glass in some cases to facilitate withdrawal of the regulator, in this case refer to Chapter 12.

27 Separate the motor from the regulator by unscrewing the three setscrews.

28 Refitting is a reversal of removal.

Relay control box

29 The relay control box is located behind the left-hand front kick panel on early cars or on later cars (including Series 2) under the centre console.

30 To remove the relay, first disconnect the lead from the battery negative terminal and then remove the kick panel or console according to type.

31 The relay is held onto its mounting by two screws. Always identify the connecting cables before removing them from the control box terminals so that they can be reconnected correctly.

Fig. 10.70. Passenger's electrically-operated window control (Sec. 45)

A Lower   B Raise

Fig. 10.7 l. A front window operating motor (Sec. 45)

Fig. 10.72. A rear window operating motor (Sec. 45)

Fig. 10.73. Window lift relay (early cars) (Sec. 45)

Fig. 10.74. Window lift relay (Series 2) (Sec. 45)

4 Relay securing screws

46 Solenoid-operated door locking system

1   Series 2 models are equipped with this system, the control switch for which is mounted on the centre console below the window lift switches.
2   Access to the switch can be gained after prising out the window lift switch panel and removing the console escutcheon (3 screws).
3   A door lock solenoid can be removed if the window is fully closed, the battery disconnected and the door interior trim withdrawn.
4   The solenoid is secured by two setscrews and its operating piston is hooked to the door lock pushrod.
5   The system circuit breakers are located above the fuse block on the driver's side of the car.
6   The door lock solenoid relays are accessible after carrying out the following operations.
7   Disconnect the battery and then push the left-hand front seat fully forward. Remove the rear seat cushion.
8   Prise the carpet and insulating material away from the rear of the transmission tunnel and the front of the box section which supports the rear seat cushion (4 in Fig. 10.78).
9   Support the relays (1 and 2) with the hand through the hole in the front crossmember while the relay securing screws are removed (6). Withdraw the relays through the hole (7) in the crossmember and disconnect the leads (8) as necessary.
10 Refitting of all components is a reversal of removal.

47 Instrument panel lighting switch (Series 2 cars) - removal and refitting

1   To remove this switch, disconnect the battery and then remove the two screws which secure the panel to which the switch is mounted.
2   Depress the spring loaded plunger and pull off the control knob.
3   Unscrew the switch retaining ring, remove the heat shield from under the locknut.
4   Disconnect the leads from the switch terminals and withdraw the switch.
5   Refitting is a reversal of removal.

48 Master lighting switch (Series 2 cars) - removal and refitting

1   Disconnect the battery.
2   Remove the fascia side panel from the driver's side.
3   Depress the spring loaded plunger and pull the control knob from the switch.
4   Unscrew the switch retaining bezel and then remove the switch shroud.
5   Push the switch through the mounting plate and disconnect the plug from the rear of the switch.
6   Refitting is a reversal of removal.

Fig. 10.75. Location of door locking switch on Series 2 cars (Sec. 46)

2   Window lift switch panel   5   Door locking switch
3   Console escutcheon

Fig. 10.76. Location of door lock solenoid (Sec. 46)

4   Securing screws   6   Door lock push-rod
                               connecting hook

Fig. 10.77. Location of circuit breakers on Series 2 cars (Sec. 46)

4   Breaker securing screws

Fig. 10.78. Door lock solenoid relays (Sec. 46)

Fig. 10.79. Instrument panel lighting rheostat (Sec. 47)

3 Knob and spring-loaded plunger 4 Ring
                                   6 Rheostat casing

Fig. 10.80. Exploded view of master lighting switch (Sec. 48)

49 Door pillar switch - removal and refitting

1 Disconnect the battery.
2 Lever the switch from the door pillar using a sharp screwdriver.
3 Disconnect the electrical lead from the back of the switch and tape it to prevent it falling into the cavity of the door pillar.
4 Corrosion is often a problem with these switches and it is a good idea to smear the switch plunger with petroleum jelly before installing it.
5 Refitting is a reversal of removal.

50 Cigar lighter - removal and refitting

1 Disconnect the battery.
2 Lever out the electric window control switch panel.
3 Withdraw the console trim panel.
4 Press together the sides of the cigar lighter bulb assembly and then remove from the bezel.
5 Disconnect the lead from the cigar lighter.
6 Unscrew the bezel and withdraw the cigar lighter from the console escutcheon.
7 Refitting is a reversal of removal.

Fig. 10.81. Door pillar switch (Sec. 49)

46 Fault diagnosis - electrical system

Symptom	Reason/s
Starter fails to turn engine	Battery discharged. Battery defective internally. Battery terminal leads loose or earth lead not securely attached to body. Loose or broken connections in starter motor circuit. Starter motor switch or solenoid faulty. Starter motor pinion jammed in mesh with flywheel gear ring. Starter brushes badly worn, sticking, or brush wires loose. Commutator dirty, worn or burnt. Starter motor armature faulty. Field coils earthed.
Starter turns engine very slowly	Battery in discharged condition. Starter brushes badly worn, sticking or brush wires loose. Loose wires in starter motor circuit.
Starter spins but does not turn engine	Starter motor pinion sticking on the screwed sleeve. Pinion or flywheel gear teeth broken or worn. Battery discharged.
Starter motor noisy or excessively rough engagement	Pinion or flywheel gear teeth broken or worn. Starter motor retaining bolts loose.
Battery will not hold charge for more than a few days	Battery defective internally. Electrolyte level too low or electrolyte too weak due to leakage. Plate separators no longer fully effective. Battery plates severely sulphated. Fan belt slipping. Battery terminal connections loose or corroded. Alternator not charging. Short in lighting circuit causing continual battery drain. Regulator unit not working correctly.
Ignition light fails to go out, battery runs flat in a few days	Fan belt loose and slipping or broken. Alternator brushes worn, sticking, broken or dirty. Alternator brush springs weak or broken. Internal fault in alternator. Regulator incorrectly set. Open circuit in wiring of regulator unit.

Failure of individual electrical equipment to function correctly is dealt with alphabetically, item-by-item, under the headings listed below

Electrically-operated windows

Complete system failure	Faulty control box. Blown fuse.
Driver's window normal, remainder inoperative	Sticking switch. Circuit earthed.
Failure of one window only	Faulty switch. Poor electrical connection. Stiff mechanism or sticking window.

Horn

Horn operates all the time	Horn push either earthed or stuck down. Horn cable to horn push earthed.
Horn fails to operate	Blown fuse. Cable or cable connection loose, broken or disconnected. Horn has an internal fault.
Horn emits intermittent or unsatisfactory noise	Cable connections loose. Horn incorrectly adjusted.

Symptom	Reason/s
Lights	
Lights do not come on	If engine not running, battery discharged. Wire connections loose, disconnected or broken. Light switch shorting or otherwise faulty.
Lights come on but fade out	If engine not running battery discharged. Light bulb filament burnt out or bulbs or sealed beam units broken. Wire connections loose, disconnected or broken. Light switch shorting or otherwise faulty.
Lights give very poor illumination	Lamp glasses dirty. Lamps badly out of adjustment.
Lights work erratically - flashing on and off, especially over bumps	Battery terminals or earth connection loose. Lights not earthing properly. Contacts in light switch faulty.
Wipers	
Wiper motor fails to work	Blown fuse. Wire connections loose, disconnected or broken. Brushes badly worn. Armature worn or faulty. Field coils faulty.
Wiper motor works very slowly and takes excessive current	Commutator dirty, greasy or burnt. Armature bearings dirty or unaligned. Armature badly worn or faulty.
Wiper motor works slowly and takes little current	Brushes badly worn. Commutator dirty, greasy or burnt. Armature badly worn or faulty.
Wiper motor works but wiper blades remain static	Wiper motor gearbox parts badly worn. Stripped splines on wheelbox spindles.

Fig. 10.82. Wiring diagram - 2.8 Litre RHD to chassis number 1G4158; 2.8 Litre LHD to chassis number 1G52012; 4.2 Litre RHD to chassis number 1L5561; 4.2 Litre LHD to chassis number 1L53096

Fig. 10.82. Wiring diagram - 2.8 Litre RHD to chassis number 1G4158; 2.8 Litre LHD to chassis number 1G52012; 4.2 Litre RHD to chassis number 1L5561; 4.2 Litre LHD to chassis number 1L53096

No.	Description
1	Alternator
3	Battery
4	Starter solenoid
5	Starter motor
6	Lighting switch
7	Headlamp dip switch
8	Headlamp outer, RH
9	Headlamp outer, LH
10	Main beam warning lamp
11	Side lamp RH
12	Side lamp LH
14	Panel lamps
15	Number plate lamps
16	Stop and tail lamp RH
17	Stop and tail lamp LH
18	Stop lamp switch
20	Interior lights
21	Door switch RH
22	Door switch LH
23	Horns
24	Horn push
25	Flash unit
26	Direction indicator switch
27	Direction indicator warning lamps
28	Flasher lamp, front, RH
29	Flasher lamp, front, LH
30	Flasher lamp, rear, RH
31	Flasher lamp, rear, LH
34	Fuel gauge
35	Fuel gauge tank unit
36	Windscreen wiper switch
37	Windscreen wiper motor
38	Ignition switch
39	Ignition coil
40	Distributor
41	Fuel pump
42	Oil pressure switch
43	Oil pressure warning lamp or gauge
44	Ignition warning lamp
46	Water temperature gauge
47	Water temperature transmitter
49	Reverse lamp switch
50	Reverse lamps
54	Foglamp RH
55	Foglamp LH
56	Clock
57	Cigar lighter
59	Interior lights switch
60	Radio
61	Horn relay
64	Bi-metal instrument voltage stabiliser
65	Boot light - switch
66	Boot light
67	Line fuse
75	Automatic gearbox safety
77	Electric windscreen washer
78	Electric windscreen washer switch
95	Revolution counter
101	Map light switch
102	Map light
113	Headlamp inner, RH
114	Headlamp inner, LH
115	Rear window demist switch
116	Rear window demist unit
139	Air conditioning/heater circuit (to)
140	Fuel tank changeover switch
146	Battery condition indicator
147	Oil pressure transmitter
150	Rear window demist warning light
152	Hazard warning light
153	Hazard warning switch
154	Hazard warning flasher unit
159	Split brake test switch and warning lamp
160	Split brake differential switch
164	Ballast resistor
165	Handbrake switch
166	Handbrake warning lamp
178	Radiator cooling fan thermostat
179	Radiator cooling fan motor
180	Automatic gearbox kickdown switch
181	Automatic gearbox kickdown solenoid
182	Brake fluid level switch
183	Ignition amplifier OPUS
185	Aerial motor
186	Aerial motor relay
187	Air conditioning relay
194	Starter solenoid/Ballast coil relay
198	Seat belt switch - driver
199	Seat belt switch - passenger
200	Seat switch - passenger
201	Seat belt warning gearbox switch
202	Seat belt warning lamp
204	Ignition protection relay
205	Fuel pump solenoid
206	Battery cooling fan motor
207	Battery cooling fan thermostat
208	Cigar lighter illumination
209	Left and right-hand dipped beam lamps
210	Panel lamps rheostat
212	Choke warning light switch
213	Choke warning light
215	Window lift master switch
216	Window lift switch, front, RH
217	Window lift switch, rear, RH
218	Window lift switch, front, LH
219	Window lift switch, rear, LH
220	Window lift motor
221	Window lift safety relay
231	Headlamp relay
244	Seat switch - driver
245	Sequential seat belt control unit
250	Inertia switch
251	Windscreen wiper relay
252	Emission control valve solenoid
253	Emission control valve switch
254	Unidirectional parking light switch
255	Fibre optics illumination lamp
256	Blocking diode - brake warning
257	Door lock solenoid
258	Door lock solenoid relay
259	Thermal circuit breaker
260	Door lock switch
285	Thermal override switch

Cable colour code

Code	Colour	Code	Colour
B =	Black	M =	Medium
D =	Dark	N =	Brown
G =	Green	O =	Orange
K =	Pink	P =	Purple
L =	Light	R =	Red
S =	Slate		
U =	Blue		
W =	White		
Y =	Yellow		

Fig. 10.83. Wiring diagram - 2.8 Litre RHD from chassis number 1G4159; 2.8 Litre LHD from chassis number 1G52013; 4.2 Litre LHD from chassis number 1L53097; 4.2 Litre RHD from chassis number 1L55562; 4.2 Litre LHD from chassis number 1L53097

Fig. 10.83. Wiring diagram - 2.8 Litre RHD from chassis number 1G4159; 2.8 Litre LHD from chassis number 1G52013; 4.2 Litre RHD from chassis number 1L5562; 4.2 Litre LHD from chassis number 1L53097

#	Description	#	Description	#	Description
1	Alternator	49	Reverse lamp switch	183	Ignition amplifier OPUS
3	Battery	50	Reverse lamps	185	Aerial motor
4	Starter solenoid	54	Foglamp RH	186	Aerial motor relay
5	Starter motor	55	Foglamp LH	187	Air conditioning relay
6	Lighting switch	56	Clock	194	Starter solenoid/Ballast coil relay
7	Headlamp dip switch	57	Cigar lighter	198	Seat belt switch - driver
8	Headlamp outer, RH	59	Interior lights switch	199	Seat belt switch - passenger
9	Headlamp outer, LH	60	Radio	200	Seat switch - passenger
10	Main beam warning lamp	61	Horn relay	201	Seat belt warning gearbox switch
11	Side lamp RH	64	Bi-metal instrument voltage stabiliser	202	Seat belt warning lamp
12	Side lamp LH	65	Boot light - switch	204	Ignition protection relay
14	Panel lamps	66	Boot light	205	Fuel pump solenoid
15	Number plate lamps	67	Line fuse	206	Battery cooling fan motor
16	Stop and tail lamp RH	75	Automatic gearbox safety	207	Battery cooling fan thermostat
17	Stop and tail lamp LH	77	Electric windscreen washer	208	Cigar lighter illumination
18	Stop lamp switch	78	Electric windscreen washer switch	209	Left and right-hand dipped beam lamps
20	Interior lights	95	Revolution counter	210	Panel lamps rheostat
21	Door switch RH	101	Map light switch	212	Choke warning light switch
22	Door switch LH	102	Map light	213	Choke warning light
23	Horns	113	Headlamp inner, RH	215	Window lift master switch
24	Horn push	114	Headlamp inner, LH	216	Window lift switch, front, RH
25	Flash unit	115	Rear window demist switch	217	Window lift switch, rear, RH
26	Direction indicator switch	116	Rear window demist unit	218	Window lift switch, front, LH
27	Direction indicator warning lamps	139	Air conditioning/heater circuit (to)	219	Window lift switch, rear, LH
28	Flasher lamp, front, RH	140	Fuel tank changeover switch	220	Window lift motor
29	Flasher lamp, front, LH	146	Battery condition indicator	221	Window lift safety relay
30	Flasher lamp, rear, RH	147	Oil pressure transmitter	231	Headlamp relay
31	Flasher lamp, rear, LH	150	Rear window demist warning light	244	Seat switch - driver
34	Fuel gauge	152	Hazard warning light	245	Sequential seat belt control unit
35	Fuel gauge tank unit	153	Hazard warning switch	250	Inertia switch
36	Windscreen wiper switch	154	Hazard warning flasher unit	251	Windscreen wiper relay
37	Windscreen wiper motor	159	Split brake test switch and warning lamp	252	Emission control valve solenoid
38	Ignition switch	160	Split brake differential switch	253	Emission control valve switch
39	Ignition coil	164	Ballast resistor	254	Unidirectional parking light switch
40	Distributor	165	Handbrake switch	255	Fibre optics illumination lamp
41	Fuel pump	166	Handbrake warning lamp	256	Blocking diode - brake warning
42	Oil pressure switch	178	Radiator cooling fan thermostat	257	Door lock solenoid
43	Oil pressure warning lamp or gauge	179	Radiator cooling fan motor	258	Door lock solenoid relay
44	Ignition warning lamp	180	Automatic gearbox kickdown switch	259	Thermal circuit breaker
46	Water temperature gauge	181	Automatic gearbox kickdown solenoid	260	Door lock switch
47	Water temperature transmitter	182	Brake fluid level switch	285	Thermal override switch

Cable colour code

B	=	Black	M	=	Medium
D	=	Dark	N	=	Brown
G	=	Green	O	=	Orange
K	=	Pink	P	=	Purple
L	=	Light	R	=	Red
			S	=	Slate
			U	=	Blue
			W	=	White
			Y	=	Yellow

Fig. 10.84. Wiring diagram - Series II models

Fig. 10.84. Wiring diagram - Series II models

No.	Description
1	Alternator
3	Battery
4	Starter solenoid
5	Starter motor
6	Lighting switch
7	Headlamp dip switch
8	Headlamp outer, RH
9	Headlamp outer, LH
10	Main beam warning lamp
11	Side lamp RH
12	Side lamp LH
14	Panel lamps
15	Number plate lamps
16	Stop and tail lamp RH
17	Stop and tail lamp LH
18	Stop lamp switch
20	Interior lights
21	Door switch RH
22	Door switch LH
23	Horns
24	Horn push
25	Flash unit
26	Direction indicator switch
27	Direction indicator warning lamps
28	Flasher lamp, front, RH
29	Flasher lamp, front, LH
30	Flasher lamp, rear, RH
31	Flasher lamp, rear, LH
34	Fuel gauge
35	Fuel gauge tank unit
36	Windscreen wiper switch
37	Windscreen wiper motor
38	Ignition switch
39	Ignition coil
40	Distributor
41	Fuel pump
42	Oil pressure switch
43	Oil pressure warning lamp
44	Ignition warning lamp
46	Water temperature gauge
47	Water temperature transmitter
49	Reverse lamp switch
50	Reverse lamps
54	Foglamp RH
55	Foglamp LH
56	Clock
57	Cigar lighter
59	Interior lights switch
60	Radio
61	Horn relay
64	Bi-metal instrument voltage stabiliser
65	Boot light - switch
66	Boot light
67	Line fuse
75	Automatic gearbox safety
77	Electric windscreen washer
78	Electric windscreen washer switch
95	Revolution counter
101	Map light switch
102	Map light
113	Headlamp inner, RH
114	Headlamp inner, LH
115	Rear window demist switch
116	Rear window demist unit
139	Air conditioning/heater circuit (to)
140	Fuel tank changeover switch
146	Battery condition indicator
147	Oil pressure transmitter
150	Rear window demist warning light
152	Hazard warning light
153	Hazard warning switch
154	Hazard warning flasher unit
159	Split brake test switch and warning lamp
160	Split brake differential switch
164	Ballast resistor
165	Handbrake switch
166	Handbrake warning lamp
178	Radiator cooling fan thermostat
179	Radiator cooling fan motor
180	Automatic gearbox kickdown switch
181	Automatic gearbox kickdown solenoid
182	Brake fluid level switch
183	Ignition amplifier OPUS
185	Aerial motor
186	Aerial motor relay
187	Air conditioning relay
194	Starter solenoid/Ballast coil relay
198	Seat belt switch - driver
199	Seat belt switch - passenger
200	Seat switch - passenger
201	Seat belt warning gearbox switch
202	Seat belt warning lamp
204	Ignition protection relay
205	Fuel pump solenoid
206	Battery cooling fan motor
207	Battery cooling fan thermostat
208	Cigar lighter illumination
209	Left and right-hand dipped beam lamps
210	Panel lamps rheostat
212	Choke warning light switch
213	Choke warning light
215	Window lift master switch
216	Window lift switch, front, RH
217	Window lift switch, rear, RH
218	Window lift switch, front, LH
219	Window lift switch, rear, LH
220	Window lift motor
221	Window lift safety relay
231	Headlamp relay
244	Seat switch - driver
245	Sequential seat belt control unit
250	Inertia switch
251	Windscreen wiper relay
252	Emission control valve solenoid
253	Emission control valve switch
254	Unidirectional parking light switch
255	Fibre optics illumination lamp
256	Blocking diode - brake warning
257	Door lock solenoid
258	Door lock solenoid relay
259	Thermal circuit breaker
260	Door lock switch
285	Thermal override switch

Cable colour code

B = Black	M = Medium	S = Slate	
D = Dark	N = Brown	U = Blue	
G = Green	O = Orange	W = White	
K = Pink	P = Purple	Y = Yellow	
L = Light	R = Red		

Chapter 11 Suspension and steering

Contents

Specifications

Front suspension

Type	Independent with wishbones, coil springs and telescopic shock absorbers and anti-roll bar
Castor angle	$2\frac{1}{4}° \pm \frac{1}{4}°$ positive
Camber angle	$\frac{1}{2}° \pm \frac{1}{4}°$ positive
Front wheel toe-in	1/16 to 1/8 in (1.6 to 3.2 mm)
Steering axis inclination	$1\frac{1}{2}°$

Rear suspension

Type	Independent with wishbone, radius arm and dual coil springs with telescopic shock absorbers
Coil spring free-length	10.59 in (26.9 cm)
Identification colour	Blue/red
Camber angle	$\frac{3}{4}° \pm \frac{1}{4}°$ negative
Wheel alignment	Parallel $\pm$ 1/32 in (0.08 mm)

Steering

Type	Power assisted (except 2.8 litre standard) rack and pinion with collapsible type column
Number of turns lock-to-lock	3 1/3
Turning circle:	
Standard wheelbase	36 ft (11 metres)
Long wheelbase	38 ft (11.6 metres)

Wheels and tyres

Roadwheels	Ventilated pressed steel 15 in diameter
Tyres	Radial ply E70VR15SP sport

Pressures (2.8 litre)*:

	Front	Rear
Driver and two passengers, speeds up to 100 mph (160 kph)	24 lb/sq in (1.68 kg/sq cm)	26 lb/sq in (1.8 kg/sq cm)
Full load plus luggage, speeds up to 100 mph (160 kph)	24 lb/sq in (1.68 kg/sq cm)	30 lb/sq in (2.1 kg/sq cm)

Pressures (3.4 and 4.2 litre)*:

	Front	Rear
Driver and two passengers, speeds up to 100 mph (160 kph)	25 lb/sq in (1.75 kg/sq cm)	26 lb/sq in (1.8 kg/sq cm)
Full load plus luggage, speeds up to 100 mph (160 kph)	25 lb/sq in (1.75 kg/sq cm)	30 lb/sq in (2.1 kg/sq cm)

*Where sustained speeds of 100 mph (160 kph) are maintained, increase the above pressures by (2.8 litres) 4 lb/sq in (0.28 kg/sq cm) and (3.4 and 4.2 litres) by 6 lb/sq in (0.42 kg/sq cm).

Torque wrench settings

	lb ft	Nm
Front suspension		
Stub axle to stub axle carrier	85	118
Steering arm to stub axle carrier	50	69
Disc to hub	35	48
Caliper to stub axle carrier	55	76
Upper swivel balljoint to stub axle carrier	50	69
Lower swivel balljoint to lower wishbone	50	69
Upper wishbone pivot shaft nuts	50	69
Lower wishbone pivot shaft nuts	45	62
Upper swivel balljoint to wishbone	30	41
Upper pivot shaft to crossmember	50	69
Spring pan bolts	30	41
Shock absorber mounting bracket	30	41
Shock absorber upper mounting	30	41
Shock absorber lower mounting	34	47
Buffers to spring pan	18	25
Upper wishbone rebound rubbers	18	25
Anti-roll bar bracket to body	30	41
Anti-roll bar to link and link to wishbone	18	25
Suspension crossmember clamp bolt	30	41
Suspension crossmember front mounting bolt	100	138
Vee mounting to body	25	35
Vee mounting to crossmember	25	35
Rear suspension		
Tie-plate to crossbeam bolts	18	25
Inner pivot bracket to final drive unit	60	83
Final drive to crossbeam	75	104
Caliper mounting bolts	50	69
Wishbone inner pivot shaft nuts	50	69
Wishbone outer pivot shaft nuts	95	132
Halfshaft inner flange bolts	50	69
Halfshaft to hub carrier	100	138
Radius rods to wishbone	65	90
Radius rods to body	40	55
Radius rod safety strap bolts	40	55
Radius rod safety strap to floor panel	30	41
Shock absorber upper mounting	35	48
Shock absorber lower mounting	35	48
Vee mounting to body	30	41
Vee mounting to cross beam	18	25
Bump stop rubber to body	18	25
Steering		
Pinion housing cover plate	18	25
Rack balljoints	50	69
Trackrod-end locknuts	140	193
Trackrod-end balljoint to steering arm	45	62
Steering gear mounting bolts	18	25
Universal joint pinch bolts	18	25
Steering wheel to shaft	28	39
Steering column to lower bracket	18	25
Lower column to body	7	10
Column to upper bracket	18	25
Fluid pipe adaptor on rack housing	50	69
Wheels		
Roadwheel nuts	45	62

1 General description

The front suspension assembly comprises a pressed steel crossmember to which is attached the steering mechanism and the upper and lower suspension wishbones.

The front suspension incorporates coil springs, hydraulic telescopic shock absorbers and an anti-roll bar fitted between the two lower wishbones. Series 2 cars have gas-pressurised hydraulic shock absorbers.

The rear suspension assembly also comprises a pressed steel crossmember, rubber mounted to the body and located by radius arms. The open driveshafts are located in the transverse plane by two links. The suspension incorporates four coil springs which enclose hydraulic telescopic shock absorbers. Series 2 cars have gas-filled shock absorbers.

The steering gear is of rack and pinion type with power assistance on all models except earlier Standard Jaguar 2.8 versions on which power steering was optionally available only. The steering column is of collapsible type incorporating shear plugs and a universal joints.

Fig. 11.1. Sectional view of one side of the front suspension

2 Maintenance and inspection

1   At the intervals specified in 'Routine Maintenance' at the beginning
of this manual, apply grease to the four top and bottom swivel
balljoints of the front suspension. When sufficient grease has been
injected, a small nylon plug on the top of the balljoint will lift (photos).
2   Remove the hub caps from the front roadwheels and apply the
grease gun to the exposed nipple. A bleed hole is provided to indicate
when sufficient grease has been injected (photo).
3   Check and adjust the front hub bearings (Section 5) and the front
wheel alignment (Section 31).
4   Grease the inner and outer pivot bearings of the rear suspension.
Remove the rear hub grease plug and fill (but do not pressurise) with
grease (photos).
5   Check the reservoir oil level in the steering pump and lubricate
sparingly the rack and pinion assembly using the nipple provided
(photos).
6   Give four or five strokes of the grease gun to the trackrod-end
grease nipple (photo).
7   Check the security of all suspension and steering nuts and bolts,
examine rubber dust excluders and gaiters for splits or cuts and renew
as necessary. Check steering linkage and balljoints for wear and adjust
or renew as described in this Chapter.

3 Front shock absorbers - removal, testing and refitting

1   The shock absorbers should be removed and tested whenever (i)
the cornering or roadholding characteristics of the car appear to have
deteriorated, (ii) there is evidence of oil on the shock absorber casing or
at 30,000 mile (48,000 km) intervals.
2   To remove a shock absorber, disconnect the upper mounting nuts
and cushions which are accessible within the engine compartment.

Fig. 11.2. Front shock absorber lower mounting disconnected (Sec. 3)

3   Unscrew and remove, the self-locking nut from the lower mounting
and withdraw the bolt.
4   Compress the shock absorber and remove it from the car.
5   Grip the shock absorber lower mounting in the jaws of a vice so
that the shock absorber is held vertically. Now fully extend and contract
the unit ten or twelve times. If there is any lack of resistance in either
direction or seizure, then the unit (which is sealed) must be renewed.
Never attempt to dismantle a shock absorber, particularly the
gas-pressurised type used on Series 2 cars.
6   Refitting the shock absorber is a reversal of removal but if the
original unit is being installed, check the rubber bushes and cushions
for deterioration and renew, if necessary.

2.1A Front suspension upper balljoint grease nipple

2.1B Front suspension lower balljoint grease nipple

2.2 Front hub grease nipple

2.4A Rear suspension inner pivot grease nipple

2.4B Rear suspension outer pivot grease nipple

2.4C Rear hub grease plug hole

2.5A Power steering reservoir

2.5B Steering rack grease nipple

2.6 Track rod end grease nipple

4 Anti-roll bar - removal and refitting

1   Place the car over a pit or raise and support it securely on stands placed under its front end.

2   Remove the two self-locking nuts which secure the anti-roll bar link to the bracket on the front suspension lower wishbone.

3   Remove the four setscrews which secure the keeper plates to the front crossmember. Lift the anti-roll bar away.

4   The link arm bush can be renewed by pressing it out of the link arm eye. The rubber support bushes are split to enable them to be removed easily. Their splits should face the rear of the car.

5   Refitting is a reversal of removal but do not fully tighten the nuts and setscrews until the weight of the car has been lowered onto the roadwheels.

5 Front hub - overhaul and adjustment

1   Apply the handbrake fully, jack-up the front of the car and remove the front roadwheel.

2   Remove the front disc caliper (see Chapter 9).

3   Prise off the dust cap from the end of the hub and extract the split pin from the castellated nut.

4   Unscrew and remove the castellated nut and thrust washer and pull the hub assembly from the stub axle.

5   Prise out the oil seal and withdraw the inner races of the tapered roller bearings. The outer tracks can be drifted from the hub if new bearings are to be fitted.

6   If the original bearings are being refitted, clean the races and dry them.

Fig. 11.3. Exploded view of the front suspension

1	Crossmember	20	Buffer	39	Insert	58	Split pin
2	Flexible mounting	21	Castellated nut	40	Spigot	59	Castellated nut
3	Flexible bush	22	Split pin	41	Ballpin	60	End cap
4	Setscrew	23	Washer	42	Ball socket	61	Locknut
6	Upper wishbone arm	24	Pivot shaft	43	Shims	62	Nut
7	Bush	25	Keeper plate	44	Cap	63	Washer
8	Washer	26	Flexible bush	45	Washer	64	Cushion
9	Self-locking nut	27	Clamp	46	Nipple	65	Cup washers
10	Shim (camber adjusting)	28	Anti-roll bar	47	Lockplate	66	Spacer
11	Pivot shaft	29	Flexible bush	48	Bolt	67	Shock absorber
12	Washer	30	Link	49	Stub axle carrier	68	Bracket
13	Bolt	31	Washer	50	Water deflector	69	Bolt
14	Upper wishbone arm	32	Cushion	51	Stub axle	70	Bracket
15	Washer	33	Distance piece	52	Oil seal	71	Bump stop
16	Self-locking nut	34	Cushion	53	Water deflector	72	Lower wishbone
17	Shim (castor adjusting)	35	Washer	54	Inner bearing	73	Spring pan
18	Upper balljoint	36	Steering arm	55	Front hub	74	Spring
19	Distance piece	37	Dust excluder	56	Outer bearing		
		38	Retaining ring	57	'D' washer		

7 Apply grease to the bearing racks and races, install them to the hub and fit a new oil seal.

8 Refit the hub to the stub axle and screw on the castellated nut with its thrust washer finger-tight.

9 Tighten the nut until while turning the hub at the same time, its rotation is felt to be slightly restricted. Unscrew the nut between one and two flats and insert a new split pin.

10 The correct endfloat of a front hub bearing is between 0.003 and **0.005 in (0.08 and 0.13 mm)** which should ideally be checked on a dial gauge.

11 Apply grease to the hub grease nipple, as described in Section 2, refit the dust cap, install the caliper and bleed the front hydraulic circuit.

12 Refit the roadwheel and lower the car to the ground.

---

6 Front coil spring - removal and refitting

1 A coil spring compressor will be needed for this operation. A suitable tool can be made up from a length of rod suitably threaded using nuts and large washers or crosspieces.

2 With the coil spring compressed, remove the six setscrews and lockwashers which secure the seat pan to the lower wishbone.

3 Slowly release the spring compressor until the tension of the coil

Fig. 11.4. Typical coil spring compressor (Sec. 6)

Fig. 11.5. Front suspension upper swivel balljoint and castor control shims (Sec. 8)

spring is relieved. Remove the compressor, spring and seat pan. On 4.2 litre models, packing pieces may be found on top of the spring or in the spring pan. These are used to adjust side-to-side riding height.
4   Refitting is a reversal of removal but align the seat pan holes with the tapped holes in the lower wishbone by using pilot studs. Withdraw these once the spring is installed.

7   Stub axle carrier - removal and refitting

1   Raise the front of the car by placing a jack under the lower wishbone. Remove the roadwheel.
2   Remove the brake caliper (Chapter 9).
3   Remove the hub/disc assembly (Section 5).
4   Remove the self-locking nut which secures the upper balljoint to the stub axle carrier.
5   Remove the nut which secures the lower balljoint to the lower wishbone.
6   Using a suitable extractor, separate the upper and lower balljoints

and withdraw the stub axle carrier.
7   Refitting is a reversal of removal.

8   Front suspension upper swivel balljoint - removal and refitting

1   The front suspension upper wishbone balljoint is a sealed unit and if worn must be renewed as a unit.
2   To remove the balljoint, jack-up the car under the lower wishbone and remove the roadwheel.
3   Remove the bolts which secure the balljoint to the upper wishbone. Take great care to retain the packing pieces and shims and to record their locations precisely as they control the castor angle.
4   Remove the self-locking nut which secures the balljoint to the stub axle carrier. Use a suitable balljoint separator to disconnect the balljoint from the stub axle carrier.
5   During the foregoing operation, restrict the movement of the stub axle carrier by tying it with a piece of wire to prevent strain on the brake flexible hose.
6   Refitting is a reversal of removal but make sure that the shims are returned to their original positions and that the balljoint securing bolts have their heads nearer the front of the car.

9   Front suspension lower swivel balljoint - overhaul and adjustment

1   Remove the stub axle carrier complete with balljoint as described in Section 7.
2   Remove the retaining ring and withdraw the flexible gaiter from the balljoint.
3   Extract the insert from around the taper pin.
4   Flatten the tab washers and remove the four setscrews which secure the ball pin cap to the stub axle carrier.
5   Remove the cap, shims, ball pin socket and the ball pin.
6   Renew any worn components and reassemble and re-shim in the following way.
7   The correct clearance of the ball pin in its socket is between 0.004 and 0.006 in (0.10 and 0.15 mm). Select shims which are available in two thicknesses until with the ball cap fully tightened, the ball pin can be moved stiffly by hand pressure.
8   Refit the stub axle carrier complete with the balljoint, as described in Section 7, and then grease the joint as described in Section 2.

10 Front suspension lower wishbone - removal and refitting

1   Remove the coil spring, as described in Section 6.
2   Remove the stub axle carrier, as described in Section 7.
3   Extract the split pin, castellated nut and washer from one end of the lower wishbone pivot shaft. Drift out the shaft.
4   The flexible bushes can be pressed out of the wishbone eyes and new ones installed if they are worn. Use soapy water or a spot of hydraulic fluid to lubricate the bushes when installing them. Check that the bushes project equally on each side of the eye.
5   Reassembly is a reversal of dismantling but do not fully tighten the pivot nut until the weight of the car has been lowered onto the roadwheel

11 Front suspension upper wishbone - removal, dismantling and refitting

1   Raise the car by placing a jack under the lower wishbone and remove the front roadwheel.
2   Remove the self-locking nut and separate the balljoint separator.
3   Tie the stub axle carrier to the suspension crossmember to prevent strain on the flexible brake hose.
4   Remove the two bolts which secure the upper wishbone pivot shaft to the crossmember. Take great care to retain and identify the locations of the shims as these control the camber angle and they must be returned to their original positions.
5   Withdraw the upper wishbone assembly.
6   Remove the self-locking nuts and their plain washers and withdraw the wishbone arms from the pivot shaft.
7   Release the locknuts and unscrew the rebound buffers from the wishbone.
8   The flexible bushes can be renewed after pressing them from the

H.5620

Fig. 11.6. Exploded view of front suspension lower swivel balljoint (Sec. 9)

1	Nut	8	Lower seat
2	Washer	9	Shims
3	Dust excluding boot	10	Cap
4	Boot retaining clip	11	Washer
5	Insert	12	Grease nipple
6	Upper seat	13	Lockplate
7	Ballpin	14	Bolts

wishbone eyes. Use soapy water or a smear of hydraulic brake fluid to facilitate pressing in the new ones.
9   Reassembly and refitting are reversal of removal and dismantling but do not tighten the castellated nuts which hold the wishbone arms to the pivot shaft until the weight of the car has once again been lowered onto the roadwheels.

12 Front suspension assembly - removal and installation

1   If major operations are to be carried out to the front suspension, it may be advantageous to remove the suspension assembly complete.
2   Disconnect the battery.
3   Jack-up the car under the suspension crossmember and remove both front roadwheels.
4   Support the car bodyframe on blocks or axle stands placed adjacent to the front jacking points. Make sure that there is at least 16 in (40 cm) clearance under the front of the car in order to be able to withdraw the suspension assembly. Do not remove the jack from under the front crossmember.
5   With a suitable hoist, take the weight of the engine without distorting the engine flexible mountings.
6   Disconnect the brake pipes at the unions on the wing valances within the engine compartment. Release the locknuts on the brake flexible pipe end fittings and pull the flexible pipes through the holes in the valances so that the pipes are under the wings. Plug all open brake pipes.
7   Disconnect the power steering flexible pipes from the steering unit. Seal the openings.
8   Detach the anti-roll bar mountings from the bodyframe.
9   Disconnect the shock absorber top mountings.
10 Remove the pinch bolt which secures the steering column lower universal joint to the steering pinion shaft.
11 Disconnect the leads from the horns.
12 Remove the nuts which secure the suspension assembly to the rear mounting rubbers. Note that the bolts are bonded to the rubbers and cannot be separated.
13 Remove the two nuts which secure the engine front mounting brackets to the support rubbers.
14 Remove the two self-locking nuts from the suspension assembly front mountings and drive out the bolts.
15 Lower the jack under the suspension crossmember and withdraw it forward from the car.
     Take great care when separating the steering column lower universal joint. Never strike it to release it from the pinion splines or the steering column shear plugs may be damaged. Prise the universal joint clamp open with a screwdriver to ease its removal.
16 Installation is a reversal of removal but the column and rack pinion will require alignment, as described in Section 26, also bleed the power steering and hydraulic brake circuits. If the suspension assembly mounting bushes are worn they can be renewed without removing the assembly. Always renew bushes in pairs, never one side only.

13 Rear spring and shock absorber - removal and refitting

1   Remove the self-locking nut from the end of the shock absorber lower mounting pivot pin.
2   Support the suspension wishbone with a jack and drive out the pivot pin.
3   Remove the spacer from the front shock absorber.
4   Disconnect the shock absorber upper mounting from the rear crossmember and withdraw the shock absorber/coil spring.
5   The coil spring must now be compressed so that the lower split type retainer can be removed and the spring removed in a downward direction.
6   Test the shock absorber as described in Section 3, paragraph 5.
7   Renew the mounting bushes if the original ones are worn.
8   Refitting is a reversal of removal.

14 Rear hubs - removal, overhaul and refitting

1   The operations are described in Chapter 8, Section 2 in conjunction with the axleshafts.

15 Rear suspension radius arm - removal and refitting

1   Jack-up and support the centre of the rear suspension unit.
2   Cut the locking wire from the radius arm safety strap and bolt.
3   Unscrew the two bolts which secure the safety strap to the body floor.
4   Unscrew the radius arm securing bolt and remove the safety strap.

Fig. 11.7. Rear shock absorber mountings (Sec. 13)

Fig. 11.8. Removing a rear suspension radius arm bush (Sec. 15)

Fig. 11.9. Tie plate to cross beam securing bolts (Sec. 16)

Fig. 11.10. Tie plate to inner pivot mounting bracket bolts (Sec. 16)

5   Withdraw the radius arm from the mounting post on the body.
6   Unscrew the self-locking nut which is nearest the front of the shock absorber lower pivot pin. Drive the pin far enough to clear the forward shock absorber and spacer. Extract the spacer, bend back the tabs of the lockwasher and remove the bolt which secures the radius arm to the lower wishbone mounting.
7   Remove the radius arm and examine the flexible bushes for deterioration.
8   Remove one of the self-locking nuts which secure the hub bearing assembly pivot shaft to the wishbone. Drive out the pivot shaft from the wishbone and hub assembly. Remove the self-locking nut and bolt which secure the radius arm to the wisbone and withdraw the radius arm. Check the condition of the mounting rubbers.
9   If inspection has proved the need for renewal of the flexible bushes make sure that the larger bush is fitted so that the two holes in it are in longitudinal alignment with the arm. When installing the smaller bush, make sure that the metal centre sleeve projects equally on each side of the bush.
10   It is recommended that a press is used to remove and install the flexible bushes.
11   Refitting is a reversal of removal but make sure that the radius arm securing bolts are tightened to the specified torque wrench settings. Use new locking wire inserted through the hole in the bolt head and secured round the safety strap.

16 Rear suspension wishbone - removal and installation

1   Drain the oil from the final drive unit, remove the rear suspension

Fig. 11.11. Driving out rear suspension wishbone outer pivot shaft (Sec. 16)

assembly (Section 19) and then invert it on a bench.
2   Remove the six self-locking nuts and bolts which secure the tie-plate to the crossbeam.
3   Now remove the eight self-locking nuts and bolts which secure the tie-plate to the wishbone inner pivot mounting brackets. Remove the tie-plate.
4   Remove one of the self-locking nuts which secure the hub bearing assembly pivot shaft to the wishbone and drive out the pivot shaft.

Fig. 11.12. Exploded view of the rear suspension

1 Crossmember	15 Grease nipple	29 Hub	43 Joint cover (outer)
2 Flexible mounting	16 Outer pivot shaft	30 Outer oil seal	44 Coil spring
3 Inner pivot mounting	17 Sleeve	31 Ring	45 Packing ring
4 Shims	18 Shim	32 Outer bearing	46 Shock absorber
5 Bracing plate	19 Bearing	33 Inner bearing	47 Dust shield
6 Wishbone	20 Ring	34 Spacer	48 Flexible bush
7 Inner pivot shaft	21 Oil seal	35 Oil seal	49 Seat
8 Spacer tube	22 Oil seal retainer	36 Ring	50 Retainer
9 Spacer tube	23 Spacer	37 Halfshaft	51 Shock absorber lower
10 Needle bearing	24 Washer	38 Halfshaft flange	mounting shaft
11 Thrust washer	25 Shim	39 Splined yoke	52 Bump stop
12 Seal	26 Hub carrier	40 Universal joint	53 Radius arm
13 Retainer	27 Grease nipple	41 Shim (camber control)	54 Flexible bush
14 Thrust washer	28 Grease retaining cap	42 Joint cover (inner)	55 Flexible bush
			56 Safety strap

5   Separate the hub carrier from the wishbone, noting any shims and their location so that they will be returned to their original positions.

6   The use of a rod as a dummy pivot shaft will keep the shims together. Place a piece of masking tape over each of the oil seals to prevent them being displaced.

7   Knock back the lockwasher tabs and withdraw the bolt which secures the radius arm to the lower wishbone mountings.

8   Remove the self-locking nut which secures the wishbone pivot shaft to the crossbeam.

9   Drive the inner pivot shaft out of the wishbone and inner pivot

mounting bracket.

10 Withdraw the wishbone assembly and collect the four outer thrust washers, inner thrust washers, oil seals and their retainers. Renew the oil seals if they have deteriorated.

11 Remove the two bearing tubes. There is no need to remove the spacer which is located between the inner pivot mounting bracket unless the mounting bracket is being renewed. If it must be removed, tap it out. The needle rollers can be extracted by tapping the cages out of the wishbone and then extracting the needle roller spacer.

12 If the needle rollers have been removed from the larger fork of

the wishbone, press one of the roller cages into position so that the numbers on the cage face outwards. Press in the second cage. Repeat the operations on the opposite side of the wishbone.

13 Insert the bearing tubes, apply grease to the four outer thrust washers, oil seals, retainers and locate them on the wishbone.

14 Offer up the wishbone to the inner pivot mounting bracket so that the radius arm mounting bracket is towards the front of the car. Align the holes and spacers. Insert a rod as a dummy shaft through each side of the crossbeam and wishbone. These rods locate the wishbone, thrust washers, crossbeam and inner pivot mounting bracket and so facilitate installation of the pivot shaft proper. The dummy shaft should be fractionally smaller in diameter than the pivot shaft itself.

15 Tap the pivot shaft into position, having smeared it with grease. As it passes through the crossbeam, the wishbone and the inner pivot mounting bracket, the temporary rods will be displaced from the opposite end. Keep the rods and shaft in contact at all times otherwise a spacer or thrust washer may drop out of position.

16 With the wishbone inner pivot shaft installed, tighten the two self-locking nuts to a torque of 50 lb/ft (69 Nm).

17 Install the eight bolts which secure the tie plate to the inner pivot mounting bracket then refit the six bolts which secure the tie plate to the crossbeam.

18 Refit the radius arm to the wishbone as described in Section 15.

19 Remove the tap which was used to hold the oil seal tracks in position and offer up the wishbone/hub assembly.

20 Again using a rod as a dummy shaft, align the wishbone hub assembly oil seal tracks and spacers. Apply grease to the wishbone outer pivot shaft and gently tap it into position so displacing the dummy shaft.

21 Slide the pivot shaft through the wishbone and hub carrier. Using feeler blades, check the clearance between the hub carrier and the wishbone. Where necessary, install shims between the hub carrier and the wishbone to centralise the hub carrier. Tighten the nuts on the pivot shaft to a torque of 95 lb/ft (132 Nm).

22 Refit the rear suspension assembly.

23 The rear suspension camber angle should be checked after a major overhaul (see Section 32).

24 Refill the final drive unit with specified oil.

25 Lubricate the wishbone grease nipples.

Fig. 11.13. Installing rear suspension wishbone inner pivot shaft (propeller shaft removed for clarity) (Sec. 16)

Fig. 11.14. Checking clearance between hub carrier oil seal retainer and wishbone of rear suspension (Sec. 16)

---

17 Rear suspension wishbone outer pivot - dismantling, reassembly and bearing adjustment

1 Support the hub carrier and wishbone securely.

2 Remove one of the self-locking nuts which secure the outer pivot shaft.

3 Drive out the pivot shaft and retain any shims which may be located between the hub carrier and the wishbone.

4 Separate the hub carrier and the wishbone.

5 Remove the oil seal retainer and prise out the oil seals.

6 Remove the inner races of the tapered roller bearings by tapping them out with a drift.

7 Remove the spacers and shims.

8 If new tapered roller bearings have been fitted, it will be necessary to adjust them in the following way.

9 Disconnect the hub from the rear axle halfshaft as described in Chapter 8, Section 2.

10 Refit the inner races for the outer pivot tapered roller bearings. Fit the spacers and a shim pack of known thickness followed by the tapered roller bearings and oil seals.

11 The bearing adjustment is controlled by shims which are located between the two pivot shaft spacer tubes.

12 To calculate the shims required to provide the specified preload of the outer pivot tapered roller bearings, drill a hole in a piece of steel plate and secure the plate in the jaws of a vice. Bolt the pivot shaft to the plate.

13 Slide an oil seal retainer onto the shaft and then install the outer pivot assembly to the shaft but without any oil seals and including an excess of shims between the spacer tubes.

14 Place an inner wishbone fork outer thrust washer onto the fulcrum shaft so that it abuts the oil seal retainer. Fill the remaining space on the shaft with washers and screw on a nut to a torque of 95 lb/ft (132 Nm).

15 Press the hub carrier assembly towards the steel support plate using a rotating motion in order to settle the tapered roller bearings. Maintain a steady hand pressure against the hub carrier and using a

Fig. 11.15. Checking rear suspension wishbone outer pivot tapered bearing endfloat (Sec. 11)

feeler blade, measure the clearance between the large diameter washer and the machined face of the hub carrier.

16 Subtract this measurement from the thickness of the shim pack which was included between the spacer tubes, or subtract the thickness of the shim pack from the clearance measured or the other way round, whichever is the greater.

The result indicates the bearing preload. The specified preload should be between 0.000 to 0.002 in (0.00 to 0.05 mm) and the shim pack should be adjusted as necessary to bring the actual preload into line with that specified.

17 Refit the hub carrier to the axleshaft, install new oil seals (lips inwards) and then fit the pivot shaft into position in the hub carrier.
18 Offer up the hub carrier to the wishbone. Ease the dummy shaft through the wishbone in conjunction with the pivot shaft. Using feeler blades, measure the gap between the oil seal retainer and the wishbone.
19 Install shims as necessary to centralise the hub carrier in the wishbone fork and to prevent the ends of the fork from closing as the pivot shaft nuts are tightened to their specified torque wrench settings.
20 It will be found easier to install the wishbone if a dummy shaft is passed through the hub carrier before offering the wishbone to the carrier.
21 Refitting is otherwise a reversal of removal. Apply grease to the lubrication nipples on completion.

18 Rear suspension wishbone inner pivot mounting bracket - removal and refitting

1   Drain the oil from the final drive unit and remove the rear suspension unit as described in Section 19. Remove the tie-plate as described in Section 16, paragraphs 2 and 3.
2   Remove the self-locking nut from one end of the wishbone inner pivot shaft, drive out the shaft.
3   Withdraw the wishbone forks from between the crossbeam and pivot mounting bracket. Collect the oil seal retainers, oil seals, inner and outer thrust washers and tubes.
4   Cut the lockwire from the two setscrews which secure the inner pivot bracket to the differential unit.
5   Remove the spacer from the mounting bracket.
6   Remove the two setscrews, noting the shims located between the bracket and the differential unit.
7   Remove the wishbone inner pivot mounting bracket.
8   Refitting is a reversal of removal but make sure that the original shims are refitted between the mounting bracket and the differential. If new components have been fitted check the clearance with feeler blades and insert shims as necessary after having passed the pivot shaft through the crossmember and the inner pivot mounting bracket.
9   Tighten the pivot bolt nut to specified torque.
10 Refill the final drive unit.

19 Rear suspension assembly - removal and installation

1   If major operations are to be carried out to the rear suspension, it may be advantageous to remove the suspension assembly complete.
2   Remove the self-tapping screws which secure the exhaust tail pipes to the rear silencers and withdraw the pipes.

H.5633

Fig. 11.16. Checking gap between rear suspension inner pivot bracket and differential casing (Sec. 18)

3   Release the clamps which secure the rear silencers to the intermediate pipes. Remove the rear exhaust silencers.
4   Release the clamps which secure the intermediate pipes to the front silencers. Withdraw the pipes from the suspension assembly.
5   Remove the locking wire from the radius arm safety straps and securing bolts. Remove the bolts which secure the safety strap to the body floor.
6   Remove the radius arm securing bolts and withdraw the safety straps.
7   Withdraw the radius arms from their mounting posts on the body.
8   Place a wooden block (9 x 9 x 1 in/22.8 x 22.8 x 2.54 cm thick) between the rear suspension tie plate and a jack, preferably of trolley type.
9   Now jack-up the rear of the car and position two chassis stands under the bodyframe members just forward of the radius arm mounting posts. Place blocks of wood between the chassis stands and the bodyframe to avoid damage.
10 Remove the rear roadwheels.
11 Disconnect the flexible brake pipe at the support bracket on the body.
12 Disconnect the handbrake cable from the caliper actuating lever which is mounted on the suspension crossbeam. Withdraw the outer cable from the trunnion on the opposite lever.
13 Remove the four bolts which secure the mounting rubbers at the front of the crossbeam to the bodyframe.
14 Remove the nuts and bolts which secure the rear mounting rubbers to the crossbeam.
15 Disconnect the propeller shaft from the differential pinion flange.
16 Lower the rear suspension assembly on the jack and withdraw it from under the car.
17 Installation is a reversal of removal but note the following points:

Renew any mounting rubbers which have deteriorated.
Tighten the radius arm to wishbone bolts after the weight of the car has been lowered onto the roadwheels.
Bleed the brake hydraulic circuit.

20 Trackrod-ends - renewal

1   If wear is found in the trackrod-end balljoints then they must be renewed as sealed assemblies.
2   Unscrew and remove the taper pin nut and separate the balljoint from the steering arm using a suitable extractor or forked wedges.
3   Hold the trackrod-end quite still with an open-ended spanner applied to its flats and unscrew the locknut one quarter of a turn. Hold the trackrod quite still and unscrew the trackrod-end from it. If the bellows are perforated, release their clips and withdraw them.
4   Screw on the new trackrod-end until it almost touches the locknut and then tighten the locknut making sure that the trackrod-end is again supported in an open-ended spanner.
5   Reconnect the trackrod-end to the steering arm.
6   The front wheel alignment must be checked and adjusted, as described in Section 31.
7   It is important that the lengths of the trackrods are equal. If for any reason they have become unequal, set the trackrod-ends on the rods so that the distance between the centre of the trackrod-end balljoint and the face of the inner balljoint is 11½ in (292.1 mm). Release the outer clip on the flexible bellows to measure and it is emphasised that this is an initial front wheel setting and precise alignment must be carried out, as described in Section 31, as soon as possible.
8   Ball pin knock which may be heard when turning right or left may be due to wear in the trackrod inner balljoints. No adjustment can be carried out and new trackrod/ball pin assemblies must be fitted. This work can be carried out without removing the rack from the car as described in the next Section.

21 Trackrod inner ball pin assembly - renewal

1   Disconnect the trackrod outer balljoint from the steering arm.
2   Remove the bellows retaining clip from the rack housing.
3   Peel the bellows back until the inner balljoint is exposed and then flatten the tabs of the lockwasher which secures the balljoint assembly to the rack.
4   Remove the inner balljoint and trackrod and extract the spring.

H.5629

Fig. 11.17. Exploded view of power steering gear

1 Valve and pinion assembly
2 Pipe union seat
3 Pipe union seat
4 'O' ring
5 Seal
6 Gasket

7 Bellows
8 Clip
9 Rack housing
10 Adaptor
11 Seal housing
12 Special 'Chevite' bearing

13 Seal
14 Seal retainer
15 Rack
16 Piston
17 Piston ring
18 'O' ring

19 Shim
20 Circlip
21 Inner balljoint assembly
22 Tab washer
23 Track rod end
24 Track rod end

25 Outlet pipe
26 Inlet pipe
27 Air tran. 'er tube
28 Rack damper assembly

168

Fig. 11.18. Exploded view of the steering upper column (Sec. 23)

1 Column
2 Steering column
3 Cowl support bracket
4 Cowl
5 Upper shaft
6 Cone
7 Grub screw
8 Split collets
9 Horn contact
10 Striker plate
11 Direction indicator switch
12 Switch cover
13 Locknut
14 Washer
15 Nut
16 Lockwasher
17 Steering wheel
18 Screw
19 Circlip

23.3 Removing steering wheel crash pad

23.4A Removing horn ring

23.4B Horn contact plunger and spring

5   Remove the trackrod-end and then discard the worn inner balljoint and trackrod.
6   Install the trackrod-end to the new rod/inner balljoint assembly, setting the components, as described in the preceding Section, paragraph 7.
7   Refit the inner balljoint to the rack, using a new lockwasher.
8   Refit the bellows, reconnect the trackrod-end to the steering arm and check the front wheel alignment (Section 31).

22 Steering gear - adjustment in-situ

1   Should rack rattle occur when travelling over rough surfaces, the rack pad requires adjustment.
2   Release the locknut which secures the rack pad adjusting screw.
3   Screw the rack adjusting screw inwards until a stiff resistance is encountered and then release the screw one flat. Tighten the locknut.

23 Steering wheel - removal and refitting

1   Unscrew the large circular locknut (13) (Fig. 11.18) until the shank at the bottom of the nut is clear of the steering column surround. The safety screw (18) which is now exposed can be extracted.
2   Withdraw the steering wheel complete with the short section of the steering shaft (5).
3   Extract the four self-tapping screws from the underside of the steering wheel hub to release the spoke crash pad (photo).
4   Remove the four self-tapping screws which secure the horn ring to the steering wheel and detach the horn ring (photo). Extract the horn contact plunger and spring (photo).
5   Unscrew the lockwasher (16) and the nut (15), withdraw the steering wheel from the shaft and extract the two halves of the split collet (8).
6   Remove the circlip (19) from the split cone (6) and withdraw the steering shaft.
7   Refitting is a reversal of removal but observe the following points.
    Check that the front roadwheels are in the 'straight-ahead' position and that the spokes of the steering wheel are horixontal before inserting the steering shaft into the upper end of the steering column assembly.
    Refit the safety screw (18) before tightening the locknut (13).
8   The steering wheel attachment components differ slightly on Series 2 cars as shown in Fig. 11.19.

24 Steering upper column - removal and refitting

1   Disconnect the battery.
2   Remove the steering wheel, as described in the preceding Section.
3   Remove the three screws which secure the direction indicator switch and cowl to the outer column.
4   Disconnect the direction indicator switch leads by separating the plug and socket.
5   Remove the speedometer and the tachometer from the instrument panel, as described in Chapter 10.
6   Disconnect the horn switch lead from the contact on the steering

Fig. 11.19. Attachment components of Series 2 steering wheel (Sec. 23)

2   Cushion rubber
3   Retaining plate and screws
4   Adaptor
5   Circlip
6   Hand locknut and grub screw
7   Cone

column.
7   Disconnect the ignition switch leads at the plug and socket connector.
8   Remove the pinch bolt which secures the upper universal joint to the steering column.
9   Remove the two nuts which secure the upper column mounting bracket to the support bracket on the body. Note the location of any packing washers under the bracket, and support the column as the bracket is released.
10 Remove the two nuts which secure the lower mounting bracket to the bulkhead and again note any packing washers which may be located under this bracket.
11 Withdraw the upper column from the universal joint splines. Take great care not to use force on the column or it may collapse due to shearing of the safety plastic plugs. A new column will then be required as no repair is possible.
12 Refitting is a reversal of removal but set the front roadwheels in the straight-ahead position and connect the upper column to the universal joint splines so that the pinch bolt holes are in alignment with the column groove. Tighten the pinch bolt to the specified torque.

25 Steering lower column - removal and refitting

1   Turn the steering wheel until the pinch bolt on the lower universal joint is accessible and then remove it (photo).
2   Reset the front roadwheels in the 'straight-ahead' position.
3   Remove the upper column, as described in the preceding Section.
4   Withdraw the lower column.

Fig. 11.20. Steering lower column components (Sec. 25)

1 Pinch bolt	4 Bush	7 Pinch bolt
2 Bottom universal joint	5 Gaiter	8 Top universal joint
3 Lower column	6 Retaining plate	9 Pinch bolt

25.1 Steering column balljoint arrangement

Fig. 11.21. Special tool being used to align steering gear (Sec. 26)

1 Attachment brackets	3 Checking levers
2 Sliding section	

5   Refitting is a reversal of removal.

---

26 Steering gear - removal and installation

1   Raise the front of the car and support it securely or place the car over a pit.

2   Remove the upper and lower steering columns as described in Sections 24 and 25.

3   Disconnect the fluid pipes from the steering housing and allow the fluid to drain into a clean container. Plug the openings.

4   Disconnect the trackrod-ends from the steering arms, as described in Section 20.

5   Remove the three bolts which secure the steering gear to the bodyframe. Note the position of the two rubber-faced thrust washers and the four plain washers for refitting.

6   Withdraw the steering gear assembly from under the car and collect the two stiffeners which are located inside the support brackets.

7   Installation of the steering gear will require the use of a special alignment tool (JD 36) and if this cannot be borrowed, then the steering gear should be refitted and the car driven to your dealer's to have it aligned at the earliest opportunity.

8   Attach the steering housing to the front suspension assembly but leave the bolts finger-tight.

9   Pull both bellows from the rack housing having first cut the securing wire.

10 The two attachment brackets of the special alignment tool must now be located on the large hexagonal heads of the lower wishbone

pivot shafts (Fig. 11.21).

11 Release the locking screw and move the sliding section of the tool (2) until the slot registers with the weld flange at the front of the suspension member. Lock the tool in this position.

12 Lift the two checking levers (3) until contact is made with one or both rack shafts. Move the position of the steering gear if necessary until both levers make contact. Tighten the three securing bolts fully and remove the tool.

13 Reconnect the flexible bellows and fit new locking wire.

14 Reconnect the fluid lines to the steering housing, refit the upper and lower steering columns.

15 Refill the steering pump reservoir to the 'FULL' mark with clean automatic transmission fluid. Bleed the system, as described in Section 29.

16 Reconnect the trackrod-ends and check the front wheel alignment, as described in Section 31.

27 Steering gear - overhaul

1 The following operations are in respect of power steering gear. On cars with manual steering assemblies, ignore any reference to the hydraulic components.

2 With the steering gear removed from the car, clean away all external dirt.

3 Remove the fluid pipes (25 and 26) (Fig. 11.17).

4 Cut the locking wire and peel back the bellows to expose the inner balljoints.

5 Flatten the tab washer and unscrew and remove the inner ball pin and trackrod as a unit. Do not dismantle th ball pin assembly. Collect the spring and spacer.

6 Remove the rack adjuster pad components.

7 Mark the relative position of the pinion housing to the rack housing also the groove in the pinion to the pinion housing. Note the position of the rack. Remove the three locknuts, remove the valve body and discard the gasket.

8 Any wear or faults occurring in the valve and pinion housing assembly can only be rectified with a new assembly. Where this action is taken then new top bad backing seals will be required, also a joint gasket.

9 Similarly if wear or faults are evident in the rack assembly then a replacement rack housing should be obtained which will contain end cap seals, 'Clevite' bearing and needle bearings.

10 Commence reassembly by placing a new sealing joint gasket over the

three studs in the rack housing.

11 Refit the pinion housing making sure that the marks made before removal are in alignment with the rack in the original relative position.

12 Refit the inner balljoints using new lockplates. Screw on the trackrod-ends and set the trackrod lengths, as described in Section 20.

13 Refit and adjust the rack pad assembly.

14 Reconnect the fluid pipes and then apply grease to the rack ball housings, fit the bellows and their clips.

15 Apply a grease gun to the nipple on the housing and inject 1 oz (28.35g) of grease. Do not inject excessive amounts of grease which would distend the flexible bellows or block the fluid transfer tube.

28 Power steering pump - removal and refitting

1 Disconnect the hose from the outlet at the rear of the pump reservoir. Allow the fluid to drain into a suitable container and then plug the openings.

2 Disconnect the second (high pressure) hose from the reservoir.

3 Disconnect the pump adjusting link from the water pump. Press the pump inwards, lift the jockey pulley against spring pressure and slip the drivebelt from the pump pulley.

4 Pull the pump outwards and disconnect the bottom pivot mounting bolt. Lift the pump and its mounting bracket from the engine compartment.

5 Refit the pump by reversing the removal operations. The pump drivebelt is automatically tensioned by the spring-loaded jockey pulley but when installing the belt, pull the pump fully away from the engine and then tighten the adjuster link bolt.

6 Reconnect the fluid hoses, and fill the reservoir to the full mark on the dipstick with Automatic Transmission fluid. Turn the pump pulley anticlockwise a few revolutions to expel any air which may be trapped in the pump.

7 Bleed the complete system, as described in the next Section.

29 Power steering system - bleeding

1 Check that the pump reservoir is full. Jack-up the front of the car.

2 With the engine idling, turn the steering wheel from lock-to-lock. Do this slowly until any lumpiness in the steering action has disappeared.

3 Top-up the pump reservoir.

Fig. 11.22. Exploded view of the power steering pump (Sec. 30)

1 Reservoir	10 Shaft	19 Spring
2 Dipstick	11 Key	20 End plate
3 Stud	12 Thrust plate	21 Clip
4 Union	13 Rotor	22 'O' ring
5 'O' ring	14 Clip	23 Flow control valve
6 Seal	15 Pump valve	24 Spring
7 Seal	16 Pump ring	25 Oil seal
8 Pump body	17 Pressure plate	
9 'O' ring	18 Pin	

30 Power steering pump - overhaul

1   In the event of a fault occurring or wear taking place, it is recommended that a replacement pump is obtained but where it is preferred to overhaul the original unit, proceed as follows making sure first that spare parts are available.

2   Drain the fluid from the pump and clean off all external dirt.

3   Remove the nut and withdraw the pulley.

4   Secure the pump carefully in the jaws of a vice and then remove the outlet union (4) (Fig. 11.22). Extract the 'O' ring from the recess.

5   Remove the two mounting studs (3) and detach the reservoir from the pump body.

6   Extract the three 'O' rings from the recesses in the pump body.

7   Remove the endplate retaining ring by inserting a pin through the hole in the pump body and then prising out the ring with a screwdriver.

8   Remove the endplate (20) and spring (19) and 'O' ring (22).

9   Remove the flow control valve (23) and spring (24).

10 Remove the Woodruff key (11) and gently tap the end of the shaft until the pressure plate, pump ring, rotor and thrust plate can be withdrawn as an assembly. Remove the pressure plate 'O' ring (22) from the pump body.

11 Separate the components taking care not to damage the pump rotor vanes.

12 Remove the clip (14), withdraw the rotor (13) and thrust plate (12). Extract the shaft oil seal (25).

13 Discard and renew all oil seals and examine components for scoring or grooves. The pump shaft and bush are supplied as a complete assembly. Check that the flow control valve slides freely in its bore, if not, renew it.

14 Commence reassembly, by smearing a new shaft seal with petroleum jelly. Install the seal to the pump body using a piece of tubing. Install the pump shaft, splined end first, from the hub end of the pump body.

15 Install the dowel pins to the pump body and then fit the thrust plate over the pins so that the face with the recesses is uppermost.

16 Fit the rotor to the splined shaft so that the countersunk side is downwards towards the thrust plate. Check that the rotor is free on the splines.

17 Fit the retaining clip to the shaft groove and then fit the pump ring to the dowel pins so that the directional arrow is uppermost.

18 Insert the vanes in the rotor slots so that the rounded end of the vane is facing outwards.

19 Apply petroleum jelly to the pressure plate 'O' ring and fit it into the lowest groove in the pump body. Smear the outside edge of the pressure plate with petroleum jelly and fit it to the dowel pin so that the spring circular recess is uppermost. Push the plate downwards using a piece of tubing applied to its outer edge. Do not tap the plate into position.

20 Install the end plate 'O' ring into its groove in the pump body, first having applied petroleum jelly to it.

21 Fit the spring (19) into the circular groove in the pressure plate.

22 Smear the edge of the endplate with petroleum jelly and place it in position so that the retaining ring is on top. Check that the gap in the clip is not opposite the hole used for removal. Apply pressure until the retaining clip can be sprung into the groove in the body.

23 Insert the valve, spring leading, into the bore in the pump. Locate new 'O' ring seals in position for the reservoir retaining bolts and the outlet union.

24 Smear the large reservoir 'O' ring seal with petroleum jelly and insert it into its groove in the pump body.

25 Fit the reservoir retaining studs, the outlet union and 'O' rings.

26 Refit the Woodruff key, pulley, lockwasher and nut.

Fig. 11.23. Fitting thrust plate to steering pump (Sec. 30)

Fig. 11.24. Fitting rotor to steering pump (Sec. 30)

Fig. 11.25. Installing pump ring (Sec. 30)

Fig. 11.26. Installing vanes to steering pump rotor plate (Sec. 30)

Fig. 11.27. Installing pressure plate to steering pump (Sec. 30)

Fig. 11.28. Installing flow control valve to steering pump (Sec. 30)

Fig. 11.29. Sectional view of power steering pump (Sec. 30)

1	Driving shaft	8	End plate
2	Pump vane	9	Spring
3	Pump ring	10	Pressure plate
4	Body	11	Flow control valve
5	Filler cap	12	Spring
6	Reservoir	13	Thrust plate
7	Oil seal	14	Rotor

31 Steering angles and front wheel alignment

1   Accurate front wheel alignment is essential for good steering and slow tyre wear. Before considering the steering angle, check that the tyres are correctly inflated, that the front wheels are not buckled, the hub bearings are not worn or incorrectly adjusted and that the steering linkage is in good order, without slackness or weat at the joints.

2   Wheel alignment consists of four factors:

Camber, is the angle at which the front wheels are set from the vertical when viewed from the front of the car. Positive camber is the amount (in degrees) that the wheels are tilted outwards at the top from the vertical.

Castor is the angle between the steering axis and a vertical line when viewed from each side of the car. Positive castor is when the steering axis is inclined rearwards.

Steering axis inclination is the angle, when viewed from the front of the car, between the vertical and an imaginary line drawn between the upper and lower suspension swivels.

Toe-in is the amount by which the distance between the front inside edges of the roadwheels (measured at hub height) is less than the diametrically opposite distance measured between the rear inside edges of the front roadwheels.

3   Due to the need for very accurate measuring equipment it is not within the scope of the home mechanic to check steering angles but the method of adjusting them is described in the following paragraphs for reasons of interest.

4   Camber angle is altered by adding or removing shims at the joint of the upper wishbone pivot and the crossmember.

5   Castor angle is altered by transposing shims from one side to the other of the upper wishbone balljoint. Whenever the castor angle is

Fig. 11.30: Location of camber angle shims on front suspension upper wishbone (Sec. 31)

Fig. 11.31. Location of castor angle shims on front suspension upper balljoint (Sec. 31)

altered, the front wheel alignment (toe-in) will need adjusting.

6   Front wheel tracking (toe-in) checks are best carried out with modern setting equipment but a reasonably accurate alternative and adjustment procedure may be carried out as follows:

7   Place the car on level ground with the wheels in the straight-ahead position.

8   Obtain or make a toe-in gauge. One may be easily made from tubing, cranked to clear the sump and bellhousing, having an adjustable nut and setscrew at one end.

9   Using the gauge, measure the distance between the two inner wheel rims at hub height at the rear of the wheels.

10 Rotate the wheels (by pushing the car backwards or forwards) through 180° (half a turn) and again using the gauge, measure the distance of hub height between the two inner wheel rims at the front of the wheels. This measurement should be from 1/16 to 1/8 in (1.6 to 3.2 mm) less than that previously taken at the rear of the wheel and represents the correct toe-in.

11 Where the toe-in is found to be incorrect, slacken the locknuts on each outer trackrod and rotate each trackrod an equal amount until the correct toe-in is obtained. Tighten the locknuts ensuring that the balljoints are held in the centre of their arc of travel during tightening.

12 It cannot be over emphasised that both during initial setting and subsequent adjustment, the effective lengths of the two trackrods must be exactly equal.

32 Rear wheel alignment

1   The rear wheels are adjustable for camber but again due to the need for precise measuring equipment and setting links (tool no. JD21) this work should be left to your Jaguar/Daimler dealer.

2   The camber angle is altered by varying the thickness of the shims which are fitted between the exleshaft inner joint flange and the brake disc.

33 Roadwheels and tyres

1   Whenever the roadwheels are removed it is a good idea to clean the insides of the wheels to remove accumulation of mud and in the case of the front ones, disc pad dust.

2   Check the condition of the wheel for rust and repaint if necessary.

3   Examine the wheel stud holes. If these are tending to become elongated or the dished recesses in which the nuts seat have worn or become overcompressed, then the wheel will have to be renewed.

4   With a roadwheel removed, pick out any embedded flints from the tread and check for splits in the sidewalls or damage to the tyre carcass generally.

5   Where the depth of tread pattern is 1 mm or less, the tyre must be renewed.

6   Rotation of the roadwheels to even out wear is a worthwhile idea if the wheels have been balanced off the car. Include the spare wheel in the rotational pattern.

7   If the wheels have been balanced on the car then they cannot be moved round the car as the balance of wheel, tyre and hub will be upset.

8   It is recommended that wheels are re-balanced halfway through the life of the tyres to compensate for the loss of tread rubber due to wear.

9   Finally, always keep the tyres (including the spare) inflated to the recommended pressures and always replace the dust caps on the tyre valves. Tyre pressures are best checked first thing in the morning when the tyres are cold.

34 Fault diagnosis - suspension and steering

Symptom	Reason/s
Steering feels vague, car wanders and floats at speed	Tyre pressures uneven. Shock absorbers worn. Spring broken. Steering gear balljoints badly worn. Suspension geometry incorrect. Steering mechanism free play excessive. Front suspension and rear axle pick-up points out of alignment.
Stiff and heavy steering	Tyre pressures too low. No grease in swivel joints. No grease in steering and suspension balljoints. Front wheel toe-in incorrect. Suspension geometry incorrect. Steering gear incorrectly adjusted too tightly. Steering column badly misaligned. Loose steering pump belt.
Wheel wobble and vibration	Wheel nuts loose. Front wheels and tyres out of balance. Steering balljoints badly worn. Hub bearings badly worn. Steering gear free play excessive. Front springs weak or broken.
Rattle on rough roads	Worn inner balljoints on ends of rack. Incorrect rack pad adjustment. Worn rack housing bushes.

Chapter 12 Bodywork and fittings

Contents

1 General description

1 The bodywork is of all steel, welded construction in either two or four door body styles. Long wheelbase versions were introduced in 1972 under the Jaguar and Daimler insignia.
2 A full air-conditioning system may be optionally specified on all models.

2 Maintenance - bodywork and underframe

1 The general condition of a car's bodywork is the one thing that significantly affects its value. Maintenance is easy but needs to be regular. Neglect, particularly after minor damage, can lead quickly to further deterioration and costly repair bills. It is important also to keep watch on those parts of the car not immediately visible, for instance the underside, inside all the wheel arches and the lower part of the engine compartment.
2 The basic maintenance routine for the bodywork is washing - preferably with a lot of water, from a hose. This will remove all the loose solids which may have stuck to the car. It is important to flush these off in such a way as to prevent grit from scratching the finish. The wheel arches and underbody need washing in the same way to remove any accumulated mud which will retain moisture and tend to encourage rust. Paradoxically enough, the best time to clean the underbody and wheel arches is in wet weather when the mud is thoroughly wet and soft. In very wet weather the underbody is usually cleaned of large accumulations automatically and this is a good time for inspection.
3 Periodically it is a good idea to have the whole of the underside of the car steam cleaned, engine compartment included, so that a thorough inspection can be carried out to see what minor repairs and renovations are necessary. Steam cleaning is available at many garages and is necessary for removal and accumulation of oily grime which sometimes is allowed to cake thickly in certain areas near the engine, gearbox and back axle. If steam facilities are not available, there are one or two excellent grease solvents available which can be brush applied. The dirt can be simply hosed off.
4 After washing paintwork, wipe off with a chamois leather to give an unspotted clear finish. A coat of clear protective wax polish will give added protection against chemical pollutants in the air. If the paintwork sheen has dulled or oxidised, use a cleaner/polisher combination to restore the brilliance of the shine. This requires a little effort, but is usually caused because regular washing has been neglected. Always check that the door and ventilator opening drain holes and pipes are completely clear so that water can drain out. Bright work should be treated the same way as paintwork. Windscreens and windows can be kept clear of the smeary film which often appears if a little ammonia is added to the water. If they are scratched, a good rub with a proprietary metal polish will often clear them. Never use any form of wax or other body or chromium polish on glass.

3 Maintenance - upholstery and carpets

1 Mats and carpets should be brushed or vacuum cleaned regularly to keep them free of grit. If they are badly stained remove them from

the car for scrubbing or sponging and make quite sure they are dry before replacement. Seats and interior trim panels can be kept clean by a wipe over with a damp cloth. If they do become stained (which can be more apparent on light coloured upholstery) use a little liquid detergent and a soft nail brush to scour the grime out of the grain of the material. Do not forget to keep the head lining clean in the same way as the upholstery. When using liquid cleaners inside the car do not over-wet the surface being cleaned. Excessive damp could get into the seams and padded interior causing stains, offensive odours or even rot. If the inside of the car gets wet accidentally it is worthwhile taking some trouble to dry it out properly, particularly where carpets are involved. **Do not** leave oil or electric heaters inside the car for this purpose.

4 Minor body damage - repair

See photo sequences on pages 182 and 183

Repair of minor scratches in the car's bodywork

If the scratch is very superficial, and does not penetrate to the metal of the bodywork - repair is very simple. Lightly rub the area of the scratch with a paintwork renovator or a very fine cutting paste, to remove loose paint from the scratch and to clear the surrounding body-work of wax plish. Rinse the area with clean water.

Apply touch-up paint to the scratch using a thin paint brush; continue to apply thin layers of paint until the surface of the paint in the scratch is level with the surrounding paintwork. Allow the new paint at least two weeks to harden, then, blend it into the surrounding paintwork by rubbing the paintwork in the scratch area with a paintwork renovator, or a very fine cutting paste. Finally apply wax polish.

An alternative to painting over the scratch is to use paint patches. Use the same preparation for the affected area; then simple, pick a patch of a suitable size to cover the sratch complete. Hold the patch against the scratch and burnish its backing paper; the patch will adhere to the paintwork, freeing itself from the backing paper at the same time. Polish the affected area to blend the patch into the surrounding paintwork.

Where a scratch has penetrated right through to the metal of the bodywork, causing the metal to rust, a different repair technique is required. Remove any loose rust inhibiting paint to prevent the formation of rust in the future. Using a rubber or nylon applicator fill the scratch with body-stopper paste. If required, this paste can be mixed with cellulose thinners to provide a very thin paste which is ideal for filling narrow scratches. Before the stopper paste in the scratch hardens, wrap a piece of smooth cotton rag around the tip of a finger. Dip the finger in cellulose thinners and then quickly sweep it across the surface of the stopper-paste; this will ensure that it is slightly hollowed. The scratch can now be painted over as described earlier in this Section.

Repair of dents in the car's bodywork

When deep denting of the car's bodywork has taken place, the first task is to pull the dent out, until the affected bodywork almost attains its original shape. There is little point in trying to restore the original shape completely, as the metal in the damaged area will have stretched on impact and cannot be reshaped fully to its original contour. It is better to bring the level of the dent up to a point which is about 1/8 inch (3 mm) below the level of the surround bodywork. In cases where the dent is very shallow anyway, it is not worth trying to pull it out at all.

If the underside of the dent is accessible, it can be hammered out gently from behind, using a mallet with a wooden or plastic head. Whilst doing this, hold a suitable block of wood firmly against the outside of the dent. This block will absorb the impact from the hammer blows and thus prevent a large area of bodywork from being 'belled-out".

Should the dent be in a section of the bodywork which has double skin or some other factor making it inaccessible from behind, a different technique is called for. Drill several small holes through the metal inside the dent area - particularly in the deeper sections. Then screw long self-tapping screws into the holes just sufficiently for them to gain a good purchase in the metal. Now the dent can be pulled out by pulling on the protruding heads of the screws with a pair of pliers.

The next stage of the repair is the removal of the paint from the damaged area, and from an inch or so of the surrounding 'sound' bodywork. This is accomplished most easily by using a wire brush or

abrasive pad on a power drill, although it can be done just as effectively by hand using sheets of abrasive paper. To complete the preparations for filling, score the surface of the bare metal with a screwdriver or the tang of a file, or alternatively, drill small holes in the affected area. This will provide a really good 'key' for the filler paste.

To complete the repair see the Section on filling and respraying.

Repair of rust holes or gashes in the car's bodywork

Remove all paint from the affected area and from an inch or so of the surrounding 'sound' bodywork, using an abrasive pad or a wire brush on a power drill. If these are not available a few sheets of abrasive paper will do the job just as effectively. With the paint removed you will be able to gauge the severity of the corrosion and therefore decide whether to replace the whole panel (if this is possible) or to repair the affected area. Replacement body panels are not as expensive as most people think and it is often quicker and more satisfactory to fit a new panel than to attempt to repair large areas of corrosion.

Remove all fittings from the affected area except those which will act as a guide to the original shape of the damaged bodywork (eg; headlamp shell etc). Then, using tin snips or a hacksaw blade, remove all loose metal and any other metal badly affected by corrosion. Hammer the edges of the holes inwards in order to create a slight depression for the filler paste.

Wire brush the affected area to remove the powdery rust from the surface of the remaining metal. Paint the affected area with rust inhibiting paint; if the back of the rusted area is accessible treat this also.

Before filling can take place it will be necessary to block the hole in some way. This can be achieved by the use of one of the following materials: Zinc gauze, Aluminium tape or Polyurethane foam.

Zinc gauze is probably the best material to use for a large hole. Cut a piece to the approximate size and shape of the hole to be filled, then position it in the hole so that its edges are below the level of the surrounding bodywork. It can be retained in position by several blobs of filler paste around its periphery.

Aluminium tape should be used for small or very narrow holes. Pull a piece off the roll and trim it to the approximate size and shape required, then pull off the backing paper (if used) and stick the tape over the hole; it can be overlapped if the thickness of one piece is insufficient. Burnish down the edges of the tape with the handle of a screwdriver or similar, to ensure that the tape is securely attached to the metal underneath.

Polyurethane foam is best used where the hole is situated in a section of bodywork of complex shape, backed by a small box section (eg; where the sill panel meets the rear wheel arch - most cars). The usual mixing procedure for this foam is as follows: Put equal amounts of fluid from each of the two cans provided in the kits, into one container. Stir until the mixture begins to thicken, then quickly pour this mixture into the hole, and hold a piece of cardboard over the larger apertures. Almost immediately the polyurethane will begin to expand, gushing frantically out of any small holes left unblocked. When the foam hardens it can be cut back to just below the level of the surrounding bodywork with a hacksaw blade.

Having blocked off the hole, the affected area must now be filled and sprayed - see Section on bodywork filling and respraying.

Bodywork repairs - filling and re-spraying

Before using this Section, see the Sections on dent, deep scratch, rust hole and gash repairs.

Many types of bodyfiller are available, but generally speaking those proprietary kits which contain a tin of filler paste and a tube of resin hardener are best for this type of repair. A wide, flexible plastic or nylon applicator will be found invaluable for imparting a smooth and well contoured finish to the surface of the filler.

Mix up a little filler on a clean piece of card or board - use the hardener sparingly (follow the maker's instruction on the pack), otherwise the filler will set very rapidly.

Using the applicator, apply the filler paste to the prepared area; draw the applicator across the surface of the filler to achieve the correct contour and to level the filler surface. As soon as a contour that approximates the correct one is achieved, stop working the paste - if you carry on too long the paste will become sticky and begin to 'pick-up' on the applicator.

Continue to add thin layers of filler paste at twenty-minute intervals until the level of the filler is just 'proud' of the surrounding bodywork.

Once the filler has hardened, excess can be removed using a file or metal plane. From then on, progressively finer grades of abrasive paper should be used, starting with a 40 grade 'wet-and-dry' paper. Always wrap the abrasive paper around a flat rubber cork, or wooden block otherwise the surface of the filler will not be completely flat. During the smoothing of the filler surface the 'wet-and-dry' paper should be periodically rinsed in water - this will ensure that a very smooth finish is imparted to the filler at the final stage.

At this stage the 'dent' should be surrounded by a ring of bare metal, which in turn should be encircled by the finely 'feathered' edge of the good paintwork. Rinse the repair area with clean water, until all of the dust produced by the rubbing-down operation is gone.

Spray the whole repair area with a light coat of grey primer - this will show up any imperfections in the surface of the filler. Repair these imperfections with fresh filler paste or body-stopper and once more smooth the surface with abrasive paper. If bodystopper is used, it can be mixed with cellulose thinners to form a really thin paste which is ideal for filling small holes. Repeat this spray and repair procedure until you are satisfied that the surface of the filler, and the feathered edge of the paintwork are perfect. Clean the repair area with clean water and allow to dry fully.

The repair area is now ready for spraying. Paint spraying must be carried out in a warm, dry, windless and dust free atmosphere. This condition can be created artificially if you have access to a large indoor working area, but if you are forced to work in the open, you will have to pick your day carefully. If you are working indoors, dousing the floor in the work area with water will 'lay' the dust which would otherwise be in the atmosphere. If the repair area is confined to one body panel, mask off the surrounding panels; this will help to minimise the effects of a slight mis-match in paint colours. Bodywork fittings (eg; chrome strips, door handles etc) will also need to be masked off. Use genuine masking tape and several thicknesses of newspaper for the masking operation.

Before commencing to spray, agitate the aerosol can thoroughly, then spray a test area (an old tin, or similar) until the technique is mastered. Cover the repair area with a thick coat of primer; the thickness should be built up using several thin layers of paint rather than one thick one. Using 400 grade 'wet-and-dry' paper, rub down the surface of the primer until it is really smooth. While doing this, the work area should be thoroughly doused with water, and the wet-and-dry paper periodically rinsed in water. Allow to dry before spraying on more paint.

Spray on the top coat, again building up the thickness by using several thin layers of paint. Start spraying in the centre of the repair area and then using a circular motion, work outwards until the whole repair area and about 2 inches of the surrounding original paintwork is covered. Remove all masking material 10 to 15 minutes after spraying on the final coat of paint. Allow the new paint at least 2 weeks to harden fully, then using a paintwork renovator or a very fine cutting paste, blend the edges of the new paint into the existing paintwork. Finally apply wax polish.

5   Major body damage - repair

Where serious damage has occurred or large areas need renewal due to neglect, it means certainly that completely new sections or panels will need welding in and this is best left to professionals. If the damage is due to impact it will also be necessary to completely check the alignment of the body shell structure. Due to the principle of construction the strength and shape of the whole can be affected by damage to a part. In such instances the services of a Jaguar/Daimler agent with specialist checking jigs are essential. If a body is left misaligned it is first of all dangerous as the car will not handle properly and secondly uneven stresses will be imposed on the steering, engine and transmission, causing abnormal wear or complete failure. Tyre wear may also be excessive.

6   Maintenance - hinges and locks

1   Oil the hinges of the bonnet, boot and doors with a drop or two of light oil periodically. A good time is after the car has been washed.
2   Oil the bonnet, release the catch pivot pin and the safety catch pivot pin periodically.
3   Do not over lubricate door latches and strikers. Normally a little oil

on the rotary cam spindle alone is sufficient.

7   Doors - tracing rattles and their rectification

1   Check first that the door is not loose at the hinges and that the latch is holding the door firmly in position. Check also that the door lines up with the aperture in the body.
2   If the hinges are loose or the door is out of alignment it will be necessary to reset the hinge positions, as described in Sections 26 or 27.
3   If the latch is holding the door properly it should hold the door tightly when fully latched and the door should line up with the body. If it is out of alignment it needs adjustment. If loose, some part of the lock mechanism must be worn out and requires renewal.
4   Other rattles from the door would be caused by wear or looseness in the window winder, the glass channels and sill strips, or the door buttons and interior latch release mechanism.

8   Bonnet - removal and refitting

1   Open the bonnet to its fullest extent and mark the position of the hinge plates in relation to the underside of the bonnet.
2   Unscrew and remove the setscrews which secure the bonnet to the hinges and with the help of an assistant, lift the bonnet from the car.
3   Refitting is a reversal of removal but align the marks made round the edges of the hinge plates before the bonnet was removed.

9   Bonnet lock - removal, adjustment and refitting

1   Slacken the locknut at the base of the dovetail bolt. Insert a screwdriver blade in the slot in the end of the dovetail bolt and unscrew the bolt complete with locknut, washers and spring.
2   To remove the lock section, slacken the nut which secures the cable and disconnect the cable from the release lever.
3   Remove the two setscrews which secure the striker and remove the striker, catch, baseplate and spacers.
4   Refitting is a reversal of removal but adjustment of the effective length of the dovetail bolt will almost certainly be required. To do this, adjust the dovetail bolt with a screwdriver until the bonnet will close smoothly and easily but without any tendency to rattle when closed. When this situation is reached, tighten the dovetail bolt locknut.

10   Bonnet hinges - removal and refitting

1   The hinge assemblies are contained in boxes located in the front subframe.
2   Remove the bonnet as previously described.
3   Unhook the bonnet counterbalance springs from their upper attachments.
4   *On all cars except Series 2*, remove the front bumper.
5   *On Series 2 cars*, remove the radiator lower grille (Section 11), then extract the four bolts from inside the wheel arch which secure the sides of the front apron panel to the body. Remove the three screws which secure the underside of the apron panel and withdraw the panel. Remove the radiator (Chapter 2).
6   The hinge assembly can now be unbolted and withdrawn.
7   Refitting is a reversal of removal.

11   Radiator grille - removal and refitting

All cars except Series 2
1   Raise the bonnet to its fully open position.
2   Remove the six nuts and remove the grille.

Series 2 cars
3   On these models, remove the two nuts and crosshead screws which secure the grille to the bonnet. Remove the grille by withdrawing it evenly.
4   The centre bar can be removed in two sections after unscrewing

Fig. 12.1. Bonnet lock striker plate (Sec. 9)

Fig. 12.2. Bonnet counterbalance springs (Sec. 10)

2   Stay bolt   4   Attachments
3   Attachments

Fig. 12.3. Bonnet hinge assembly (Series 2 cars) (Sec. 10)

the retaining nuts.

5   The lower grille is secured by two screws located behind the spotlamps. To remove the grille, withdraw the screws and lift the grille upwards to disengage its locating pegs at the lower edge.

6   Refitting in all cases is a reversal of removal but do not tighten the grille securing screws fully until the grille has been aligned squarely in the body aperture.

Fig. 12.4. Luggage compartment lid lock (Sec. 13)

Fig. 12.5. Door capping screws (early cars) (Sec. 14)

12 Luggage compartment lid - removal and refitting

1   Raise the lid to its fullest extent.
2   Disconnect the reversing lamp cables.
3   Mark the position of the hinge plates in relation to the underside of the lid.
4   Remove the securing setscrews and with the help of an assistant lift the lid from the car.
5   Refitting is a reversal of removal.

13 Luggage compartment lid lock - removal and refitting

1   Open the lid to its fullest extent.
2   Remove the clip which secures the link to the lock control and disconnect the link.
3   Remove the three securing screws and withdraw the lock.
4   The lock control can be removed from the lid if the retaining plate is first slid to one side.
5   Refitting is a reversal of removal, any adjustment can be made by slackening the two striker screws and moving the striker within the limits of the elongated screw holes.

14 Front door lock - removal and refitting

Early cars

1   Remove the four countersunk screws which secure the wood capping

14.3A Removing blanking plate from ventilator control knob

14.3B Withdrawing ventilator control knob

14.5 Removing door armrest

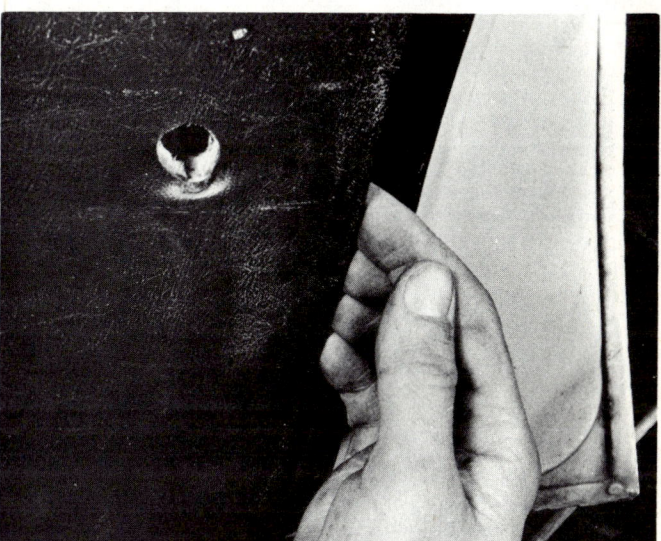

14.7 Removing door interior panel

Fig. 12.6. Front door lock mechanism (early cars) (Sec. 14)

1   Lock   2   Remote control (front view)   3   Remote control (rear view)

to the door interior waist rail.

2   Four more screws will be exposed once the wood capping is removed and these should be unscrewed and the padded waist rail removed.

3   Prise out the centre plate (using a thin blade) from the swivelling ventilator control knob. The screw now exposed should be removed and the knob withdrawn (photos).

4   Remove the centre screw from the window regulator handle and pull off the handle (cars without electric windows).

5   Remove the two securing screws from its lower edge and withdraw the armrest (photo).

6   Carefully peel away the interior trim panel covering, where it is stuck to the edge of the window glass aperture.

7   Insert a wide blade or rule between the trim panel and the door and prise off the panel which is secured by spring clips. Work the fingers round the edge of the trim panel until all the spring clips are released (photo).

8   Temporarily refit the window regulator handle and wind the window up to its fullest extent.

9   Lift the insert from the bottom of the glass rear channel and remove the screw now exposed.

10 Remove the lower section of this channel by drawing it downward.

11 Release the two link rods which connect the exterior handle pushbutton and the key-operated lock by detaching the spring clips and prising the rods from the nylon bushes in the levers.

12 Remove the link rod which connects the remote control handle to the latch from its nylon coupling block and withdraw the nylon bearing from the door panel.

13 Disconnect the link rod which connects the inside safety locking lever to the latch lever after first releasing the locknuts and withdrawing the rod through the slot in the lever.

14 Remove the three screws which secure the latch and dovetail plate to the door and withdraw the latch through the aperture in the door panel.

15 The exterior handle can be removed after withdrawing the two securing screws.

16 The remote control unit can be removed after withdrawing its three securing screws.

17 The private lock is held in position by a spring clip which is accessible from inside the door cavity.

18 Refitting is a reversal of removal but observe the following points.

19 Check that the operating lever on the key-operated lock is towards the rear of the car when installed.

20 Adjust the outside handle pushbutton lever link rod by turning the trunnion so that there is a slight free-movement of the pushbutton when the link rod is connected to the latch. It is important that the screw in the pushbutton (which is located behind the pivoted lever) should be screwed in to its fullest extent.

21 Reconnect the link rod to the locking lever on the latch but do not tighten the adjuster nuts (B) (Fig. 12.8) until they have been set to provide a slight free-movement in the lock lever before corresponding

moverment in the latch locking lever takes place. The link rod lever should be connected to the rear hole in the latch lever.

22 Check the operation of the latch lever in the remote control unit. Slight free-movement must be provided by screwing the link rod in or out of the nylon adjuster block (A) which is attached to the handle.

23 The door should close smoothly and positively without rattle or any tendency for the striker plate to force the door upwards or downwards as it is closed. Adjust the position of the striker plate (by releasing its securing screws) until this situation is achieved.

Later cars

24 On later cars, disc type door locks are fitted which differ from earlier assemblies by the fact that the locks can only be locked by the use of the key.

25 Access to the lock mechanism is as described for the earlier type lock but the attachment details are as shown in Fig. 12.19.

Fig. 12.7. Front door lock push-button and latch adjustment points (early cars) (Sec. 14)

Fig. 12.8. Front door lock remote control adjustment points (early cars) (Sec. 14)

Fig. 12.9. Front door lock and latch (later cars) (Sec. 14)

Fig. 12.10. Door latch outer unit disc in open position (Sec. 14)

Fig. 12.11. Rear door courtesy lamp switch plate removed (Sec. 14)

14.29 Front door trim panel removed showing loudspeaker leads and power operated window connections

Fig. 12.12. Rear door lock mechanism (early cars)(Sec. 15)

4 Lock (arrow indicates child safety latch)   5 Remote control (rear view)

Fig. 12.13. Rear door latch on later cars (child safety catch arrowed) (Sec. 15)

Fig. 12.14. Rear door lock mechanism (later cars) (Sec. 15)

This sequence of photographs deals with the repair of the dent and scratch (above rear lamp) shown in this photo. The procedure will be similar for the repair of a hole. It should be noted that the procedures given here are simplified - more explicit instructions will be found in the text

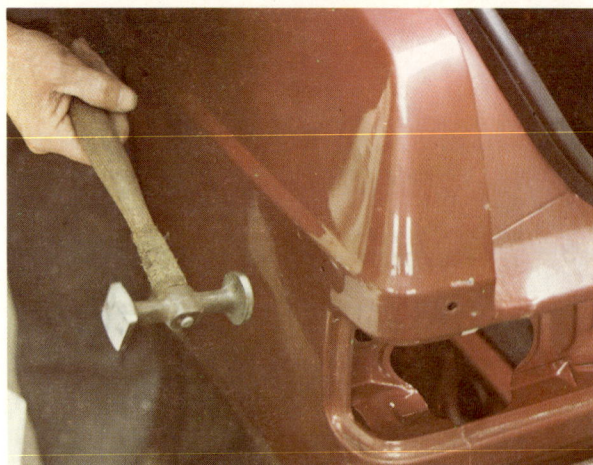

In the case of a dent the first job - after removing surrounding trim - is to hammer out the dent where access is possible. This will minimise filling. Here, the large dent having been hammered out, the damaged area is being made slightly concave

Now all paint must be removed from the damaged area, by rubbing with coarse abrasive paper. Alternatively, a wire brush or abrasive pad can be used in a power drill. Where the repair area meets good paintwork, the edge pf the paintwork should be 'feathered', using a finer grade of abrasive paper

In the case of a hole caused by rusting, all damaged sheet-metal should be cut away before proceeding to this stage. Here, the damaged area is being treated with rust remover and inhibitor before being filled

Mix the body filler according to its manufacturer's instructions. In the case of corrosion damage, it will be necessary to block off any large holes before filling - this can be done with zinc gauze or aluminium tape. Make sure the area is absolutely clean before ...

... applying the filler. Filler should be applied with a flexible applicator, as shown, for best results: the wooden spatula being used for confined areas. Apply thin layers of filler at 20-minute intervals, until the surface of the filler is slightly proud of the surrounding bodywork

Initial shaping can be done with a Surform plane or Dreadnought file. Then, using progressively finer grades of wet-and-dry paper, wrapped around a sanding block, and copious amounts of clean water, rub-down the filler until really smooth and flat. Again, feather the edges of adjoining paintwork

The whole repair area can now be sprayed or brush-painted with primer. If spraying, ensure adjoining areas are protected from over-spray. Note that at least one-inch of the surrounding sound paintwork should be coated with primer. Primer has a 'thick' consistency, so will fill small imperfections

Again, using plenty of water, rub down the primer with a fine grade of wet-and-dry paper (400 grade is probably best) until it is really smooth and well blended into the surrounding paint-work. Any remaining imperfections can now be filled by carefully applied knifing stopper paste

When the stopper has hardened, rub-down the repair area again before applying the final coat of primer. Before rubbing-down this last coat of primer, ensure the repair area is blemish-free - use more stopper if necessary. To ensure that the surface of the primer is really smooth use some finishing compound

The top coat can now be applied. When working out of doors, pick a dry, warm and wind-free day. Ensure surrounding areas are protected from over-spray. Agitate the aerosol thoroughly, then spray the centre of the repair area, working outwards with a circular motion. Apply the paint as several thin coats.

After a period of about two-weeks, which the paint needs to harden fully, the surface of the repaired area can be 'cut' with a mild cutting compound prior to wax polishing. When carrying out bodywork repairs, remember that the quality of the finished job is proportional to the time and effort expended

26 When refitting this type of lock, make sure that the remote control lock lever is forward and the latch outer unit disc is in the open position.

27 Offer the latch outer unit to the latch mechanism so that the mounting holes are in alignment and then set the mechanism so that the pawl pin is beside the pawl operating lever. This is most important as the lock will be damaged if the latch outer unit and the latch mechanism plate is secured while the components are in opposing positions.

28 The striker plate on later model cars can only be removed from inside the door pillar. Access is obtained by disconnecting the battery and removing the rear door courtesy lamp switch plate. Adjustment of the striker plate can be carried out simply by releasing the two securing screws.

Series 2 cars

29 Access to the door locks on these cars is similar to the procedure described earlier in this Section except that radio speakers may be built into the armrests. In this case withdraw the screws from the lower edge of the armrest and withdraw it far enough to be able to disconnect the speaker leads (photo).

30 Disconnection of the remotely controlled exterior mirror is described in Section 53, and the crash roll which is fitted to the door interior panel is held in position by four screws and locating pegs.

15 Rear door lock - removal and refitting

Early cars

1 The operations are similar to those described in the preceding Section, paragraphs 1 to 23, except for the following differences.

2 There is no ventilator control or armrest to be removed from the interior trim panel.

3 The screw located in the pushbutton operates the contactor directly on the lock latch and no link rod is fitted.

Later cars

4 On later cars, disc type door locks are fitted which incorporate a child safety locking device.

5 To remove this type of lock, wind the window up to its fullest extent and remove the link rods which connect the remote control unit to the latch mechanism (at the latch end).

6 Remove the exterior handle link rod from the handle.

7 Prise the safety lever from the latch mechanism lever.

8 Extract the four screws which secure the latch to the door edge and withdraw the latch from the door cavity.

9 Refitting is similar to the procedure described in Section 14, paragraphs 26 and 27 for the front door locks, except it is not necessary to set the latch plate mechanism although the latch outer unit disc must be in the open position as shown in Fig. 12.9.

10 The rear door lock striker plate can only be removed after withdrawing the panel edging trim and peeling away the adhesive tape which covers the access hole. Adjustment of the striker plate can be carried out simply by releasing (but not removing) the securing screws.

16 Front door swivelling ventilator - removal and refitting

1 Remove the door interior trim panel as described in Section 14.

2 Remove the two screws and withdraw the ventilator gearbox.

3 Remove the two setscrews and detach the buffer and bracket from the bottom of the door panel.

4 Remove the single setscrew and the two screws from the glass frame front channel.

5 Wind the window fully down and withdraw the ventilator from the door frame.

6 Refitting is a reversal of removal.

17 Front door glass (4 door cars) - removal and refitting

1 Remove the door interior panel (Section 14) and the swivelling ventilator (Section 16).

2 Prise out the weatherstrip from the doorframe.

Fig. 12.15. Method of access to rear door striker plate (later cars) (Sec. 15)

Fig. 12.16. Swivelling ventilator frame setscrew (early cars) (Sec. 16)

Fig. 12.17. Swivelling ventilator frame securing screws (early cars) (Sec. 16)

Fig. 12.18. Window regulator connection to glass channel (early cars) (Sec. 17)

3 Wind the glass up to the halfway position, slide it forward to clear the regulator arm and remove it from the door.
4 Refitting is a reversal of removal.

18 Rear door glass (4 door cars) - removal and refitting

1 Remove the door interior trim panel, as described in Section 14.
2 Remove the four screws and nuts and withdraw the detachable top section of the glass frame channel.
3 Wind the window fully up and then slide it forward to disengage the regulator arm and channel and then withdraw the glass upwards from the door cavity.

19 Rear door fixed quarter light (4 door cars) - removal and refitting

1 Remove the door interior trim panel, as previously described.
2 Remove the three screws which secure the bottom of the quarter light frame to the door panel.
3 Remove the two screws which secure the top of the frame to the window channel and then withdraw the quarterlight glass and frame.
4 Refitting is a reversal of removal.

20 Door glass and carrier (Series 2, two door cars) - removal and refitting

1 Remove the crashroll from the door interior panel. The crashroll is secured by four screws.
2 Remove the door interior trim panel (Section 14).
3 Remove the three screws which secure the glass bezel guide to the front of the door.
4 Remove the five screws which secure the crashroll retaining plate.
5 Prise away the anti-rattle pads which are located between the door frame and the glass.
6 Carefully remove the waterproof sheet clear of the window lift mechanism.
7 Lower the window sufficiently to be able to extract the four screws which secure the window mounting plate.
8 Slacken the two nuts which secure the window lift quadrant guide channel to the glass mounting.
9 Raise the window to its fullest extent then extract the two screws which secure the glass to the mounting plate.
10 Remove the rubber weatherstrip from the glass edge (closing face).
11 Ease the glass from the mounting plate and lift it from the door.
12 To remove the glass carrier assembly, extract the chrome beading and weatherstrip from the door and then raise the carrier to its fullest extent. Disengage the spring from the glass carrier plate.
13 Lower the carrier plate enough to permit access to the guide channel which locates the lift motor quadrant.
14 Remove the two nuts which secure the guide channel to the glass carrier, slide the channel from the lift motor quadrant and lift the guide from the door.
15 Disengage the spring assembly from the spigot mounting and lift the spring assembly from the door.
16 Remove the nylon pads from the top corners of the pulley mechanism frame.
17 Move the glass to give access to the four setscrews which secure the carrier plates, remove the setscrews and separate the outer plate from the inner one and withdraw the plates from the door.
18 Remove the four setscrews which secure the pulley mechanism to the door, retain the washers and then remove the carrier/pulley assembly from the door.
19 Refitting is a reversal of removal but observe the following points.
20 Make sure that the longer setscrews are located in the outer ends of the glass carrier plates.
21 Do not fully tighten screws on the carrier/pulley assembly until the glass is installed and the window fully raised.
22 When fitting the glass, close the door and adjust the glass to give a 9/32 in (7 mm) clearance between the drip rail and the edge of the glass.

Fig. 12.19. Rear door glass frame channel screws (Sec. 18)

Fig. 12.20. Glass securing details (Series 2, two door cars) (Sec. 20)

2 Glass bezel guide screws
3 Crash roll plate screws
6 Window mounting plate screws
8 Window light quadrant guide unit
10 Glass to mounting plate securing screws

Fig. 12.21. Door glass carrier details (Series 2, two door cars)

6 Guide channel nuts
7 Spring assembly
8 Nylon anti-rattle pad screw
9 Carrier plate screws
10 Carrier plate
11 Pulley frame brackets

21 Rear quarter glass and carrier (Series 2 - two door cars) - removal and refitting

1   Remove the rear quarter trim panel, as described in Section 25.
2   Remove the rear quarter crashroll (two screws) and its mounting (five screws).
3   Peel away the waterproof sheet from the door and remove the two bolts which secure the glass buffer to the quarter panel, withdraw the buffer.
4   Lower the glass to its halfway position and support it at its lower edge.
5   Remove the four setscrews which secure the window lift motor to the quarter panel. Move the motor to the rear while disengaging the quadrant arm from the glass guide channel.
6   Withdraw the motor from the door aperture.
7   Pull the glass into the fully closed position and disengage the glass guide rollers from the carrier plate. Withdraw the glass completely.
8   To remove the glass carrier, extract the two bolts which secure the carrier to the lower mounting bracket, also the single bolt which secures it to the side mounting bracket.
9   Remove the two crosshead screws which secure the upper section of the glass carrier to the quarter panel.
10 Lower the glass carrier and disengage the upper section from the chrome beading. The carrier can now be withdrawn.
11 Refitting of the carrier and the glass is a reversal of removal but apply grease to the guide channels.

22 Electrically-operated windows

1   Refer to Chapter 10, Section 45, for details of this system

23 Solenoid-operated door locks

1   Refer to Chapter 10, Section 46, for details of this system fitted to Series 2 cars.

24 Window regulator (early cars) - removal and refitting

1   Remove the door interior trim panel as previously described.

2   Remove the four screws which secure the regulator mechanism to the door and then disengage the regulator arm and withdraw the mechanism from the door cavity.
3   Refitting is a reversal of removal.

25 Rear quarter trim panel (Series 2 - two door) - removal and refitting

1   Push both front seats fully forward and remove the screw from each side of the transmission tunnel. These screws secure the rear seat cushion to the seat pan crossmember.
2   Draw the seat cushion forward and remove it from the car.
3   Remove the two screws which secure the lower edge of the rear seat squab to the seat pan. Push the squab upwards and disengage it from its upper securing clips. Remove the squab.
4   Release the screws and remove the door sill tread plate.
5   Pull away the edging strip from the front edge of the quarter trim panel.
6   Remove the bolt which secures the seat belt lower anchor plate noting carefully the sequence of washers and spacers.
7   Prise off the plastic cover plate from the upper anchor plate and unbolt the seat belt.

Fig. 12.23. Window regulator securing screws (early cars) (Sec. 24)

Fig. 12.22. Rear quarter glass details (Series 2, two door cars) (Sec. 21)

2	Crash roll screws	9	Glass carrier to panel screws
4	Glass buffer bolts	10	Glass carrier to side mounting
7	Window lift motor setscrews		bracket screws
8	Window lift quadrant arm	11	Glass carrier to lower mounting bracket screws

Fig. 12.24. Rear quarter trim panel details (Series 2 two door cars) (Sec. 25)

4	Seat belt lower anchorage	8	Edging trim
5	Seat belt upper anchorage	9	Quarter trim panel
6	Armrest bezel	10	Seat belt
7	Armrest screw		

Fig. 12.25. Front door hinge locations (early cars) (Sec. 26)

Fig. 12.26. Door hinge (Series 2 cars) (Sec. 27)

3 Under wing access panel   *5 Wing to body pillar bolts*
4 Wing to sill bolts

8 Remove the chrome bezel from the front of the armrest by extracting the screw and sliding the bezel forward. Remove the screw exposed by the removal of the bezel.
9 Peel the trim from the lip of the door aperture and prise the quarter trim panel from the car body.
10 Feed the seat belt through the hole in the panel and lift the panel from the car.
11 Refitting is a reversal of removal.

26 Front door (except Series 2 cars) - removal and refitting

1 Extract the split pin and the clevis pin from the door check strap bracket.
2 Mark the outline of the hinges on the door.
3 Open the door to its widest and support it under its lower edge on blocks covered with pads of rag.
4 Unscrew and remove the six bolts which secure the hinge plates to the door edge. Lift the door away.
5 If the hinges must be removed from the body pillar, mark the outline of the hinge plates before removing them. The wing will have to be separated from the lower sill and the valance before the hinge plate bolt heads can be unscrewed; see the next Section, paragraph 2.
6 Refitting is a reversal of removal and if the hinge plates are aligned with the marks made before removal, there should be no need for adjustment. However, where new components have been installed, do not tighten the hinge bolts until the door has been correctly aligned within the frame to give equal gaps all round. In extreme cases of mis-alignment shims may be required to be inserted under the hinge plates.
7 Finally, adjust the door lock striker plate to provide smooth positive closure.

27 Front door (Series 2) - removal and refitting

1 The procedure is similar to that described in the preceding Section except that spring type door checks are used instead of straps.
2 Access to the hinge bolts is obtained by removing the under wing panel and extracting the bolts which secure the lower edge of the wing to the sill and the rear of the wing to the body pillar. Prise the wing from the body pillar by driving in two wedges so that sufficient space is provided to engage a spanner on the hinge bolt heads.

28 Rear door - removal and refitting

1 The operations are similar to those described in the previous Sections 26 or 27, except that the hinges are secured to the door by two bolts and a special screw.

29 Windscreen - removal and refitting

This is a job best left to professionals but where it is decided to carry out the work yourself, proceed in the following way with the help of an assistant.
1 Where a windscreen is to be renewed then if it is due to shattering, the fascia air vents should be covered before attempting removal. Adhesive sheeting is useful to stick to the outside of the glass to enable large areas of crystallised glass to be removed.
2 Where the screen is to be removed intact then an assistant will be required. First release the rubber surround from the bodywork by running a blunt, small screwdriver around and under the rubber weatherstrip both inside and outside the car. This operation will break the adhesive of the sealer originally used. Take care not to damage the paintwork or cut the rubber surround with the screwdriver. Remove the windscreen wiper arms and interior mirror and place a protective cover on the bonnet. Remove the bright trim from the rubber surround.
3 Have your assistant push the inner lip of the rubber surround off the flange of the windscreen body aperture. Once the rubber surround starts to peel off the flange, the screen may be forced gently outwards by careful hand pressure. The second person should support and remove the screen complete with rubber weatherseal.
4 Before fitting a windscreen, ensure that the rubber surround is completely free from old sealant, glass fragments and has not hardened

Fig. 12.27. Windscreen removal (Sec. 29)

Fig. 12.28. Metal section rear bumper and fittings (Sec. 30)

Fig. 12.29. Impact absorbing type bumper (Sec. 30)

1   Impact absorbing cover   4   Bumper bar

Fig. 12.30. Energy absorbing strut used with impact absorbing type
bumper (Sec. 30)

2   Strut to mounting tube nut   5   Rubber insulating sleeve
3   Strut to bumper bolt

or cracked. Fit the rubber surround to the glass and apply a bead of suitable sealant between the glass outer edge and the rubber.

5   Cut a piece of strong cord greater in length than the periphery of the glass and insert it into the body flange locating channel of the rubber surround.

6   Apply a thin bead of sealant to the face of the rubber channel which will eventually mate with the body.

7   Offer the windscreen to the body aperture and pass the ends of the cord, previously fitted and located at bottom centre into the vehicle interior.

8   Press the windscreen into place, at the same time have an assistant pulling the cords to engage the lip of the rubber channel over the body flange.

9   Remove any excess sealant with a paraffin soaked rag.

10   Removal and installation of the rear window glass is carried out in an identical manner but (if fitted) disconnect the leads to the heating element in the glass.

30 Bumpers - removal and refitting

1   Removal and dismantling standard type metal section bumpers is simply a matter of removing the securing bolts and lifting the bumper assembly from the car.

2   Impact-absorbing type bumpers installed on later cars supplied to North America must be renewed if deformed and great care must be taken to set their height and alignment correctly.

3   This type of bumper is dismantled by first unbolting and then peeling the absorbent cover from the bumper bar.

4   Unbolt and remove the bumper bar and then withdraw the telescopic strut assemblies. If the struts are damaged or offer little or no resistance when compressed then they must be renewed as units.

31 Heating and ventilation system - description

1   The heating system comprises the necessary intake and ducting to direct air to the windscreen, front interior and rear passenger compartment by passing the air over a matrix which is heated from the engine cooling system.

2   The necessary controls are provided to regulate the air temperature and the volume and direction of flow of the air. On earlier cars, the controls are operated by vacuum from the engine. On Series 2 cars, the controls are of vacuum and mechanically actuated type. A vacuum tank provides a reserve to enable six operations of the controls to be carried out after the engine has been switched off.

3   A two-speed booster fan is provided for use in conditions when the car is not moving forward fast enough to provide the normal ram effect.

4   An independent fresh air supply is provided from outlets on the fascia panel and on later cars a further fresh air outlet at lower level is positioned for both front seat occupants.

Fig. 12.31. Heater controls (Sec. 31)

A   Fresh air   C   Air distribution
B   Heat   D   Fan

32 Heater vacuum servo system components (except Series 2 cars) - removal and refitting

1   Failure of any one of the components of the vacuum control system will normally require renewal of the unit. Before taking this action however, always check the connecting hoses for security of joints and for perforation.

Flap actuator
2   This flap allows fresh air to be drawn into the heating system.
3   To remove it, prise off the air intake grille from the scuttle by inserting two small screwdrivers at opposite sides of the grille (photo).
4   Raise the bonnet and detach the vacuum pipe from the actuator unit.
5   Remove the two nuts which are accessible from within the plenum chamber and withdraw the actuator securing bolts.
6   Disconnect the coupling rod from the flap and then remove the actuator unit.
7   Refitting is a reversal of removal but make sure that no preload is placed on the diaphragm when connecting the coupling rod to the flap. The rod length can be adjusted to avoid this situation by screwing the rod in or out.

32.3 Air intake grille removed

Fig. 12.32. Heater vacuum servo system (early cars) (Sec. 32)

1   *Air flap modulator*
2   *Actuator*
3   *Heat control modulator*
4   *Heater sensing unit*
5   *Water valve*
6   *Vacuum tank*
7   *Non-return valve*
A   *To manifold*
B   *Water inlet*
C   *Water outlet*

H.5735

Flap control quadrant modulator

8 This is mounted centrally in the panel above the radio aperture and is a conical valve which controls the degree of vacuum which exists between the vacuum tank and the flap actuator.
9 To remove the modulator, withdraw the knobs from the three heater control levers, also the knobs from the heat control rotary modulator and the radio.
10 Insert a small screwdriver behind the lever escutcheons and lever them from the nylon bush retainers. Remove the control panel fascia.
11 Extract the four screws and withdraw the heater control panel to the rear in order to gain access to the modulator securing screws.
12 Disconnect the vacuum pipes, remove the two securing screws and lift out the modulator.
13 Refitting is a reversal of removal.

Water valve servo unit

14 This is a diaphragm valve which, controlled by a combination of the vacuum tank, heat control rotary modulator and heat sensing unit, regulates the flow of water through the heater matrix.
15 To remove the unit, drain the cooling system, as described in Chapter 2.
16 Disconnect the hoses from the unit and remove it.
17 Refitting is a reversal of removal.

Heat control rotary modulator

18 This device is very similar to the flap control modulator except that it has a rotary type control knob. Refer to paragraphs 8 to 13, of this Section for removal and refitting operations.

Heat sensing unit

19 This unit is located in the air ducts below the instrument panel and is basically a valve which automatically controls the coolant flow through the water valve irrespective of the engine water pump speed.
20 Access to this component is obtained in the same way as described for the flap control modulator (paragraphs 8 to 11).
21 Disconnect the three vacuum pipes from the unit, remove the two securing screws and lift the unit away.
22 Refitting is a reversal of removal but install a new joint between the sensing unit and the duct if necessary.

Fig. 12.33. Location of heater water valve servo unit (Sec. 32)

Fig. 12.34. Heater fans (early cars) showing direction of rotation (Sec. 33)

33 Heater fans (except Series 2 cars) - removal and refitting

1 The twin heater booster fans are speed controlled by resistance units wired in series. In the event of wear or a fault occurring in the fan motors, they must be renewed as units.
2 To remove a fan/motor assembly, disconnect the leads from the resistance units on the engine compartment rear bulkhead.
3 Remove the motor mounting plate screws, lift the motor/fan assembly from the bulkhead, detaching the electrical leads from their clips as it is withdrawn.
4 Remove the mounting plate and impeller for fitting to the new motor. It must be noted that the units are handed for left and right-hand rotation; do not interchange them and check that the correct type has been obtained as a replacement.
5 Refitting is a reversal of removal but renew the motor mounting plate sealing gasket, if necessary, to provide a tight joint.

34 Heater matrix (except Series 2 cars) - removal and refitting

1 The heater matrix is located on the engine compartment rear bulkhead and it is retained in position by the compression of foam rubber pads which takes place when the heater/air duct assembly is installed.
2 Drain the cooling system (Chapter 2).
3 Disconnect the battery.
4 Disconnect the coolant hoses from the matrix.
5 Remove the radio/heater control panel as described in Section 26 paragraphs 9, 10 and 11.
6 Disconnect the radio and the heater control vacuum pipes having first marked them so that they can be correctly reconnected.
7 Remove the side fascia panels as described in Section 47.
8 Remove the instrument panel as described in Chapter 10.
9 Remove the centre console as described in Section 45.
10 Remove the four nuts and detach the two struts which support the fascia assembly.
11 Remove the left and right-hand air ducts (four screws).
12 Remove the plenum chamber from the bulkhead (eight screws).
13 Withdraw the heater matrix. If the matrix is leaking have it professionally repaired or renew it. If the matrix is blocked, try reverse flushing it or use proprietary cleansing compound strictly in accordance with the manufacturer's instructions.
14 Refitting is a reversal of removal but renew the foam pads instead of refitting the original deformed ones.

35 Heater controls (Series 2 cars) - removal and refitting

1 Disconnect the battery and remove the centre console (Section 46).
2 Remove the two bolts which secure the control panel mounting plate to the heater (Fig. 12.35).
3 Remove the three screws which secure the vacuum switches to the mounting plate. Identify the vacuum pipes and disconnect them from the switches.
4 Extract the circlip from the shaft of the temperature control switch.
5 Remove the mounting plate from its studs.
6 The micro or vacuum switches can be removed from the mounting plate after extracting the securing screws.
7 Refitting is a reversal of removal.

36 Heater temperature control cable assembly (Series 2 cars) - removal and refitting

1 Disconnect the battery and remove the centre console (Section 46).
2 Remove the under scuttle casing.
3 Remove the radio/heater control mounting panel from the left-hand side of the heater.
4 Remove the four self-tapping screws which secure the air outlet duct in the right-hand footwell.
5 Remove the three self-tapping screws which secure the duct assembly in the right-hand footwell and at the rear outlet. One of these screws is located behind the control mounting panel and needs the use of a right-angled crosshead screwdriver.
6 Set the temperature control knob in the vent position, loosen the

Fig. 12.35. Heater control mounting plate (Series 2) (Sec. 35)

3 Mounting plate to heater nuts
4 Vacuum switch screws

6 Airflow and temperature
   control switch shafts

Fig. 12.37. Heater flap linkage (Series 2 cars) (Sec. 37)

A Locking screw
B Locking screw
C Locking screw
N Lever operating flap

Q Lever operating flap
R Lever
T Eccentric pivot

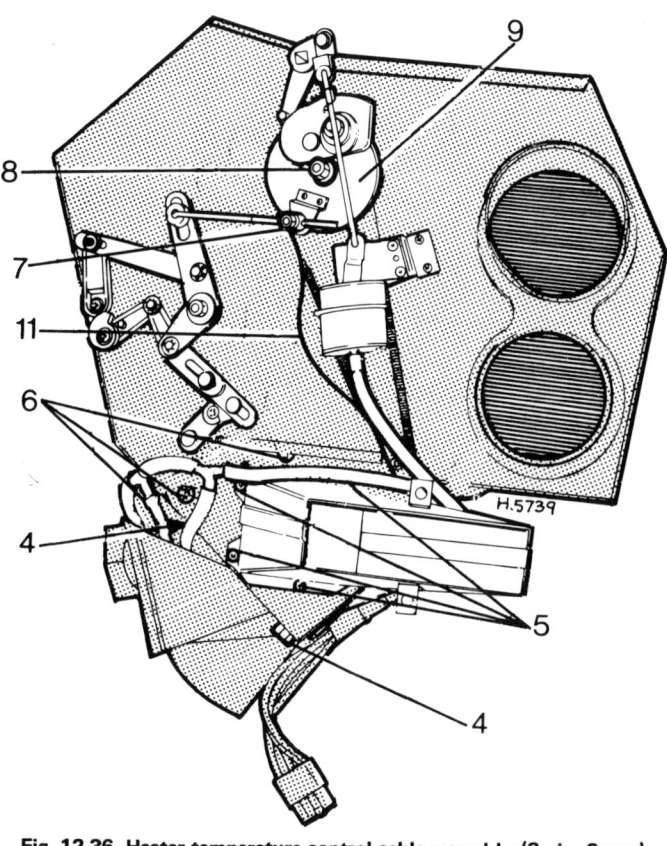

Fig. 12.36. Heater temperature control cable assembly (Series 2 cars)
(Sec. 36)

4 Control panel to heater
   securing unit
5 Footwell air outlet duct
   screws
6 Rear air outlet screws

7 Flap link rod nut
8 Drive wheel pivot nut
9 Main drive wheel
11 Temperature control cable

flap link operating rod locknut on the main drive wheel. Remove the
nut and washer from the pivot of the main drive wheel.
7 Lift the jockey pulleys against the tension of the springs and
withdraw the main drive wheel from its pivot.
8 Ease the radio/heater control panel and the right-hand footwell
outlet assembly away from the heater.
9 Disconnect the control cable.
10 When refitting the cable, wind it round the main drive wheel 3½
times. Make sure that the cable can be locked to the bollard on the
wheel by the washer under the locking screw but do not tighten it at
this stage.
11 Set the temperature control at the 10 o'clock position and locate
the cable round the jockey pulleys in such a way that the upper strand
of the cable leaves the bollard and passes round the forward pulley.
Pull the ends of the cable as far as possible horizontally and then adjust
the cable until the nipples are level with each other.
12 Tighten the bollard locking screw and fit the cable end nipples into
the main driving wheel making sure that the ends of the cable do not
cross.
13 Refit the radio/heater control panel and the footwell outlet assembly.
14 Keeping the cable taut, refit the main driving wheel to the pivot and
screw on the nut and washer.
15 The flap linkage should be adjusted as described in the next Section.
16 Complete the refitting by reversing the rest of the removal operations.

37 Heater flap linkage (Series 2) - adjustment

1 Turn the temperature control knob to vent.
2 Refer to Fig. 12.37 and slacken the locking screws 'A', 'B' and 'C'.
3 Turn the lever 'R' to a fully clockwise position and hold in this
position using firm finger-pressure. Tighten locking screw 'A'.

4   Press flap 'N' to a fully clockwise position and tighten locking screw 'C'.

5   Turn the temperature control knob to defrost. Using a screwdriver engaged in the slotted end of the adjusting link, push the operating flap 'Q' fully clockwise and tighten lockscrew 'B'.

6   The eccentric pivot 'T' on the upper flap actuating cam is adjustable through 180° to vary the level of face level air temperature.

38 Heater air intake and outlet grilles (Series 2) - removal and refitting

Demister duct outlets

1   These can be removed by levering them from their surround.

2   Refit by pressing firmly into place.

Demister flap and actuator

3   Remove the crash roll from the fascia (Section 51).

4   Remove the two nuts which secure the flap assembly to the screen rail.

5   Disconnect the plastic ducting and the vacuum tube and lift the flap/actuator assembly from the screen rail.

6   Refitting is a reversal of removal.

Ventilator fascia outlets

7   Disconnect the battery.

8   Remove the fascia (Section 51).

9   Unclip the side outlets at the rear of the fascia or remove the four securing screws from the centre outlet.

10 Refitting is a reversal of removal.

Rear ventilator

11 Raise the console glovebox lid and extract the two screws which secure the lid retaining bar.

12 Withdraw the three screws which secure the hinge plate to the glovebox.

13 Extract the three screws which secure the glovebox liner.

14 Pass the hand under the glovebox liner and grip the bayonet type locking ring of the air vent assembly. Press in and rotate the vent anticlockwise until the locking ring releases. Withdraw the air vent assembly.

15 Refitting is a reversal of removal.

Fig. 12.40. Ventilator fascia outlet (Series 2 cars) (Sec. 38)

Fig. 12.38. Demister duct (Series 2 cars) (Sec. 38)

Fig. 12.39. Demister flap and actuator (Series 2 cars) (Sec. 38)

2 Securing nuts	4 Vacuum tube connection on actuator
3 Plastic ducting	5 Flap assembly

Fig. 12.41. Rear ventilator (Series 2 cars) (Sec. 38)

1 Lid retaining bar screws	4 Air vent locking ring
2 Hinge plate screws	5 Air vent assembly
3 Liner screws	

Fresh air intakes
16 To remove the grille from the scuttle just in front of the windscreen, prise it out with a sharp screwdriver.
17 Disconnect the washer tube from the washer jet.
18 To remove the intake grille located above the outer headlamp lens, withdraw the screw and lift the embellisher upwards to clear the lower retaining tags.

---

39 Heater motor/fan units (Series 2) - removal and refitting

1 Disconnect the battery.
2 Remove the under scuttle casing from the right-hand side if access to the right-hand motor is required or from the left-hand side if the left-hand motor is to be removed.
3 Remove the fusebox and move it to one side or alternatively remove the glovebox liner dependent upon whether the car is LHD or RHD and to which motor access is required. Inspection will enable the correct procedure to be adopted.
4 Pull the pliable air duct from the outlets at the side of the heater unit.
5 Remove the side fascia panels.
6 Extract the two screws which secure the fresh air outlet control bracket.
7 Unscrew and remove the two motor mounting nuts, disconnect the vacuum tube from the actuator, disconnect the electrical leads and withdraw the motor/fan assembly.
8 Reassembly is a reversal of removal but the top air flap should be closed so that it can enter into its aperture and seal. To close the flap apply vacuum to the actuator by connecting a length of tubing between the open end of the original tubing and the actuator.

Fig. 12.42. Fresh air intake grille (Series 2 cars) (Sec. 30)

1 Grille   2 Washer tube

Fig. 12.43. Headlamp fresh air intake (later cars) (Sec. 38)

---

40 Heater motor resistance unit (Series 2 cars) - removal and refitting

Left-hand drive cars
1 Disconnect the battery and remove the fascia under scuttle casing from the driver's side.
2 Remove the side panel from the centre console.
3 Mark the cables and disconnect them from the resistance unit.
4 Remove the three securing screws and withdraw the resistance unit from the heater casing.

Right-hand drive cars
5 Disconnect the battery.
6 Remove the glove compartment liner.
7 Repeat operations described in paragraphs 3 and 4.
8 Refitting is a reversal of removal.

---

41 Heater motor relays (Series 2 cars) - removal and refitting

1 Disconnect the battery.
2 Remove the left-hand side casing from the centre console.
3 Remove the left-hand air outlet duct (four screws) from the footwell.
4 Mark the electrical leads and disconnect them.
5 Remove the securing nuts and withdraw the relay unit.
6 Refitting is a reversal of removal but make sure that the earth lead is secured under one of the relay securing nuts.

Fig. 12.44. Heater motor mounting (Series 2 cars) (Sec. 39)

3 Fuse block mounting nuts
8 Heater motor assembly mounting nuts
9 Vacuum actuator

Fig. 12.45. Heater motor resistance unit (Series 2 cars) (Sec. 40)

Fig. 12.46. Location of heater motor relays (Series 2 cars) (Sec. 41)

3   Footwell air outlet duct   4   Heater relay

Fig. 12.47. Heater securing nuts on bulk head (Series 2 cars) (Sec. 42)

Fig. 12.48. Heater securing nuts on top rail (Series 2 cars) (Sec. 42)

42 Heater unit (Series 2 cars) - removal and refitting

1   Disconnect the battery and drain the cooling system.
2   Carry out the following operations described in other Sections of this Chapter:

Remove the fascia crash roll.
Remove the fascia side panel from the driver's side.
Remove the fascia side panel from the passenger's side.
Remove the glove compartment liner.
Remove the centre parcels shelf.
Remove the centre console.
Remove the fascia panel.

3   Disconnect the heater hoses from the nozzles on the engine compartment rear bulkhead.
4   Remove the two large nuts from the centre of the bulkhead within the engine compartment.
5   Remove the two retaining nuts from the centre of the top rail.
6   Remove the bayonet fixing type stub pipes from the sides of the heater unit.
7   Disconnect the vacuum control tubes but first mark them clearly for reconnection.
8   Disconnect the multi-pin connectors at each side of the heater unit.
9   Ease the heater unit out and lift it from the car. Take care to protect the carpet against coolant which may be spilled during removal. The gearlever on manual gearbox cars should be in 2nd, 4th or reverse and on automatic transmission cars in '1' to prevent obstruction during removal of the heater.
10   Refitting is a reversal of the removal operations.

43 Heater matrix (Series 2 cars) - removal and refitting

1   Remove the heater unit, as described in the preceding Section.
2   Using a quick drying paint, mark the relative positions of all the heater control rods, knobs and cams.
3   Disconnect the tensioning springs from the heater matrix control flap operating arms.
4   Disconnect the operating rods.
5   Disconnect the inlet and outlet pipes from the heater casing.
6   Remove the heater matrix cover plate (six screws).
7   Remove the single screw which secures the cam and the operating arm to the footwell outlet flap shaft and remove the arm.
8   Withdraw the heater matrix from the side of the heater casing using a steady pull.
9   If the matrix has been leaking, do not waste your time trying to solder it as the heat must be localised otherwise more damage will be caused. It is better to renew the matrix on an exchange basis. If the matrix is blocked, try reverse flushing with a cold water hose. In extreme cases use a proprietary descaler and cleanser. If this fails, renew the matrix.
10   Refitting is a reversal of removal but make sure that the shock absorbing pads are correctly positioned and that the control rods are connected with their paint marks in alignment.

44 Air-conditioning system

1   This is a factory-fitted option and operations must be restricted to those described in this Section. On no account disconnect any part of the system as the gases and chemicals contained in the circuit can cause injury if released. If it is essential to remove one of the system components in order to gain access to other parts or assemblies always have the air-conditioning system discharged and later re-charged by your Jaguar/Daimler dealer or a professional refrigeration engineer.
2   At the intervals specified in 'Routine Maintenance' check the compressor drivebelt tension. This should be ½ in (12.7 mm) total deflection at the centre of the belt.
3   Any adjustment should be carried out on the threaded adjuster rod which is accessible from under the car.
4   During the Winter when the air-conditioner is not normally in use, it is recommended that the system is operated for about ten minutes per week in order to maintain the components in good order.
5   If bubbles or foam appear in the sight glass (which is located

Fig. 12.49. Diagrammatic view of the air conditioning system (Sec. 44)

A Compressor
B Discharge valve
C Suction valve
D Condensor

E Sight glass
F Bobbin
G Dessicant

H Receiver/drier
J Evaporator
K Hot vapour line

L Liquid
M Cold vapour line
N Heat exchanger

adjacent to the compressor) when the system is operating, the system requires servicing by your dealer.

6   Every 12 months or before the Summer have the oil level in the compressor checked by your dealer. This is a job requiring special equipment.

7   Water condensate is discharged from the air-conditioning system evaporator casing soon after the car stops and the blowers are switched off. This is a normal characteristic and a pool of water observed under cars fitted with these systems need cause no alarm.

45 Centre console (except Series 2) - removal and refitting

1   Disconnect the battery.
2   Disconnect and remove the overdrive switch from the control lever (see Section 10).
3   Remove the gearlever knob.
4   Remove the two screws from the front of the top finisher plate, remove the plate and disconnect the cigar lighter lead.
5   Remove the heater/radio control panel, as described in Section 32, paragraphs 8 to 11.
6   Remove the rear ashtray support panel (two screws).
7   If electrically-operated windows are fitted, remove the switch control panel and disconnect the leads from the switches. The control panel is secured by pegs located in nylon bushes and it should be prised away from them.
8   Remove the two screws which secure the rear of the console to the support brackets, also the two screws located in the top outer corners of the parcel tray.
9   Withdraw the console and detach the two rear heater duct pipes
10 Refitting is a reversal of removal.

46 Centre console (Series 2) - removal and refitting

1   Disconnect the battery.
2   Remove the console side trim. These are retained by two screws on the ventilation louvres.
3   Pull off the heater and ventilation control knobs and withdraw the panel far enough to be able to unscrew the four screws which secure the centre shelf to the console and fascia. Take care not to damage the opticell fibre elements.

Fig. 12.50. Centre console side trim panel (Series 2 cars) (Sec. 46)
1   Ventilator louvre screws   2   Panel

4   Detach the temperature air sensor pipe from the centre shelf and move the tray clear of the console.
5   Prise the window lift control panel clear of the top finisher.
6   Remove the three screws which secure the top finisher to the console, raise the top finisher and detach the leads from the cigar lighter and the door lock switch.
7   Feed the window lift switch panel and switches through the aperture in the top finisher. Lift the finisher from the console.
8   Remove the front seat cushions. To do this, extract the securing screws from the brackets at the front edge of the cushions. Raise the front of the cushion and pull forward. If a seatbelt warning system is fitted, disconnect the leads from the switch.
9   Push the front seats fully forward and extract the screws which

Fig. 12.51. Centre console top finisher (Series 2 cars) (Sec. 46)

7 Window lift switch panel   9 Cigar lighter and door lock
8 Securing screws   switch
                               11 Finisher panel

Fig. 12.52. Side fascia panel details (Series 2 cars) (Sec. 48)

1 Sill tread plate   4 Trim
2 Underscuttle casing   5 Side fascia panel
3 Weatherseal

Fig. 12.53. Windscreen pillar trim details (Sec. 48)

2 Mounting screw   4 Angle bracket   5 Trim
3 Mounting screw

secure the rear window lift switch pedestal. Raise the pedestal and disconnect the electrical leads.

10 Extract the two screws which secure the rear of the centre console to the transmission tunnel.

11 Disconnect the multi-pin connector which is exposed by withdrawal of the pedestal. Raise the rear of the console and extract the two screws which secure the wiring harness to the air duct.

12 Slide the console towards the rear, detach the wiring harness from the clips and then feed the radio and ventilation panel through the aperture in the front of the console. Slide the console away from the fascia, disengaging the heater air duct pipes from the outlets.

13 Lift the centre console over the gear control lever and remove it.

14 Refitting is a reversal of removal.

47 Side fascia panel (except Series 2) - removal and refitting

1 Disconnect the battery.
2 Remove the speedometer and tachometer, as described in Chapter 10.
3 Remove the fresh air outlet from the side fascia panel.
4 Remove the steering wheel and upper shaft, as described in Chapter 11.
5 Remove the direction indicator switch and cowl, as described in Chapter 10.
6 Detach the ignition switch escutcheon (two screws).
7 Remove the cover from the warning lamp cluster.
8 Hinge the instrument panel downward having first removed the knurled thumb screws.
9 Remove the two hexagon headed setscrews which are now visible, also the single nut which is accessible through the air vent aperture. The side fascia panel can now be withdrawn.

48 Side fascia panel (Series 2) - removal and refitting

1 Remove the tread plate from the door sill.
2 Remove the under scuttle casing (see Section 51, paragraph 4).
3 Pull off the weatherseal from the edge of the door opening.
4 Extract the two screws from the base of the panel in the footwell.
5 Disengage the side panel from the air vent regulator control and lift the panel from the car.
6 The windscreen pillar trim can be removed if required by first withdrawing the crash roll from the fascia (Section 51) and then extracting the right-angled bracket screws located at the base of the pillar and then prising the trim from its retaining clip.
7 Refitting is a reversal of removal.

49 Glovebox panel (except Series 2) - removal and refitting

1 Disconnect the battery.
2 Remove the fresh air outlet from the panel.
3 Hinge the instrument panel downward having first removed the two screws from the upper corners.
4 Remove the two hexagon headed setscrews now visible, also the single nut which is accessible through the air vent aperture. The glovebox panel can now be withdrawn.

50 Fascia panel (except Series 2) - removal and refitting

1 Disconnect the battery.
2 Lever up the loudspeaker grille using a thin screwdriver or blade.
3 With the grille removed, remove the two screws which are now visible.
4 Remove the two self-tapping screws from the underside of the fascia safety roll. These are located just above the fresh air outlets. The fascia panel may now be detached.
5 Refitting is a reversal of removal.

Fig. 12.54. Fascia panel (Series 2 car) (Sec. 51)

2 Demister vent   4 Map reading lamp
3 Crash roll screws   5 Lamp terminals

Fig. 12.55. Underscuttle details (Series 2 cars) (Sec. 51)

2 Speedometer trip control   4 Rheostat leads
3 Fascia support bracket   6 Underscuttle casing

Fig. 12.56. Exterior rear view mirror (remote controlled - Series 2 cars) (Sec. 53)

1 Screws   4 Mirror mounting screws
2 Escutcheon plate   5 Mirror
3 Grub screw

51 Fascia panel (Series 2) - removal and refitting

1 Disconnect the battery.
2 Prise the demister air vents from the crash roll and then unscrew the four screws which secure the crash roll.
3 Prise the map light from its housing in the crash roll and disconnect the leads. Remove the crash roll.
4 Remove the underscuttle casing from the driver's side. To do this, the speedometer trip control securing ring will have to be unscrewed, the casing securing screws removed and the rheostat switch leads disconnected.
5 Remove the four screws which secure the fascia to the screen rail.
6 Remove the two nuts which secure the outer ends of the fascia to the lower mounting brackets.
7 Pull off the heater and ventilation control knobs.
8 Withdraw the radio panel far enough forward to permit access to the screws which secure the centre tray.
9 Remove the four screws which secure the centre shelf to the console. Detach the temperature air sensor pipe from the centre tray and move the tray clear of the fascia.
10 Remove the two nuts which secure the fascia to the heater unit.
11 Slacken the clamp screws which secure the ignition and light switch shrouds. Withdraw the shrouds and clamps and detach the opticell unit.
12 Slacken the steering column upper mounting bolts but do not completely remove them.
13 Remove the direction indicator switch shroud (three screws) and then ease the fascia panel forward and disconnect the multi-pin connectors which supply the instruments.
14 Disconnect the cable from the rear of the speedometer.
15 Remove the fascia panel complete with air ventilator ducting.
16 Refitting is a reversal of removal but it will be an easier job if the demister duct nuts are slackened.

52 Instrument panel - removal and refitting

1 Reference should be made to Chapter 10, Section 40, for a description of removal and refitting of the instrument sub-panel.
2 If the hinged instrument panel must be removed, extract the hinge pins and lift the panel away.
3 Refitting is a reversal of removal.

53 Exterior mirror (Series 2) - removal and refitting

1 The mirror on these cars is remotely controlled.
2 Remove the two screws which secure the control lever escutcheon plate to the inside of the door.
3 Partially withdraw the control lever and the plate from the door and slacken the grub screw which secures the escutcheon plate to the control lever.
4 Remove the two screws which secure the mirror to the door.
5 Withdraw the mirror and the mounting pad, pulling the control cable through the door.
6 Refitting is a reversal of removal.

Metric conversion tables

Inches	Decimals	Millimetres	Millimetres to Inches		Inches to Millimetres	
			mm	Inches	Inches	mm
1/64	0.015625	0.3969	0.01	0.00039	0.001	0.0254
1/32	0.03125	0.7937	0.02	0.00079	0.002	0.0508
3/64	0.046875	1.1906	0.03	0.00118	0.003	0.0762
1/16	0.0625	1.5875	0.04	0.00157	0.004	0.1016
5/64	0.078125	1.9844	0.05	0.00197	0.005	0.1270
3/32	0.09375	2.3812	0.06	0.00236	0.006	0.1524
7/64	0.109375	2.7781	0.07	0.00276	0.007	0.1778
1/8	0.125	3.1750	0.08	0.00315	0.008	0.2032
9/64	0.140625	3.5719	0.09	0.00354	0.009	0.2286
5/32	0.15625	3.9687	0.1	0.00394	0.01	0.254
11/64	0.171875	4.3656	0.2	0.00787	0.02	0.508
3/16	0.1875	4.7625	0.3	0.01181	0.03	0.762
13/64	0.203125	5.1594	0.4	0.01575	0.04	1.016
7/32	0.21875	5.5562	0.5	0.01969	0.05	1.270
15/64	0.234375	5.9531	0.6	0.02362	0.06	1.524
1/4	0.25	6.3500	0.7	0.02756	0.07	1.778
17/64	0.265625	6.7469	0.8	0.03150	0.08	2.032
9/32	0.28125	7.1437	0.9	0.03543	0.09	2.286
19/64	0.296875	7.5406	1	0.03937	0.1	2.54
5/16	0.3125	7.9375	2	0.07874	0.2	5.08
21/64	0.328125	8.3344	3	0.11811	0.3	7.62
11/32	0.34375	8.7312	4	0.15748	0.4	10.16
23/64	0.359375	9.1281	5	0.19685	0.5	12.70
3/8	0.375	9.5250	6	0.23622	0.6	15.24
25/64	0.390625	9.9219	7	0.27559	0.7	17.78
13/32	0.40625	10.3187	8	0.31496	0.8	20.32
27/64	0.421875	10.7156	9	0.35433	0.9	22.86
7/16	0.4375	11.1125	10	0.39370	1	25.4
29/64	0.453125	11.5094	11	0.43307	2	50.8
15/32	0.46875	11.9062	12	0.47244	3	76.2
31/64	0.484375	12.3031	13	0.51181	4	101.6
1/2	0.5	12.7000	14	0.55118	5	127.0
33/64	0.515625	13.0969	15	0.59055	6	152.4
17/32	0.53125	13.4937	16	0.62992	7	177.8
35/64	0.546875	13.8906	17	0.66929	8	203.2
9/16	0.5625	14.2875	18	0.70866	9	228.6
37/64	0.578125	14.6844	19	0.74803	10	254.0
19/32	0.59375	15.0812	20	0.78740	11	279.4
39/64	0.609375	15.4781	21	0.82677	12	304.8
5/8	0.625	15.8750	22	0.86614	13	330.2
41/64	0.640625	16.2719	23	0.90551	14	355.6
21/32	0.65625	16.6687	24	0.94488	15	381.0
43/64	0.671875	17.0656	25	0.98425	16	406.4
11/16	0.6875	17.4625	26	1.02362	17	431.8
45/64	0.703125	17.8594	27	1.06299	18	457.2
23/32	0.71875	18.2562	28	1.10236	19	482.6
47/64	0.734375	18.6531	29	1.14173	20	508.0
3/4	0.75	19.0500	30	1.18110	21	533.4
49/64	0.765625	19.4469	31	1.22047	22	558.8
25/32	0.78125	19.8437	32	1.25984	23	584.2
51/64	0.796875	20.2406	33	1.29921	24	609.6
13/16	0.8125	20.6375	34	1.33858	25	635.0
53/64	0.828125	21.0344	35	1.37795	26	660.4
27/32	0.84375	21.4312	36	1.41732	27	685.8
55/64	0.859375	21.8281	37	1.4567	28	711.2
7/8	0.875	22.2250	38	1.4961	29	736.6
57/64	0.890625	22.6219	39	1.5354	30	762.0
29/32	0.90625	23.0187	40	1.5748	31	787.4
59/64	0.921875	23.4156	41	1.6142	32	812.8
15/16	0.9375	23.8125	42	1.6535	33	838.2
61/64	0.953125	24.2094	43	1.6929	34	863.6
31/32	0.96875	24.6062	44	1.7323	35	889.0
63/64	0.984375	25.0031	45	1.7717	36	914.4

1 Imperial gallon = 8 Imp pints = 1.16 US gallons = 277.42 cu in = 4.5459 litres

1 US gallon = 4 US quarts = 0.862 Imp gallon = 231 cu in = 3.785 litres

1 Litre = 0.2199 Imp gallon = 0.2642 US gallon = 61.0253 cu in = 1000 cc

Miles to Kilometres		Kilometres to Miles	
1	1.61	1	0.62
2	3.22	2	1.24
3	4.83	3	1.86
4	6.44	4	2.49
5	8.05	5	3.11
6	9.66	6	3.73
7	11.27	7	4.35
8	12.88	8	4.97
9	14.48	9	5.59
10	16.09	10	6.21
20	32.19	20	12.43
30	48.28	30	18.64
40	64.37	40	24.85
50	80.47	50	31.07
60	96.56	60	37.28
70	112.65	70	43.50
80	128.75	80	49.71
90	144.84	90	55.92
100	160.93	100	62.14

lb f ft to Kg f m		Kg f m to lb f ft		lb f/in^2: Kg f/cm^2		Kg f/cm^2: lb f/in^2	
1	0.138	1	7.233	1	0.07	1	14.22
2	0.276	2	14.466	2	0.14	2	28.50
3	0.414	3	21.699	3	0.21	3	42.67
4	0.553	4	28.932	4	0.28	4	56.89
5	0.691	5	36.165	5	0.35	5	71.12
6	0.829	6	43.398	6	0.42	6	85.34
7	0.967	7	50.631	7	0.49	7	99.56
8	1.106	8	57.864	8	0.56	8	113.79
9	1.244	9	65.097	9	0.63	9	128.00
10	1.382	10	72.330	10	0.70	10	142.23
20	2.765	20	144.660	20	1.41	20	284.47
30	4.147	30	216.990	30	2.11	30	426.70

Castrol GRADES

Castrol Engine Oils

Castrol GTX

An ultra high performance SAE 20W/50 motor oil which exceeds the latest API MS requirements and manufacturers' specifications. Castrol GTX with liquid tungsten† generously protects engines at the extreme limits of performance, and combines both good cold starting with oil consumption control. Approved by leading car makers.

Castrol XL 20/50

Contains liquid tungsten†; well suited to the majority of conditions giving good oil consumption control in both new and old cars.

Castrolite (Multi-grade)

This is the lightest multi-grade oil of the Castrol motor oil family containing liquid tungsten†. It is best suited to ensure easy winter starting and for those car models whose manufacturers specify lighter weight oils.

Castrol Grand Prix

An SAE 50 engine oil for use where a heavy, full-bodied lubricant is required.

Castrol Two-Stroke-Four

A premium SAE 30 motor oil possessing good detergency characteristics and corrosion inhibitors, coupled with low ash forming tendency and excellent anti-scuff properties. It is suitable for all two-stroke motor-cycles, and for two-stroke and small four-stroke horticultural machines.

Castrol CR (Multi-grade)

A high quality engine oil of the SAE-20W/30 multi-grade type, suited to mixed fleet operations.

Castrol CRI 10, 20, 30

Primarily for diesel engines, a range of heavily fortified, fully detergent oils, covering the requirements of DEF 2101-D and Supplement 1 specifications.

Castrol CRB 20, 30

Primarily for diesel engines, heavily fortified, fully detergent oils, covering the requirements of MIL-L-2104B.

Castrol R 40

Primarily designed and developed for highly stressed racing engines. Castrol 'R' should not be mixed with any other oil nor with any grade of Castrol.
†*Liquid Tungsten is an oil soluble long chain tertiary alkyl primary amine tungstate covered by British Patent No. 882,295.*

Castrol Gear Oils

Castrol Hypoy (90 EP)

A light-bodied powerful extreme pressure gear oil for use in hypoid rear axles and in some gearboxes.

Castrol Gear Oils (continued)

Castrol Hypoy Light (80 EP)

A very light-bodied powerful extreme pressure gear oil for use in hypoid rear axles in cold climates and in some gearboxes.

Castrol Hypoy B (90 EP)

A light-bodied powerful extreme pressure gear oil that complies with the requirements of the MIL-L-2105B specification, for use in certain gearboxes and rear axles.

Castrol Hi-Press (140 EP)

A heavy-bodied extreme pressure gear oil for use in spiral bevel rear axles and some gearboxes.

Castrol ST (90)

A light-bodied gear oil with fortifying additives

Castrol D (140)

A heavy full-bodied gear oil with fortifying additives.

Castrol Thio-Hypoy FD (90 EP)

A light-bodied powerful extreme pressure gear oil. This is a special oil for running-in certain hypoid gears.

Automatic Transmission Fluids

Castrol TQF

(Automatic Transmission Fluid)

Approved for use in all Borg-Warner Automatic Transmission Units. Castrol TQF also meets Ford specification M2C 33F.

Castrol TQ Dexron®

(Automatic Transmission Fluid)

Complies with the requirements of Dexron® Automatic Transmission Fluids as laid down by General Motors Corporation.

Castrol Greases

Castrol LM

A multi-purpose high melting point lithium based grease approved for most automotive applications including chassis and wheel bearing lubrication.

Castrol M33

A high melting point lithium based grease containing molybdenum disulphide.

Castrol BNS

A high melting point grease for use where recommended by certain manufacturers in front wheel bearings when disc brakes are fitted.

Castrol Greases (continued)

Castrol CL

A semi-fluid calcium based grease, which is both waterproof and adhesive, intended for chassis lubrication.

Castrol Medium

A medium consistency calcium based grease.

Castrol Heavy

A heavy consistency calcium based grease.

Castrol PH

A white grease for plunger housings and other moving parts on brake mechanisms. *It must NOT be allowed to come into contact with brake fluid when applied to the moving parts of hydraulic brakes.*

Castrol Graphited Grease

A graphited grease for the lubrication of transmission chains.

Castrol Under-Water Grease

A grease for the under-water gears of outboard motors.

Anti-Freeze

Castrol Anti-Freeze

Contains anti-corrosion additives with ethylene glycol. Recommended for the cooling systems of all petrol and diesel engines.

Speciality Products

Castrol Girling Damper Oil Thin

The oil for Girling piston type hydraulic dampers.

Castrol Shockol

A light viscosity oil for use in some piston type shock absorbers and in some hydraulic systems employing synthetic rubber seals. It must not be used in braking systems.

Castrol Penetrating Oil

A leaf spring lubricant possessing a high degree of penetration and providing protection against rust.

Castrol Solvent Flushing Oil

A light-bodied solvent oil, designed for flushing engines, rear axles, gearboxes and gearcasings.

Castrollo

An upper cylinder lubricant for use in the proportion of 1 fluid ounce to two gallons of fuel.

Everyman Oil

A light-bodied machine oil containing anti-corrosion additives for both general use and cycle lubrication.

Index

Printed by
Haynes Publishing Group
Sparkford Yeovil Somerset
England